The Best
AMERICAN
ESSAYS
1989

The Best
AMERICAN
ESSAYS
1989

Edited and with an Introduction
by GEOFFREY WOLFF

ROBERT ATWAN,
Series Editor

TICKNOR & FIELDS   NEW YORK   1989

ISSN 0888-3742
ISBN 0-89919-891-0
ISBN 0-89919-892-9 (PBK.)

Printed in the United States of America

M 10 9 8 7 6 5 4 3 2 1

"Playing Chess with Arthur Koestler" by Julian Barnes. First published in *The Yale Review*. Copyright © 1988 by Julian Barnes. Reprinted by permission of the author. The essay was also published in the London *Observer*.

"A Snapping Turtle in June" by Franklin Burroughs. First published in *The Georgia Review*. Copyright © 1988 by Franklin Burroughs. Reprinted by permission of the author.

"Think About It" by Frank Conroy. First published in *Harper's Magazine*. Copyright © 1988 by *Harper's Magazine*. Reprinted by permission of the publisher.

"Insider Baseball" by Joan Didion. First published in *The New York Review of Books*. Copyright © 1988 by Joan Didion. Reprinted by permission of the author.

"Schedules" by Annie Dillard. First published in *Tikkun*. Copyright © 1988 by Annie Dillard. Reprinted by permission of the author. The essay also appears in the author's collection *The Writing Life*, published by Harper & Row in 1989.

"The Muses Are Heard" by Stanley Elkin. First published in *Harper's Magazine*. Copyright © 1988 by Stanley Elkin. Reprinted by permission of the author.

"Confessions of a Low Roller" by Joseph Epstein. First published in *The American Scholar*. Copyright © 1988 by Joseph Epstein. Reprinted by permission of the author.

"Accommodations" by Richard Ford. First published in *Banana Republic Trips*. Copyright © 1988 by Richard Ford. Reprinted by permission of the author. "Accommodations" also appeared in altered form in *Harper's Magazine*.

"Parade March from 'That Creaturely World'" by Albert Goldbarth. First

Contents

Foreword

THIS YEAR'S VOLUME — the fourth in the annual series — is made up largely of personal writing. These essays are intimate, candid, revealing, close to the pulse of human experience.

But "personal" has another, shiftier, side. Its roots reach back to the Latin *"persona,"* the literal term for "mask" and, by metonymic extension, a theatrical character *(dramatis persona)*. Thus, oddly enough, the term we automatically use to convey intimacy and sincerity has hidden overtones of disguise and performance. Readers may overlook this double sense, but personal essayists rarely do. They know that the first-person singular is not a simple unmediated extension of a self, that the "I" of the sentence is not always the same as the "I" who writes the sentence.

It's this polarization at the heart of the word that makes the personal essay such a complex literary item. Who is the "I" of the essay — a real person or a literary *persona?* Is what the essayist tells us fact or fiction? Did George Orwell actually shoot an elephant one miserably overcast day in Burma? Did E. B. White really preside over the death of a sick pig? And did Virginia Woolf truly watch a moth expire on a window ledge? Or did they make these moments up? Who knows for sure? Some enterprising scholar might track down an official Burmese report citing the dead elephant; another might even find a Maine veterinarian's note about the dead pig; but that dead moth will never be the subject of anyone's fact check. We'll always have to take Virginia Woolf's word for it.

Yet isn't that finally the issue, taking the writer's word? Admittedly, it's easier for us to do this when the essay proceeds along the lines of reflection or opinion (though Jonathan Swift's first-person singular is a savagely duplicitous affair). But once the essayist steps into the flow of personal narrative and anecdote, the writer's word begins to sound dangerously like fiction, especially when episodes are developed with dialogue, dénouement, the whole bag of tricks. Here is where the personal essayist confronts the toughest challenge of the form: telling stories that are at once artful, true, and *believable*.

This is ultimately a matter of craft and credibility, a delicate balance of literary *persona* and literal person. Observing how it's done — how the essayist successfully merges these often contradictory roles — is one of the pleasures of the genre. Self-effacement is, of course, one crafty way to establish narrative credibility. Montaigne pioneered this technique; he knew readers would be skeptical of self-serving anecdotes but would instinctively trust anyone who admitted to faults and foolishness, confusions and embarrassments. Since Montaigne, personal essayists have not had an easy time assuming heroic poses. From its first sentence to its last, Orwell's great essay shrugs off self-importance. Why *did* he shoot the elephant? "I had done it," he confesses, "solely to avoid looking a fool." A nobler motive and we might have raised our eyebrows.

Essayists understand, too, that a true story doesn't usually come packaged in a compellingly dramatic shape but rather tends to disperse itself into observation or anticlimax. Which is fine, since essayists love to pause. They frequently feel the need to pull in the reins of narrative, take a careful look around, note the intellectual terrain, and offer some unabashed exposition and commentary. (Readers who see such essayistic moments as unnecessary "digressions" are probably the same people who think the funny lines in *Hamlet* are examples of "comic relief.") Personal essayists can even take some compositional delight in the shape of something not happening. "The writer in me," says Frank Conroy parenthetically in "Think About It," "is tempted to create a scene here — to invent one for dramatic purposes — but of course I can't do that." What better illustration of an essay knowing itself.

The personal essay has long existed in a literary twilight zone.

Because it presumes to tell a true story yet often uses fictional techniques, it stands awkwardly with one foot in and one foot out of so-called imaginative literature. Unlike fiction, drama, and poetry, the essay doesn't come equipped with an impressive critical vocabulary and thus hasn't acquired the proper credentials demanded by university English departments for literary certification. But the climate has recently begun to change as writers and even critics are growing increasingly enchanted with the form. "Don't spread it around," Joseph Epstein said a few years ago, "but it's a sweet time to be an essayist." Geoffrey Wolff's collection proves how sweet a time it truly is.

The Best American Essays features a selection of the year's outstanding essays, essays of literary achievement that show an awareness of craft and a forcefulness of thought. Roughly 300 essays are gathered from a wide variety of regional and national publications. These essays are then screened and turned over to a distinguished guest editor, who may add a few personal favorites to the list and who makes the final selections.

To qualify for selection, the essays must be works of respectable literary quality intended as fully developed, independent essays (not excerpts or reviews) on subjects of general interest (not specialized scholarship), originally written in English (or translated by the author) for first appearance in an American periodical during the calendar year. Publications that want to make sure their contributions will be considered each year should include the series on their subscription list (Robert Atwan, *The Best American Essays*, P.O. Box 1074, Maplewood, New Jersey 07040).

For this volume I'd like to thank Donald McQuade for all the encouragement he has given this series since its inception; in his courses at Berkeley he is helping to change the ways in which essays are read and taught. Without the editorial assistance of Laurie Parsons at Ticknor & Fields these volumes would most likely come out every *two* years. A number of people made sure Geoffrey Wolff and I saw some of the year's outstanding essays; we thank especially Daniel Kelly (under whose editorship *Minnesota Monthly* published many remarkable essays), Alexander Butrym, and Eric Ashworth for having first called our attention to three of the selections that appear in this book. In his own writing, Geoffrey Wolff has consistently explored the moral and literary complexities of the first-person singular. These deeply important concerns are at the center of this year's collection.

R.A.

Introduction: An Apprentice

THERE RECENTLY ARRIVED in my mailbox a *billet-doux* from my little brother. More specifically this was a five-page letter to him, from me, with his Post-it self-stick memo stuck to page 1. The letter was dated "13/xi/63" — à la European mode — and post-marked Cambridge, England, mailed to an eleventh grader. Single-spaced elite, without margins, it was typed with such manifest urgency that words fly truncated off the right edge of the tissue-thin foolscap; the keys must have been righteously rapped — *o*'s are little holes.

The tone of this document owes much to austere dogma, a religion of literary Art. It answers a letter in which Toby seems obscurely to have offended me by an expression of enthusiasm for his country, and some of its contemporary and popular prose writers. At that time he was too young to drive a car, and I wasn't, so I took it upon myself to tell the stripling a thing or two:

"We live in an age when contraception and the Bomb and rejected opportunities usurp each other [*sic*] as negative functions . . . the cliché governs by executive function . . . in the ruined warrens are pockets of beautiful life . . ." The bulk of my letter consists of a suggestion that before Toby read another word of William Styron or Norman Mailer (for whom he had confessed such provocative admiration) he turn at once to Donne, Eliot on Donne, Sophocles, Aristotle, John Jones on Aristotle, Racine, Hegel (on tragedy), and I don't know who all else. In short: "Begin at the beginning and familiarize yourself with literature." To this end he was to write weekly essays for me, who had been old enough to drive almost seven years now, and I would lead him across the ages, "working through language and time until you learn how to read, and may discover whether you wish to write."

Jeepers! Or, as Toby noted on the yellow Post-it: "I *still* don't know any of the stuff in here, and I'm a Full Professor, Mr. Smarty Pants!! (I thought you might want this back.)" (Well, better that the document be revealed by me — don't you think? — than by Tobias's biographer.)

For a letter so passionately typed, mine has an oddly distanced air, save for its *ad hominem, ad extremum,* and *ad absurdum* assertion that "every backward glance at our family tree reveals a body hanging from the withered limbs." I think I understand the abstracted character of these declarations: whatever the provenance of my athletically typed (and no doubt plagiarized) maxims, all I can now say with confidence is these were thoughts never thunk by me, or never in just these words, or so I think.

Let's say Toby has me by the shorts on this one; it's in his archive still — he sent a photocopy, damn him! Alas, there's more: I tell my young brother "I've finally [!] quite decided to become Bunny [Wilson] rather than Scott." (That would be F. Scott Fitzgerald.) Oh boy. Boy oh boy.

But there's more on Toby's Post-it annotation: "It's a sweet letter. I was touched by it." In the spirit of confession may I disclose that I too am touched by my jejune gospel of a literary calling? My correspondence with my brother launched gaudy little vessels of language; my sentences didn't go forth carrying cargo, but in a hope of netting something out there on the vasty deeps. At the end of my *magnum opus* to my baby brother, my *dogma summa,* my whatever-the-hell-I-should-call-it, I signed off: "I'm sorry I have no news; I have little to talk of other than my work. That is everything."

It's simple enough to poke fun at the patchwork boy I was, the ill-matched concoction of attitudes and characteristics I aspired to be. At twenty-three I dressed in motley: three-piece blue pinstripe with gravy stains on the vest (a touch of Edmund Wilson in the waistcoat?), suspenders, wire-rimmed glasses to add even more years to my solemn face, already pallid from bad diet and irregular habits. (My God, I'd already had my first gout attack!) My Cambridge college tie beneath my Cambridge gown offset bohemian footwear, army surplus boots. The Greeks, Jacobeans, and Metaphysicals shared my bookshelves with modern poets, William Burroughs, Harold Pinter, Jean Genet, and *Europe on Five Dollars a Day.* Parked in front of my digs stood a cherry-red 750 cc Royal Enfield Constellation with full racing fairing, hell of a bike. George Steiner, my Churchill College tutor, my reason for being at Cambridge, was satisfied with the (literary) books but sore about the motorcycle. Let's call the ragout of my conflicting circumstances a mess.

But for all the hotchpotch of my circumstances and styles, for all the egregious posturing and borrowed sentiment and faked-up lingo of my lugubrious letter to my brother, there was also something there I will not now disavow. In those overwrought homilies about the long littleness of life and eternal uplift of Art was a felt passion, a longing for something that mattered, might stay, be firm. I was forever pressing books on friends ("Have you read this? You *must* read that!"); I pitched woo saying poems — nice conceit — by heart. (For their periodic drive and lonely outcasts caught in implied sensual contact I favored the closing lines of *Paradise Lost:*

> The world was all before them, where to choose
> Their place of rest, and Providence their guide:
> They hand in hand with wand'ring steps and slow
> Through Eden took their solitary way.)

I knew then — had known since before *I* was licensed to drive — that a life lived reading and writing could be a life well lived, in good company. That may have been all I knew, but I would not unknow it now.

I was an eager little student back then, avid to please, twenty-three going on sixty. The teachers whose good reports I cherished were cultural and literary critics — R. P. Blackmur, George Steiner, F. R. Leavis — for whom it seemed to me (if not them) that literature of imagination was a secondary artifact, the rough ore from which the precious alloy of criticism might be fabricated. To me, then, the self-consciously impenetrable essays in *Scrutiny, Encounter, Partisan Review,* and *Kenyon Review* were primary texts, and to read them was to belong to an exclusive guild whose members shared a dense jargon, a chastening insistence on commitment to text, a call to arms in some arcane combat in which a solemn band of initiates guarded the True Faith's gates against a vulgar gang of middlebrow, midcult vandals. (Leavis was an especially ferocious and unyielding enemy of popularizers of Culture, those Sunday Supplementarians among whom he numbered his Cambridge colleague George Steiner.)

I wished to stand stringent sentry among the few initiates. Why? I was a sucker for pulpit oratory (as long as it came delivered from a secular pulpit, say a lectern), and I was a sucker for whatever was inside the place I was outside. Also: I was skeptical of all faiths save bookishness; I was bone idle except around books. Around books I worked like a Turk, reading with a pencil in my hand, reading three or four things at a clip, a Dickinson poem between chapters of *Bleak House,* which I'd been led to by a Leavis essay, which I'd taken up to balance a study of I. A. Richards's *Practical Criticism.* I'd read headlong and helter-skelter since I'd plowed as a kid through Albert Payson Terhune simultaneously with the Hardy Boys. To read compulsively and to write about reading were my only appetites (of too many appetites) sanctioned as virtues rather than condemned as vices.

The poet Stanley Kunitz has remarked, reviewing his life's work for a collection of his poems, that evolution is a delusion. We change, but always at a cost: to win this you lose that. I feel sharp-witted these days, like to believe I know the score, would as soon laugh at myself as laugh at another, value lowlife idiom at least as preciously as high sentiment, have a quick way with the vocabulary of deflation. When my brother recently forwarded to me that old letter, I paraphrased (shame would not countenance full quotation) its rhetoric and presumptions to a friend of many, many years who had herself been on the receiving end of my bygone puffed-up gravitas. I said to my friend with what I took to be irony, "Jesus, I sure was learned then."

"Yes," she said. "You were."

I paused quite a good pause there, and let this soak in, and realized that I was lingering in the dangerous domain of a truth, and I wanted to laugh my way to a comfier neighborhood. "What do you think happened?" I asked. "Wisdom, or just too much television?"

"Nah," she said. "You could say car payments. You could blame kids, or the appeal of a good night's sleep after a sensible day's work. Basically you eased up is all. Got to like horseplay and being happy better than thinking till your head hurt."

She was part right, I'm afraid. To be the Man of Letters I aspired to be, avuncular at twenty-three, a virtuoso of the well-timed *harrumph,* able to contextualize, perspectivize, plumb the subtexts, incite chums and bully a younger brother to do the same — this was, in the age just before the age of the Beatles, dark and lonely work, sober work, hard work. My friend was also part wrong, for a plunge into language was not joyless work, which is why — I guess — I still spend my hours reading and writing sentences.

A final note about that letter to my brother: it was mailed a little more than a week before President Kennedy was murdered. I know it's recollection's merest commonplace to suggest that what happened to him and to America had something to do with me, but it did have something to do with me, or with how at bedrock I wanted to regard myself. Think how many of our countrymen gave up this to take up that, left law school to paint or quit painting to study law. It was as though the narrator of Frank O'Connor's "Guests of the Nation," in the immediate aftermath of a political assassination, was speaking for Americans: "And anything that happened me afterwards, I never felt the same about again."

Fact is, on the stroke of Dallas I no longer wanted to be a knockoff of Edmund Wilson, or F. Scott Fitzgerald, or R. P. Blackmur, or John Milton, or even of George Steiner. I inexplicably and all at once aspired to experience acts I might verify as being important; I meant to find a voice, apart from the remnants of conflicted idioms in my schoolboy collection, that I might convince myself was truly mine, and to give up proselytizing writing to a captive audience of correspondents in favor of learning how to write. In brief, an old story: I was an unhappy graduate student, woe was me. So I quit. Graduated. *Commenced,* as they nicely say.

*

I had what seemed to me a dandy cee-vee: Choate, a postgrad-
uate year at an English public school, Princeton *(summa cum
laude)*, a couple of years teaching literature in Turkey at Istan-
bul University and Robert College, Fulbright at Cambridge . . .
Moreover, after having decided at Princeton that I was too exquisite to waste on that suburban New World my roughneck
country, I was coming home! With arms outstretched! Willing
to shake and make up! Put my shoulder to the wheel of American culture where my conspicuous gifts could count, as a journalist in the nation's capital. How was it then that *The Washington
Post* personnel office imposed on me a typing test, which I
failed? Never mind. I taught myself to type fast enough to get
an interview "upstairs" and was tentatively hired by a managing
editor who had a soft spot for Turkey (he was building a vacation house there), and soon (despite my failure of a psychologi-
cal test in which I declared — what *could* I have been thinking?
— I would rather be a florist than a baseball manager, which I
wouldn't rather be, but I had blackened the wrong rectangle on
the answer sheet, and try explaining that to an alarmed personnel director while you're wearing an English shirt of peach
broadcloth with a white detachable collar) I was at useful work,
making a difference, writing about a dozen obituaries a day.

"I don't suppose you're secretly writing a novel during your
time off?"
    How could Bill Brady, night city editor, have guessed, my
first afternoon on the death shift? Was it written on my face?
Had he unriddled my furrowed brow, translated my sad eyes,
explicated my gnawed fingernails? The man was a seer. He saw
more than I could possibly show because, yes, while I *meant* to
dream up a novel when I wasn't retailing the deaths of civil
servants and merchants, and who had survived them, and what
kinds of Masons they were . . . while I had every intention —
when I wasn't tracking down pix to accompany my little essays
("Wolff! Have we got art with the Makepeace obit?") — of doing
art, I hadn't yet done art.
    I was not, that is, after all, a Writer. Now that's been said, and
I feel better. I was a would-be writer. Today such a distinction
cannot exist. To want to be a writer is to be one, done and done.

If I ask a dozen undergraduate students in a fiction workshop how many think of themselves as writers, they are confused by the question. I read what they write, don't I? What else is writing? What's the question, again? (Not that these young writers take everything for granted: quite a few ask, midway through their second semester as artists, whether they will someday be "first rate." More than a couple have requested my warranty: will I certify, if they work hard, read the books I have suggested they read, mend the errors of usage I have located, that they will — soon — become "great"? Because if labor were to make them merely "good," what's labor's point?)

In my day we defined ourselves as Writers by no more logical a measure: when you were published by a disinterested, consequential (read *grown-up*) publication, then you were a Writer. By this measure, a couple of stories in the Choate literary magazine, a couple of excerpts from a novel in the *Nassau Literary Magazine,* and some polemic from the left in *Cambridge Forward* did not a Writer make. Lest I seem to claim for Kids Back Then proportion and humility superior to the feral ambition of Kids Today, let me confide that I wanted to be a Writer long before I had the dimmest notion what story I wished to write. Let's call the phenomenon, then as now, careerism.

For someone not a Writer, however, I had sure done a gang of writing. In addition to all those school papers and independent projects and critical essays and book-length college theses I had taken a year off from Princeton to complete a novel, *Certain Half-Deserted Streets;* I have dined out a time too often on the sad story of that prolonged bit of make-believe, so *requiescat in pace, Certain Half-Deserted Streets;* I'll trouble your quiet no more.

But until I hit the glory hole of material that is any obituary essayist's estate, the principal vessel into which I poured my art was the letter. Love letters were best, but any letters would do. Letters were my apprenticeship. I used them as my commonplace book, as tryouts for characters, to get a purchase on what mattered to me and how I might articulate what mattered. I wrote weather reports and geography lessons, how snow touched the black waters of the Bosporus, how the sun bore down on Lindos, what a ninth consecutive day of rain did to

Paris. Hundreds of these letters, most unanswered. What was the recipient to say? This was not correspondence (as my amused brother now realizes); these were finger exercises, and just about as welcome to the addressee at the other end as a sixth, ninth, fifteenth run-through of "Heartaches" by a first-year student of the tenor sax.

Letters at least gave the illusion of a reader. Journals never panned out for me, and the reason touches character rather than genre. Hidden by the privacy of a journal, I was too free to display my worst self. I look back over journal entries from years back — entries that I taught myself to write as though they were public, in which I obliged myself to develop characters as though I were meeting them every time for the first time, in which no information was short-handed or privileged — and I discover a whiner. Awful. My characteristic voice is aggrieved or furious, condescending or monstrously generous. To the degree that journals have showed this bellyacher plain, have urged me to repair at the root of my temperament what was revealed by the ill symptom of my most private voice, I thank them.

My voice was of no interest to *The Washington Post.* To stamp a Geoffrey A. Wolff imprimatur (I hadn't yet the good sense to drop the middle initial that distinguished me from all those other Geoffrey Wolffs writing death notices for Washington's morning newspaper) on an obituary begged too much novelty even from a would-be writer raring to make a mark. How many ways can one say this late person was born, was educated, worked for a living, had kids, joined associations, lived in a house or apartment, grew infirm, moved to a rest home, and died? Not that I didn't labor to make even the oldest of stories new: "The world yesterday lost a good man: 'There was never a better dad,' said Trixie A. of the gentle-fingered chiropractor lying this morning in Hulbert's Funeral Parlor."

"Come off it, Wolff! You've got the embalmer spelled wrong! *Hubert!* Get the stuff right, give me a new lead, hold it to eight inches, where's the art?"

This was good for me. The demented urgency of deadline taught me never again to fear blank paper (although sometimes, later, I should have feared it more, should have simply shut up); the knowledge that every obituary is read with a jeweler's loupe by the survivors made me imagine those few readers at my back, peering over my shoulder as I composed: "No, you moron! It's 2021 Hillyer Place, not 2201! And he was deputy assistant secretary, not assistant deputy!" And so many dozens gone! The cry was still, They go! So many little essays so quickly composed! As a result, to paraphrase the boast of a newspaper colleague who must have been thinking of me: "I can type faster than anyone who can write better, and write better than anyone who can type faster."

For the poet form is self-imposed, the parabolic net across which one plays Frost's legendary game. For the journalist form is mere circumstance. For me form was prison, and to be its hostage — in an obituary, news story, book review, police report — was to long to escape. I graduated from obituaries to night police, and in a ceremony of initiation my predecessor (freed by my elevation to tell stories of zoning in Montgomery County) took me back to the clip files to show me the Gabbett Lede (newspaperese for first — leading — sentence, what jargon-meisters now call The Attack). Harry Gabbett worked night rewrite. If you know your *Front Page*, I need tell no more of him than that he was all five and a half feet an ace, that he later, when I was on final probation at the *Post* and six weeks short of marriage, "re"wrote stories about events I neglected to attend because of some small trouble with alcohol, that he got these stories (about conventions of librarians and disputes between city planners and how many meals can the Washington Hilton prepare in how many minutes for a banquet) on the front page, under my byline, and that he wore, in the newsroom, a Borsalino hat.

The Gabbett Lede began a story that had been phoned in from police headquarters about a pissant holdup at a movie theater. The desperado got away with small change. Gabbett, laconically, requested details, perpetrator description, mode of arrival, path of flight, the usual. The reporter, bored by the tedious usual, eager to knock off at three A.M., gave Gabbett what meager intelligence he had, and Gabbett wrote his lede: "A man carrying a briefcase to show he was in business, and pointing a revolver to show what business he was in . . ."

The ceremonial display of the Gabbett Lede was to suggest

that there's a great story in anything. It's an old American notion. I was first told back in junior high that in each of God's
creatures is a great novel. Huey Long was wrong: every man is
not a king; neither is each a Flaubert. Harry Gabbett, for example, was not Montaigne, or Samuel Johnson, or John McPhee.
Harry Gabbett wrote a honey of a lede, not a great essay. He
caught the reader's attention, sure enough, but to what end? It
is one thing to want and win a reader's attention, quite another
to have a reason to want and hold the reader's attention. Ambition is ubiquitous, purpose rare.

Ambition showed a pleasant face at *The Washington Post*. To
work there as a young would-be seemed honorable, was a hoot.
I've not had a happier job of work, except writing in solitude
from felt need something nobody asked me to write, and that's
only a happy way to put in hours when it's a happy way to put
in hours, when it seems to be going well, and it rarely seems to
be going well, which sense of dissatisfaction is one of the ways a
writer may know it might, just might, be going well, going okay,
going not so bad. Of course a sense of dissatisfaction can also be
simple discrimination, a commonsense response from a commonsense craftsman to a botched piece of work.

Anyway, at the *Post* there was a large-heartedness to my colleagues, a pervasive decency. My friends among the reporters
were greenhorns like me, and old pros, but they shared an
appealing irreverence unsoiled by cynicism, a capacity to be
surprised, an affection for our mutual enterprise, a seriousness
(without solemnity) about newspapering. They were undriven
to shinny the greasy pole of the masthead, except the few office
politicians who thought of themselves as "people persons," and
for those few bozos poles were erected that dead-ended in an
assistant managing editor's office, shut off from both the editor's office and the newsroom. The poles were easier to slide
down than up, so there was always an empty desk to be sat at by
a new time-serving striver.

Among the beat reporters, people who by God gave a day's
work for a day's pay, I mingled as an apostate, a curiosity. To a
good beat reporter a story was not form but material. Good
reporters didn't kick against the box of form except to make it
longer by inches, so it could hold more facts, bring newer news.

Pro newsmen had a different relationship with time than mine. For them augury was all. It mattered less what they knew than when they found it out. Divination was chronology, being wired in *pronto*, wised up *first*, having the *breaking* inside skinny, knowing now what the future held.

As a night police reporter I meant to write for the ages, labored to make a mark as a poet of the mean streets, long on the atmospherics of violent death, writing blowhard Miltonic sentences: "Beneath a spill of mustard light from the broken streetlamp, in a wet gutter choked with last week's racing forms, wearing a pair of mis-matched shoes, lay the victim. Stabbed." (And to hell making his solitary way?)

Bill Brady would read; Bill Brady would shout across the newsroom: "Wolff! How about a domicile for the stiff! And maybe an age. And perhaps an approximate time of death. And while you're digging, maybe you can let us know his name?"

This was not meant to be. When I got sent from police headquarters to chase ambulances, and sometimes caught the ambulances, I wouldn't — couldn't — do the next thing, which was report. The *Post* had a year-long crusade on its editorial page, exhorting drivers to buckle up. To support this campaign, reporters covering automobile accidents were instructed to learn whether victims had worn seat belts. I chanced on a catastrophe one night in a suburban Virginia emergency room, a mother and father dragged from a movie and brought to that hospital to be told that all three children — eldest fourteen, youngest eight — were dead. The eldest had taken his brother and sister for a spin in the family sedan. I was told to ask the parents whether their children had buckled up. I would ask those parents nothing. A reporter was sent to report, and I was fetched back to the newsroom and told how it was, that maybe this was for the best, maybe I'd get down to that novel after all.

"What novel?" I asked.

"Come on, Wolff," the city editor said, "every cub has a novel."

To tell the truth, I had stolen some time on the job to write a little fiction. Sent to cover the dead Herbert Hoover, lying in state at the Capitol Rotunda (and a stately thing he was in that place at that time, believe me), I had done some creative writing on the response aspect of that sober story. I was instructed to get "responses" from the well-wishers passing puzzled by the late personage, and if you put a gun to my head, I'll have to admit my college roommates weren't really there that afternoon, shaking their heads, saying, "This was a tragedy; they broke the mold when they made Herbert Hoover; the world is a poorer place without him."

But the city editor was wondering about my novel. Well, if the city editor had read Philip Roth's landmark *Commentary* essay in 1961, "Writing American Fiction," he'd have known that fact — awful, sensational, numbing, intimidating fact, the fact of the Bomb, the fact of Holocaust — was where it was at. Who better than a city editor to recognize the limitless bazaar of the bizarre *mondo weirdo* every morning? Roth wrote, famously: "The American writer in the middle of the 20th century has his hands full in trying to understand, and then describe, and then make *credible* much of the American reality. It stupefies, it sickens, it infuriates, and finally it is even a kind of embarrassment to one's own meager imagination."

During that way-back time death was modish. Remember? God was dead, the American Dream was, likewise the novel. That may have been why this cub didn't "have a novel" to take up the slack of imminent unemployment. I had elected to become Bunny instead of Scott, right?

In the event, I wasn't sacked after all. Ben Bradlee saved my sorry ass and made me the *Post*'s book editor. I wrote book reviews for *The Washington Post*, hundreds of book reviews, hundreds, five years of book reviews, three a week, many hundreds. Add two years of book reviews twice weekly for *Newsweek*. Let's not forget five years of book reviews, every two weeks, for *New Times*. (Notice how *new* everything was?) A dozen or so for *The New Leader*. Book reviews for *The New Republic*. Have we hit a thousand yet? Oh, and *The New York Times Book Review*, and at the end of this sequence *Esquire*, who found my book reviewing — how may I put this more delicately than *Esquire* put it — stale. For fifteen years without a break (except to teach about eleventy zillion semesters, except to write three novels, a biography and an autobiography, except to write essays) I wrote about writing.

I came to have opinions about writing. Casual opinion-mongering, standing hunch on stilts, is the curse of the critic and teacher, deepening his voice an octave, encouraging his vigorous nod of agreement with his own abruptly contrived axiom, lightning-bolt theorem. I do declare I developed almost (but not quite) as many opinions about writing as I read books (the shortfall caused the condition I call stale and *Esquire* called b-o-r-i-n-g), but my overruling opinion was simple enough: I loved what I liked and hated what I didn't, and what I liked took as many forms as what I didn't: verse, short stories, novels, reporting, biography, autobiography, just about everything that came from the heart (as I understood the heart to have a location *close to the bone*), that came to the page felt. At some point shy of a thousand compositions accounting for what I loved and loathed, I realized that I had not had much occasion to love book reviews, collected or uncollected, yours or mine. (I'm a slow learner: quite a few years after *Esquire* suggested I holster my critical pens, I found myself quick-drawing literary opinions for a new periodical, *New England Monthly*. As I write, I've been opinion-free almost a year: one day at a time; it's easier than I thought to say no, opine nothing, read without a pencil in my hand, read to learn or enjoy rather than to mark a pub date, which to inklings means *publication date* rather than an assignation in a tavern.)

I look back now at those desiccated, pulpy clips, a quarter century of them, and my heart leaps up, and my heart falls. Where did I find the time? My God, I was always up to something; did I ever say no? Much of my longer, more arduous criticism was written in the early days for *The New Leader*. Calvin Trillin has boasted that his piecework wage from a similarly high-minded periodical was in the low two figures. *The New Leader* paid me less, considerably less, if you catch my drift. And telephoned collect to copy-edit the work, and copy-edited it skillfully and respectfully, as though what I had written and they would publish mattered. Writing for such a periodical was to write for an audience of two, for me and an editor. It was to cast work down a well, no response from the world, not a whisper, yet I would not now undo what I did.

Neither would I bind it between hard covers. For the book

reviewer, or for this book reviewer, judgment is everlastingly interim, occasional, hedged by duty. Still the eager-beaver student, I boned up on Haiti, the fall of the Third French Republic, the fall of Algeria (the *Britannica* was my friend), Sir Walter Raleigh and Sir Walter Scott, a world of plenty or stew-pot of trivia, depending on my vantage; my vantage shifted glacially from contentment *(What a nice position I have!)* to imbalance *(What am I doing here?)*.

Looking back at all that discourse, I find plenty to respect, little to love. If my sentences were ornamentally purse-proud my first year as the *Post*'s book critic, my letter from Cambridge had foretold no less. I got better, plainer, quicker, briefer, smarter. The *Post* (or the *Post* in the person of Ben Bradlee) was patient, let me make mistakes of rhetorical excess (as long as they came in at length, Size Small), didn't second-guess my selections of first books of poets, translations of up-to-the-minute French *nouvelles* from the *Ecole du Regard;* the *Post* gave me leave to polemicize and deplore, speculate and assert. I read those ancient efforts and hear now, a word one week, a dependent clause the next, a parenthetical a little later, the discovery of a voice.

That voice, increasingly intimate, almost thrustingly candid, was coming in closer contact with the reality of my temperament. It was willing to lighten up, to giggle, to play the fool. A scholar who made fart noises in the Choate chapel, who laughs at fart jokes still, is a scholar who cannot lay permanent claim to a grave voice. The writers I came to admire, to write about again and again until I became — stale? — have sassy voices, spritz, pizzazz. The John Barth of *The Sot-Weed Factor,* the Robert Coover of *Public Burning,* everything by Stanley Elkin, *Portnoy's Complaint, Catch-22* . . .

And not long after I didn't have a novel — not for what Philip Roth lamented but because I had nothing novelistic on my mind — bingo, I had one. Looking back twenty and more years at *Bad Debts,* I see its reason for being is fog-bound. I recollect how pinched I felt by reviewing, how dead-ended by the responsibilities inherent in the form. As much as I burned to speak, I had the rudimentary decency to realize I was in print principally to listen and translate. It is tautological to rehearse the review's iron imperatives: its debt to the text, its obligation submissively to compress what is complex without dishonoring that book's integrity. Perimeter, the hedge, duty, equity, perspective . . . the high-mindedness (not to mention a limit of 800 words plus or minus 2) was suffocating. To progress (as it seemed) from pint-sized to bottomless, from institutional accountability to unimpeded will — that was the ticket! A novel was open-ended, obliged to no deadline, owed debts only to itself, could be fresh, unfair, low-minded, new, mine alone! My early working title for *Bad Debts* was *Accounts Past Due*, as though I owed the thing to an impatiently waiting world; this is the kind of tacky sentiment that puts fulfillment names — *At Last!, Finally!* — on the transoms of boats. (While I've got boat names front and center, while I'm swearing off book reviews, let me note the name of a pocket yacht in a nearby port, *Never Again VI*.)

Me, myself, and I were tall in the saddle those late years of the sixties. Remember when Miss Bartlett told us in seventh grade that each of our lives would make a great novel, and how next year's homeroom teacher advised us to write only from experience, and how the very next year we were instructed *Never, never, never begin a letter or an essay with the first person singular?* Well, writers back in the time I'm telling about began many a sentence with "I." In those days, believe me, Willie Loman wouldn't have waited for his widow to insist: *Attention must be paid!* If you don't have a dog, Delmore Schwartz observed, bark for yourself. Mailer's *Advertisements for Myself* was merely the leading-edge breeze of serial tempests of self-inflation, good storms, fine furies, mischief. The writers I most admired then were working way, way up the register and a full crank of the volume knob beyond the Eric Sevareidish sonorities, all hush and long view, that Tom Wolfe described in his preface to *The New Journalism* as the voice of a "radio announcer at a tennis match." The sixties made a high-voltage, high-pitched, bully great ruckus — confrontational, profane, immediate, assertive — and hooray for it!

What, after all, is the pleasurable purpose of this calling if it isn't music? What we agree to call voice? I can't remember why I read comic books, but I suspect it was for the noise that racketed in my inner ear, drowning the dead stillness of a rainy

rural Connecticut afternoon. I'm willing to concede that plot —
outcome — was my quarry in Albert Payson Terhune: *Won't
somebody make this collie happy?* Fancy provoked me to read F. W.
Dixon's Hardy Boys: the young gangbusters secretly owned a
speedboat and a motorcycle; this was like reading an Evinrude
catalogue. But by the time I got to Jim on his raft, Mister Pick-
wick on his high horse, by the time I was learning poems and
passages by heart, I was there to listen, to ride the riffs and
changes, hear the solos: *Listen to me!*

Not every voice a great soliloquy makes, a truth at odds with
the education of many an American writer, with the education
of *this* American writer. I remember (see how difficult, even
now, to break the habit of that pronoun, that solipsistic verb), at
boarding school in England, writing about Cordelia in the moment when she recognizes how mistaken is her father's mea-
surement of affection. I spent the greater part of my allotted
space telling about a tangled misunderstanding between my dad
and myself: "So I understand just how Cordelia felt." Of course
my teacher wrote "who cares?" Of course he was right to write
that: to filter all data through the mesh of personal relevance is
the voice's tyrannical sway over listener and speaker alike.
Sometimes it should be okay to take facts in, quietly manipulate
them behind an opaque scrim, and display them as though the
arranger never arranged. It should be all right to mediate, let
another voice speak through your spirit medium, pretend as a
writer not to be front and center on stage.

It should be okay. (We have John McPhee, for example, and
we have . . . Be patient, and I'll remember who else we have.
Oh, yes, we have — Hang on just a sec . . .) But the music that
drew me to the club was the virtuoso solo, the timed bomb of a
joke, an unexpected change-up of delivery, the driving cadence
of a long list of nouns, a juxtaposition of the decorous with the
vulgar, Hamlet on how to deliver a speech, Hamlet on Yorick's
skull, Bessie Smith singing "Up on Black Mountain," or Billie
Holiday doing a new spin on an old ballad, or Edward Hoagland's description of a leopard dropping from a tree on the dog
hunting him, "as heavy as a chunk of iron wrapped in a flag,"
good Anglo-Saxon music, tough, weighty, cargoed with conso-
nants. Or Michael Herr getting the sound of America's Vietnam

pitch-perfect, right on the button: "What they say is totally true, it's funny the things you remember. Like a black paratrooper with the 101st who glided by and said 'I been *scaled* man, I'm *smooth* now,' and went on into my past and I hope his future, leaving me to wonder not what he meant (that was easy), but where he'd been to get his language."

Americans, having been to so many odd schools to get our language, want to be heard. I want to. Why? Why write *Kilroy was here?* Is the declaration selfish, designed to drown out rival claims? (Kilroy was here and you weren't.) Is it mistakenly self-important? (You'll surely wish to know Kilroy once stood where you now stand: please note the plaque.) Is it generous, an attempt to connect with who comes after?

I dunno.

Hunter Thompson. Nora Ephron. Frank Conroy. Frederick Exley. Tom Wolfe! Listen up!!! It wasn't lost on me that I was using my nice-mannered cameo reviews to bring news that Tom Wolfe (who did a bit of hard time himself for *The Washington Post,* out in the suburbs, good responsible work) had decided the novel (the second of which I worked on when I wasn't writing nice-mannered cameo reviews) was . . . moribund.

This stung, and so did Wolfe's cock-of-the-walk exclusion from happening literature of everyone not among his band of a score of brothers (and two sisters), his hot-shot New Journalists. This was something apart from the clubby High Table we students of literature had thought to form. Tom Wolfe referred to himself and his fellow guerrilla essayists as "aces," as though they were Great War flyboys, up there in the ether of derring-do, looking down at us earthbound, stick-in-the-mud *pedestrians!* Of course Wolfe wrote with irony — he cannot write without irony (which can get to be a drag) — but still . . . Aces! The combat motif puzzled me then and grates me still. Those dumb bullfighter conceits, this penman *mano a mano* against that one, yackety-yak . . . Top dogs! Prizefighters! Hem in the ring with Tolstoy, Mailer with Betty Friedan. Come off it! Who's keeping count? To be *numero uno* is always to be *numero uno* for the time being — ¿*verdad?* I'm the king of the castle, you're a dirty rascal. Until we switch places. Sure seems temporal, sure throws a monkey wrench into immortality's works. Who's the best writer? Who's the ace? Am I to believe that serious writers seriously write to duel serious banjos with other serious writers? Seriously?

More to the point of Wolfe's account of the origins and prospects of what he reluctantly agreed to call New Journalism, what's the tippy-top genre? Does sestina fight welterweight against epic's light heavy? Many an ace (and perhaps the Tom Wolfe of *Bonfire of the Vanities?*) regards fiction as a more highly evolved form than the literature of fact. This antique prejudice seems to regard experience as unworthy of fancy, as though to imagine were not itself an act, as though to think were not itself (cf. Eliot on Donne) an experience.

I mean to testify, as one who has written fiction, biography, autobiography, personal essays, and other stuff that taxonomical hierarchy is writing's least interesting property. Now, personal best — that has some spin on it. Personal best, regardless of genre, is a measure, and a provocation, and a scourge. I guess I've been circling, sniffing at, putting off speaking plain about ambition. From before the time I sermonized my brother from the elevation of Cambridge, I had been encouraged to get with the program, get a wiggle on, get in print. Having confessed so much, perhaps I will be believed when I claim never to have gotten the point of getting in print, just to get there.

Let's put payday to one side for a moment. Byline doesn't race my pulse, never has. So how can I account for what crowds my files? The reviews? A report — much, much longer than this account of apprenticeship — on the making of an encyclopedia ("*Britannica 3*, History Of"). This piece of work for *The Atlantic* inspired its editor at the time to boast, in my presence, with the aim of cheering me, that his pride in that magazine stemmed in no small measure from its willingness to publish material other publications might dismiss as "dull," as "without sex appeal." (I also wrote for *The Atlantic* a sequel, "*Britannica 3*, Errors Of"; it was not as compelling a read as my original report, and I didn't get to keep a second set of review copies, thirty volumes, leatherette-bound. As I say, I learn slow, like *The Atlantic*.) I have written three essays about fire: wood-burning stoves, the art of laying a fire, the prospect of whole-tree harvesting and wood-chip combustion.

These essays I wrote between the end of *Black Sun* (a biography of Harry Crosby, unsuccessful poet and spectacularly successful suicide) and the beginning of an account of my childhood with my father, *The Duke of Deception,* at a time when I was professing literature at Middlebury, Columbia, and Princeton. I might have been expected to know better. What could have been on my mind? I think fire was, heaven help me; I think I must have been interested in fire, just as I was later interested in writing an essay about windmills. Now I haven't the least interest in windmills or in the energy potential of wood chips.

Nobody made me write that stuff. If my experience with editors has not always been happy, so what? Most have left my voice alone, have not sought to regularize the jitter and rumble of my idiom or to file smooth the burred edges of my syntax. I like commas better than editors like them, but we generally fight to a draw. In two years at *Newsweek* no one urged me to write like a committee or commanded me to review this instead of that. (The sorry truth: *Newsweek* didn't have to tell me what to review; I knew, without knowing I knew, just what the magazine wanted. When I recognized what I had learned too well, I slunk off to unlearn it.)

No sooner had I left institutional writing for the *Post* and *Newsweek* than my loyalty to deadlines trembled. With every year I write slower, research deeper, overprepare, won't let a piece go, fiddle with it past all reason. When the work turns out to have mattered to me, all to the good. So what if *The Duke of Deception* required a year more than I planned, while I researched my own sweet self! The sweat of day labor gives my voice the only authority I can hope for it; if I can trick myself into believing I know everything about my subject, I can hope to choose from the welter of the matter's chaotic possibility just that narrow band of fit sound that might enable a persuasive voice. Simply, unoriginally: hard, calculated donkey work — no friend of deadlines — may win an illusion of easy discourse.

My discords with editors have been over issues of length and design, which usually wear down to a single issue: my pace and route. I like to back into my subject, loop around it, take some time, explore byways. Like a wolf, I need range room; increas-

ingly, I write increasingly. Editors don't like this. Editors, from
my vantage, are often wrong not to like this. (At *New Times*
Jonathan Larsen gave his critics all the space they needed; I
wrote my best for *New Times;* however good my criticism would
get, that's where freedom got it that way, until *New Times*
folded.) Let's say an editor and I agree I'll write about J. D.
Salinger. His lawsuit. His solitude. What solitude might do to as
well as for a writer. Salinger's work. How it felt to read it then.
How it looks now. Length? About a thousand words. I say okay
. . . and write a couple thousand words, about a thousand too
few, and the piece is cut — with payday looming — by five
hundred.

I wonder about my choices, my compromises, that history of
okay-let-it-go-and-could-you-rush-the-check at my back. Let's
ask it: Was I a hack? Am I? I think not; I let myself off with a
not-guilty on this one because however misbegotten, however
strenuously willed my engagement, I cared then about what I
wrote then.

But I don't care about wood chips ("The Phoenix of the Forest") now, and couldn't. I ask more of myself now, and that's
the form my ambition has taken: a contest with some previous
self. I raise the stakes of my work by looking in and reporting
what I think I've found. I often recoil from what I find in here,
but experience has taught me that to try to find words to tell
with emotional precision what I've found is an enterprise I can
live with. I want — who does not? — to say words that count,
sentences that I mean.

I'm not crazy; I know how this sounds. "Who cares?" comes
as quick to me as to my long-ago teacher, as to you. "Who does
he think he is?" That's a just question. The essays I've saved, the
essays I'm happy to have my sons read, are personal and then
some: accounts of my childhood (I had the good luck as a writer
of mixed luck back then), of my follies (Boy Scouting, fast cars
and boats, destructive drinking, having earned a place in my
headmaster's estimation as "the weak link in an otherwise strong
Choate chain"), my education (a fluid knack for self-invention
stamped for better or worse in the Wolff DNA), simple passions
(sailing, skiing, mountain climbing), complex passions (friends,
wife, sons, the very work that tells these things) . . . Failures too:

unrequited fourth-grade love (a broken heart), physiological ruin (a broken heart), and certain humiliations.

Stanley Kunitz, wise man, knows another thing I've listened to: "You can say anything as long as it is true, but not everything that's true is worth saying. . . . You need not be a victim of your shame, but neither should you boast about it." Of course he's right, and sometimes I feel so powerfully the simple truth of this judgment that I shut up shop, or simply shut up, or throw my voice to a fictional character, or get an exit visa to another world, Harry Crosby's, Herman Melville's, anyone's life but this one. I know that the self can be too easy a subject, that candor without the restraint of reticence is just so much cheap talk. I know that it's as ugly a lie to be disarmingly hard on oneself as to be charmingly easy.

Because: Who *does* he think he is? Like many another personal writer — Frank Conroy, Frederick Exley, Harry Crews, Maureen Howard — the tale I tell carries (or fails to carry) its only reason for being: itself. I live and work on faith, that while cheap talk won't connect, careful candor might.

Providing I honor my contract with you. I work by Hemingway's precept that a writer's root charge is to distinguish what you really felt in the moment from the false sentiment of what you now believe you should have felt. The personal essay, autobiography, has been a red flag to professional classifiers and epistemologists; a critical industry has flourished for the refinement of generic protocols (many in French, with as much fine print as an installment purchase agreement), subcontracted principally to skeptics. In the judgment of Northrop Frye, for instance, a piece of work is shelved with autobiography or with fiction according to whether the librarian chooses to believe it.

Well. I've written one, and I've written the other, and I'm here to testify that the issue is at once weightier and simpler: a personal essayist means to tell the truth. The contract between a personal essayist and a reader is absolute, an agreement about intention. Because memory is fallible, and point of view by its nature biased, the personal essayist will tell a slant tale, willy-nilly. But not by design. Here's an artless instance: an old friend once a best friend, an ex-friend fallen out during the Vietnam miseries, came to my house years later to forgive me, in front of my children, for having been a deep-cover CIA agent and FBI informer. Neither of which, the dull truth to tell, I am, was, or had been. I wrote about the experience of his visit, the effect of his wretched forgiveness. "The Company Man and the Revolutionary," like any story of failed friendship, is a text bristling with paradox, special pleading, flawed understanding, skewed interpretation. One aspect of my account is *not* open to textual exegesis: I either was or was not a government agent. Simply. One truth, take it or leave it. Not a question of memory. A reader of that essay — a philosophy professor, for God's sake — an acquaintance, said he had scrutinized my narrative and found in it a subtext that persuaded him I had indeed been just the mole my ex-friend believed me to have been. I say to that reader, as I said to that reader: Fuck you.

If I now believe that there are in life matters more compelling than the deconstruction of such a text as my denial of treachery, likewise I believe that the presumptively impermeable membrane placed between a personal writer and his text is there to be penetrated. I believe time has earned me the right to penetrate it, to sound off. If personal writing may be (tautologically?) distinguished from fiction in the intractability of some matters of fact, so may the personal writing I favor license *tell* to modify *show*. Having made Hemingway's distinction between what it felt like then and what it now feels it should have felt like, why not pipe up and account for the discrepancy? The caveats against authorial intrusion are so reflexively assumed now that I feel simple-headed to question them, but the fact is, I can't get the point of shutting up about my own case. The illusion in fiction of letting facts speak exclusively for themselves is a convention merely, a trick of design. As a personal essayist, acts preoccupy me, properly; they make the only map of motive I know how to read, but isn't it niggardly to cut oneself off from context and acountability, to repudiate what hard-won meditation years have tried to teach? Isn't it sullen, after all, to show a skein of events and tell of what's been shown . . . nothing?

Age is on the personal writer's side, I hope. Writing about being a son, it helps to be a father. To have wrestled in novels with competing points of view is to have learned — oh so slowly!

— to see myself through the eyes of characters (mother, father, brother) I once regarded as bit players in my heroic drama. I'm less cocksure, I think, more sociable (on the page). I'm less fiercely alien, not so determined to be exotic. By inches, reality reveals its ruthless yardstick; a character at a time, the writer populates his personal world. If the personal writer gives up over time the sprightly energy of self-interest, he may win in its place a generosity that gives good work nothing but good service. Not Hallmark sentiment, of course, but a capacity — having been so many distinct and special cases — to regard others too as special cases.

Raymond Carver's last great story is "Errand." It seems to be about Chekhov's final days and his death from consumption in a Black Forest resort hotel. A Great Man, great events, the stuff of major biography. Toward the end of the account a bellboy enters the action, summoned to bring champagne to mark the final moment. The bellboy's perspective is not literary history's perspective: he wonders about his tip, frets about his wrinkled uniform and a cork littering the rug. He has ambition, longs to be a successful bellboy. He doesn't know Chekhov from Geoffrey Wolff, but he's alive, alert to life, complicated, fecund. A quarter century back, when I wrote my brother from Cambridge, I wouldn't have understood that bellboy: why he was there or what he was worth — worth to himself, let alone to the writer who made him. But I recognize him now, and that's what I've learned in twenty-five years.

GEOFFREY WOLFF

The Best
AMERICAN
ESSAYS
1989

JULIAN BARNES

Playing Chess with
Arthur Koestler

FROM THE YALE REVIEW

Game 1

WE PLAY not on a board but on a curious rubber traveling mat.
Perhaps it was originally magnetized to make the pieces hold
firmly to their squares, but if so, the magnetism has long worn
off. The mat has been rolled up for many years and does not
flatten out properly, despite Arthur's smoothings. The surface
dips and sways like undulating meadowland: bishops look even
more threatening as they cant toward you at twenty degrees to
the perpendicular. Those who play chess know how in the
course of a game that bland grid of sixty-four squares becomes
charged with lines of energy, pockets of power, backwoods do-
mains of stagnancy and despair. As the isobars of control and
vulnerability develop, this ruckled mat throws in some extra
uncertainties, some distracting bits of dream and surrealism.

We begin cautiously: neither of us has played for some time.
Every so often I am interrupted by the thought, *I'm playing chess
with Arthur Koestler!* While it's normal to imagine how your opponent is assessing your game (will he buy that bluff? does he
know I prefer bishops to knights?), it's less helpful to start worrying about what your opponent will think of you off the board
because of what you do on it. But these considerations are hard
to put aside when playing someone you have long admired,
whose work spoke with a personal clarity during your intellec-

tually formative years — and someone, after all, who reported the Fischer-Spassky match in Reykjavik for the London *Observer*. What does such a man think as I swap knights to double a pawn on his KB file? Is he judging this a crude maneuver that achieves a petty, vulgar advantage when one ought to be aiming for elegance, beauty, and finesse? Or is he saying to himself, like any other normal chess-playing human, "Oh damn, why did I let this whippersnapper double my pawns like that?"

Our rustiness, the joke "board," and the normal half-ludic, half-social uncertainties of playing an unfamiliar opponent are compounded by Arthur's physical condition. He is now seventy-seven, and known to be suffering from Parkinson's disease. When I arrive he remarks, in front of his wife, Cynthia, how much he has deteriorated in the last twelve months. "Zis Parkinson's — it knocks me sidevays," he says in that almost parodic Middle European accent which still comes as a surprise because you somehow expect mastery of written and spoken English to go together. (But of course they don't. See Nabokov: "I think like a genius, I write like a distinguished author, and I speak like a child.") Arthur's hand movements have lost their precision, and perhaps his eyesight is not so good anymore, because occasionally during our five games he starts to put a piece down on an impossible square, awarding himself, for example, two bishops on the same diagonal. Usually he notices; once or twice I have to point it out (and do not like to ask whether the fault is one of hand or eye). Each time, he apologizes courteously: "Zis Parkinson's, it knocks me sidevays."

The game is tedious and barely competent until I get a useful pawn pin. He struggles to shift it and loses another pawn, then I rack up the pin, he semi-blunders, and I win rook for bishop. This, I know, is the key breakthrough: queens are already off, and my two rooks look unstoppable. Then it's my turn to blunder. Like many average players, I have a visceral fear of the opponent's knight. Bishops, queens, and rooks move in that straightforward undeceitful way of theirs; the knight — well, the opponent's knight — is sneaky and treacherous. Predicting the piece's behavior more than two moves ahead is almost impossible. So suddenly, without any decent notice at all, Arthur's whinnying horse is right in where it shouldn't be, forking my rook and king. All that hard work wasted, I think. "Analyzing the position" (as we describe sitting there and worrying a lot), I see that when he takes my rook, I recapture the knight, and we're level on material again. A long, grim struggle to come. So I move my king and *bang*, his next move is not, as I expect, to take off my rook, but to contrive a very neat mate with two bishops and knight. Ouch. You do like to be allowed at least to foresee the manner of your impending defeat. Oh well. 1–0.

Game 2

It's the summer of 1982, and I am down at the Koestlers' farmhouse in Denston, Suffolk, for a week. I seem to be writing two novels at the same time, one of which is about Flaubert. Writers divide into those who happily talk about their work in progress and those who squirm in embarrassment at the prospect. I am a squirmer (of course, it's not just embarrassment; it's also caution that someone might steal the idea for your book, plus sheer vanity — however good you make it sound, you probably won't be able to convey the full originality, daring, and brilliance of the project). Three or four times over the last year or so Arthur has asked me what I am working on, and each time I answer, with tight-lipped paranoia, "A book about Flaubert." Each time — preferring, as is his style, the challenging question to the mollifying expression of interest — he responds, "Why not Maupassant?" I never really find an answer. I suppose I should just say "Flaubert's better."

I stay in the visitor's flat at the end of the farmhouse. I write in the morning, have lunch, read, play chess with Arthur, and go for a run in the early evening (I am in what I hopefully refer to as "training" for the London Marathon, which is a safe nine months away). The weather stays fair, and a satisfying balance is held between work, exercise, and pleasure. The only bogus thing about my day is the "training." I have decided to avoid an overhasty buildup to the twenty-six miles, and so jog around the unfrequented Suffolk lanes for twenty minutes or so, each day making it to a slightly more distant tree, a different patch of cow parsley. All kinds of mental stratagems have to be employed

(dreaming up dinners, playing through sexual fantasies) to keep
my legs moving, to rebuff the tempting voice which says, "What
are you doing this for, you don't need this running shit, nobody
can see you, come on, give up . . ." But I just about don't give
up in my low-level quest for a certain healthiness.

Arthur, as it later turns out, is worse than he lets on: he has
leukemia as well as Parkinson's. Both diseases are to some extent
controllable, though one or the other will get him in the end.
One example of his "deterioration," he says, is that his voice is
no longer reliable. It tires quickly and he can't always control
the register; recently he's been turning down requests for radio
and television interviews, and won't do any more. I fail to notice
any fluctuations in his voice over two and a half hours the first
evening, so am only half-convinced of his supposed decline, but
he knows better. As it transpires, he is already planning his
suicide. He has always been a firm and public believer in what
is — either euphemistically or accurately, I can never quite decide — referred to as "self-deliverance." EXIT, the British organization founded to promote the cause of euthanasia, has
produced a booklet offering practical advice. Arthur, in his me-
thodical way, has already annotated his copy of a précis of what
to do: "1. An hour and a half before your meal . . ." He sum-
marizes the amounts of drink and drugs specified, and notes
for future use the shelf life of barbiturates ("eight years").

The second game lasts longer than the first, about an hour
and three-quarters. Playing white, I open with a fianchettoed
bishop. There is occasionally some mild surprise value in this
beginning, though I use it mainly because it tends to lead to
open, attacking chess. I hate and fear those clogged games with
a great ball of pawn tension in the middle of the board; one
minor miscalculation and the whole thing will suddenly unravel
in your face. I remind myself that Bent Larsen, the Danish
grand master famous for his attacking style, frequently opens
with a fianchettoed bishop. As I play P-QN3 followed by B-N2,
I dream of a pair of bishops on neighboring diagonals aiming
their crossbows into the heart of black's defensive nest. But it
seems I am not as good a chess player as Bent Larsen. A lot of
pins and semi-pins hinder the bold maneuvers I have imagined.
My diagonal threats peter out. Another loss. 2–0.

Game 3

After the second game, I mention to Arthur that I've never played the King's Gambit. Whenever I try it out by myself, it always seems to lead to a lost position for white: it is suicidal. I know only one person — a reckless, pressing daredevil on the board — who ever plays this sharp, aggressive, old-fashioned gambit. So I oought to be less surprised when Arthur, as white, opens p-K4, p-KB4. I think, *Oh shit, the King's Gambit! I should never have told him how unfamiliar I am with it.* I picture him sneaking off the previous evening to his chess manuals and running through all the subtleties of this violent opening. Such thoughts don't help black's defenses; also, the suicidal tendencies implicit for white whenever I rehearse the King's Gambit seem mystifyingly absent for my opponent.

Now, toward the very end of his life, Arthur is mellowed by weakness. In the three or four years I have known him, he has become much less combative. I met him first at his house in Montpelier Square, at one of those London dinners at which most of those present have two houses and yet (and therefore) spend a lot of time complaining about the trade unions. It seems *de rigueur* on these occasions to have in your wallet a cutting from the *Daily Telegraph* about some obscure restrictive practice whereby workers with metal-boring drills are bringing the country to its knees by refusing to use their drills for boring wood. I was working for the *New Statesman* at the time (and living in a bed-sitter), so was unsusceptible to the inference that if only these recalcitrant workers would allow themselves to be pushed around a bit more, then people with two houses could afford a third house (which conclusion has been well borne out as Mrs. Thatcher's Britain continues). There was much disgust and dismay expressed that evening about the behavior of the National Graphical Association — the printers then being the particular object of fashionable odium among right-thinking people. (Quite by chance, I had spent that day at a small printing works in Southend, supervising the going-to-press of the *Statesman*'s back half. Everyone there had been hardworking, cooperative, and entirely lacking in a forked tail.) Not long after Mrs.

Thatcher became leader of the Conservative party, she paid a visit to Arthur. A previous prime minister, Harold Wilson, had recruited two famous Hungarian economists, Balogh and Kaldor, to his staff of special advisers. Arthur recalled that he was flattered by Mrs. Thatcher's attention but declined her casting: "I will not be your Hungarian guru."

Now he sits in the sunshine, with Mozart on the radio and a bottle of Moselle in a wine cooler before him, looking rather like a wise squaw. He walks with a stick and seems weary of his reputation for belligerence. I have recently read a new biography of Camus, and mention — thinking it might amuse him — that the historical record is confused. Some authorities maintain that he gave Camus a black eye only once; others assert that it was twice. But he is not particularly amused. "Only once," he says wearily. "It was a drunken brawl."

Despite my trepidation when faced with the King's Gambit, I seem to have chances at first; then Arthur establishes a strong center. A potential weakness is that he leaves his queen and knight on the same diagonal. But how to exploit this without being obvious? Gratifyingly, the weakness exploits itself: a forced defensive pawn-push on my part sets up a square for my bishop, which leaps out from the back rank into a killer pin on knight and queen. The queen falls. Some peril remains, as Arthur has two attacking rooks, two bishops, and a knight, plus a pawn on the sixth rank, but once all chances of a breakthrough are headed off he gently topples his king. 2−1.

Afterwards, I go for a run, light-headed and light-hearted. *Hey, I've beaten Arthur Koestler at chess!* There is nobody, alas, to tell; but I run for twenty-eight minutes nonstop, the longest for ages, without feeling too bad. When my calves begin to ache, I imagine lush country wives with throbbing décolletages who drive up alongside and implore me to take a lift; then I don't think of my calves for a while. But reality being what it is, there are no beckoning *chauffeuses;* I seem to have chosen a road driven only by careless and surly males.

Game 4

While we are on the subject of literary brawls, there's something else to clear up. That famous occasion Arthur threw a bottle at Sartre, was it the same brawl as when he gave Camus a black eye, or a separate one? "I *never* threw a bottle at Sartre," he replies. The record on that, he insists, is false. He adds that his friendship with Sartre was "poisoned" by "Simone."

I open p-QB4, which Arthur says he has never played against (can this be true? well, it will be in this sense, that my first few moves are always divertingly ungrounded in open theory). After a tense beginning, Arthur gradually puts on the K-side pressure and establishes — revenge for the last game — an unbreakable pin on knight and queen. For a while, I am forced into a mixture of last-ditch defense and a series of waiting moves (never good for morale). Then I see the chance for a possible breakthrough: I give up the pinned knight for two central pawns, which opens routes to his isolated king, which he has overconfidently neglected to castle. Gradually, I increase the pressure and cram him into back-row submission. After an hour and a half of unremitting tension, I pummel my way to victory. 2–2.

With the game over, Arthur puts the pieces back on the board and dismisses one of his moves as a blunder — or rather, given his joke-shop pronunciation, "a blonder." If I hadn't mated him, he points out, he would have mated me. So far we have played four times, he has won twice and "blondered" twice. Tomorrow will be the decider.

Afterwards, another record-breaking run: a whole thirty minutes nonstop. Arthur's postmatch exercise is of a different nature. If he sits down for too long he gets dizzy; so while I glide puffingly past the cow parsley dreaming of delinquent wives, he walks slowly twice around the house to clear his head. "Zis Parkinson's, it knocks me sideways." His attitude to his illness seems mainly one of interest. He mentions other famous people who have suffered from Parkinson's. It is a distinguished disease (a disease for people with two houses, perhaps). His response to old age is also scientific and practical. The brain needs exercise like any other muscle. He writes five hundred words a day. He does the *Times* crossword. No doubt his chess games with me are designed not just for pleasure.

Domestically, he is a frail dictator. The telephone rings while he is in the house and Cynthia is gardening. Arthur gets up and walks slowly to the front door. "Ooo-oo," he goes, an Indian brave's call now reduced, in old age, to a squaw's call. "Telephone, angel." And Cynthia comes running from the garden. Neither seems to find this system unusual. One year, my wife and I are staying at Denston on Arthur's birthday. The telephone rings several times; Cynthia screens the callers. Perhaps he takes one birthday greeting out of six. Nor is there, for the rest of that day, any acknowledgment of the date. He is devoid of sentimentality or nostalgia. In the same way, he is interested only in what he is working on now, not what he wrote thirty years ago. In another writer this might spring from irritation at being praised for your backlist while doubts are raised about your current preoccupations; with him it seems quite genuine. He once showed me a garage at Denston which he mockingly referred to as his "archive": I remember rows of steel shelving and large numbers of foreign editions. "Do you have a copy of your first book?" (I remembered it as an encyclopedia of sex written under a rather transparent pseudonym.) "Of course not," he replied. "That would be an enormous vanity."

He is a very courteous man. I quiz him about his name being on a board outside the local church: there is "Arthur Koestler" amidst a lineup of English officers, gentry, and clergymen appealing for funds. "It is expected," he replied defensively and a little stiffly, as if I should not be so openly surprised at an agnostic Hungarian Jew taking up his squirearchical responsibilities. At dinnertime he always rises to pour the first glass of wine for everyone — with however trembling a hand. His courtesy, however, should not be mistaken for indulgence. "You won't mind if I slip away after dinner?" he inquires most evenings, almost as if it were your house and his tiredness were making him a bad guest. But when, after dinner, you attempt to bid him good night as it is only a quarter past nine and your glass has just been refilled, he responds with a slightly firmer emphasis, "I think we all go to bed now, yes?" Yes, Arthur. He needs

Cynthia to help him: he has a contact lens, for instance, which he is no longer able to handle himself; she puts it in and takes it out for him. No doubt he also doesn't want you sitting up and discussing him with his wife.

Game 5

Six in the morning. High cloud and light summer air. Moorhens are processing from the pond to the corn field; two young rabbits are rolling on their backs in a dust heap where an elm has been removed; tits and sparrows are already in overdrive, all motion and babble. Nature is parodying itself for a city dweller charmed by the simplest country sights; and the sound of Arthur's voice is in my head as I watch the exuberant, carefree, normal scenes. "Zis Parkinson's, it knocks me sidevays."

It is our final game of the series, the decider. I am thirty-six and in full health; he is seventy-seven and very ill; the score is 2–2. Perhaps he will never play chess again. Perhaps I should lose, perhaps I should make a deliberate blonder. Like every chess player, Arthur delights in victory and loathes defeat: surely, out of gratitude for his writing, and out of affection, I should throw this last game?

Such reflections seem patronizing and irrelevant after only a couple of moves. Has any chess player *ever* thrown a match? Chess is a game of courteous aggression — and therefore very suitable for Arthur — but the courtesy and formality only serve to sharpen and focus the aggression. As Arthur's first attack develops, he immediately stops being a seventy-seven-year-old invalid who may never move p-K4 again; he becomes a ferocious assailant trying personally to damage me, to overthrow and humiliate me. How dare he! Gradually, I neutralize his first thrust, then begin a dogged pawn-march of my own. At first the maneuver is purely defensive — I push a pawn, he is obliged to retreat a piece — but its nature slowly changes. I realize that a huge advancing arrowhead of pawns with one's pieces undeveloped behind them is hardly recommended by any reputable chess strategist, but in this particular game the ploy seems unfaultable: with every pawn-move he is getting more and more cramped. His pieces are pushed back until they have barely a single square left to go to: in one corner, for instance, he has a rook's pawn, doubled pawns on the knight file, plus a knight in the corner square, all of which are locked up by a mere two pawns of mine. His queen darts out, but I lay a trap and plan my final push. I move a knight, which discovers a double attack on his queen. He must resign — yes, he must lose his queen, and then he must resign! I've got him beaten!

At this point an alarm clock goes off somewhere in the house. It is set for regular intervals throughout the day and designed to remind Arthur to take his medicines. Cynthia has gone out, so we set off around the house looking for the alarm, which is still buzzing. For some reason this proves difficult; eventually we track it down in Arthur's study and turn it off. He dutifully swallows a pill and we return to the board.

My inevitable feelings of pity and tenderness during this interruption do not affect my planned ruthlessness on the board. The game, afer all, is serious (on move 7 Arthur attempts to vault one of his bishops over the top of a pawn; he doesn't spot the illegality, I point it out, he apologizes — "It's my eyes, you know"). Now we settle back into our chairs again. Yes, that's right, his queen is attacked by two of my pieces. There is no free square for it to run to. I must win! But then, quite unexpectedly, Arthur finds a place for his queen: on a square currently occupied by one of my pawns. Fuck! Damn! A blonder! Worse, I'm clearly due to lose another pawn (in fact, the two pawns cementing down his K-side corner). Ah well, nothing to do but push on. Arthur, having prized away one little finger of my stranglehold, is able to begin an attack; I counter by grubbing out some of his seventh-rank pawns with my rook. Queens are now off, we have one rook each, I have bishop for knight (good), but am two pawns down. Even so, I have chances, incredibly strong chances: a pawn on the seventh rank, defended by a rook, and with its queening square covering my bishop. Yes, I must surely queen, and then win his rook. How can this not happen? Victory soon! And yet, somehow, I don't manage to queen (I can't quite work out why not — his king just lolloped over and messed me up, I should never have allowed it). I lose rook and pawn for rook, and though I still have bishop for knight, I'm three pawns down. Nothing for it. *Resigns.* 3–2.

Afterwards, despite the result, I don't feel as depressed as I normally would: it has been a fluctuating, violent, eccentric game in which we both had chances, and I played as well as I could. That Arthur won makes me feel, in the circumstances, a more or less grudgeless admiration. An hour and a half, a titanic struggle, and I feel shattered: what a testament to the old fighter that he overcame the young (well, youngish) whippersnapper . . . But this magnanimity in defeat is not allowed to lie undisturbed. Arthur has the true chess victor's talent for rubbing things in: over dinner, an hour or so later, he changes the conversation to remark wistfully, "Of course, I am only fifty percent vot I vos at chess." I'm not exactly cheered by this not exactly tactful remark. But a little later I am partially restored. Cynthia says she can't remember when Arthur last had a series of daily games like this — surely not since he played George Steiner at Alpbach. That must have been interesting; what, I ask, was Steiner's game like? Arthur, a small man, has a way of puffing up his chest like a pouter pigeon at moments of pride. "He played like a *schoolboy*." Well, that's some consolation. Oh, and did you tend to beat him, Arthur? More puffed chest: "Alvays."

Analysis

We oscillate, Koestler recognized, between *la vie triviale* and *la vie tragique*. I was preparing to run the marathon; he was preparing to die. I failed (well, the winter snow interfered with my training schedule — and besides, in the end my application was rejected, probably because I put "journalist" on the form and they decided they had far too many journalists running already and didn't need any more coverage); he succeeded. We met over chess, that trivial pursuit which refers to nothing else in life, to nothing significant, and yet which engages our full seriousness. George Steiner, who like Koestler covered the Fischer-Spassky match, strove in his report to convey the powerful emotions involved in a chess match. What he wrote is certainly unforgettable:

The poets lie about orgasm. It is a small, chancy business, its particularities immediately effaced even from the most roseate memories, compared to the crescendo of triumph in chess, to the tide of light and release that races over mind and knotted body as the opponent's king, inert in the fatal web one has spun, falls on the board.

Steiner had the grace (and humor) to add: "More often than not, of course, it is one's own king." Without this rider, sated Casanovas would probably have been rushing to the local chess club to try out a more passionate sport.

Later that year my wife and I went down to Denston. Arthur said to us quietly, "Here is a conundrum which I cannot express to Cynthia. Is it better for a writer to be forgotten before he is dead, or dead before he is forgotten?" We nodded, and I remember thinking, *Well, that's hardly a conundrum for you, Arthur, obviously your work is going to survive your death* . . . Except, of course, that this was not his question. He was asking which was *better*.

In late February of the following year Cynthia telephoned. We had a long-standing arrangement to take him to a Hungarian restaurant; she was canceling for the second time in a fortnight. She said Arthur had the flu, and whenever he got mild secondary illnesses it made his Parkinson's worse. She sounded nervous and apologetic, but no more so than usual; we agreed to fix a new date when Arthur was feeling stronger. "We're not going to let you get out of this, Cynthia," I said.

They did get out of it. Four days later Arthur and Cynthia killed — or delivered — themselves. I was standing in the newsroom of the *Observer,* one Thursday after lunch, and saw it on a television routinely emitting Ceefax news. A journalist standing nearby glanced at the screen and commented with casual knowledgeability, "He killed her and then did himself in." I wanted to knock the journalist down, or at least insult him violently, but said nothing. There wasn't any point in being angry with the fellow himself (saying the first thing that comes into our heads on such occasions wards off the reality, denies that death will call for us too in due course); what made me angry was the realization that Arthur was finally passing into untender hands (FAMOUS AUTHOR IN SUICIDE PACT, etc.), that he would no longer be there to correct things, get annoyed, or even just laugh. He had moved from "Arthur" to "Koestler," from present to past tense. He had been handed irretrievably into the care of others: how well would they treat him? (No more accurately than he would have predicted. All his life Arthur had been sternly opposed to having children: the *Times* obituary, in its final paragraph, invented a daughter for him and Cynthia.)

The note Arthur left was dated the previous June — before I played chess with him. In it he spoke of his clear and firm intention to commit suicide before he became too enfeebled to make the necessary arrangements. He reassured his friends that he was leaving them in a peaceful frame of mind, and "with some timid hopes for a depersonalised after-life beyond due confines of space, time and matter and beyond the limits of our comprehension."

His death was exemplary, well managed, and, from the evidence, easy. Cynthia's death was, from the evidence, difficult, and causes problems. That she lived entirely for him nobody doubted; that he could be tyrannical was equally clear. Did he bully her into killing herself? This was the unmentionable, half-spoken question their friends came up against. I did not know him very well, but I seldom met anyone with less obvious romanticism or sentimentality; I would judge that a suicide pact would strike him as foolish, vulgar, and anachronistic. Indeed, I can imagine him getting irritated with Cynthia for wanting to join him: if his death, like his life, was to be part of a campaign, if it was intended to change people's minds about self-deliverance, what could be more counterproductive as propaganda than for his healthy fifty-five-year-old wife to kill herself as well? Which provokes the slimy follow-up question: if he didn't bully her into it, why didn't he bully her out of it? It seems to me that at this point speculation becomes impertinent, unless you can imagine yourself as a seventy-seven-year-old suffering from Parkinson's and leukemia and no longer able to rely on prolonged spells of lucidity. If you can do that, then I'll listen to you.

Cynthia, in the note she left, said that she didn't think much of double suicides as a rule. She wasn't a dramatic woman; she was shy, nervous, birdlike, capable of seeming in the same day both twenty-five and fifty-five. She moved awkwardly, like an adolescent unhappy with her body, who expects at any moment to knock over a coffee table and be sent to her room for doing so. I liked her, but her character evaded me: it was as if she would not show you what she was like for fear that something (what?) might happen to make her realize she'd been a fool for showing herself to you. On warm summer afternoons at Denston she used to clear the pond of weed, with a dog occasionally and unhelpfully at her heels. She had a long garden rake with a piece of rope attached to the end of the handle. She would throw the rake into the pond, haul it out with the rope, scrape the weeds off the teeth of the rake, pile them on the bank, and throw the rake back in. It looked a slow and awkward business. She herself looked awkward, liable to overbalance into the pond at any moment; but she kept at it with what looked a childlike doggedness. Splash, pull, scrape, pile; splash, pull, scrape, pile; splash, pull, scrape, pile. That last summer I played chess with Arthur she didn't clean the pond.

FRANKLIN BURROUGHS

A Snapping Turtle in June

FROM THE GEORGIA REVIEW

ALL THAT CAN usefully be said about New England weather has
been said. It is arbitrary, precipitate, and emphatic, less certain
than a baby's bottom. Like the mind, it isn't necessarily bound
by chronology. April can suddenly hearken back to February; a
few hours in January will be as balmy as a May afternoon —
that is, as one of those rare May afternoons that aren't recollect-
ing March or daydreaming about September. Here on an overcast Tuesday morning late in June, it is summer sure enough,
yet we must depend more upon the floral calendar than the
thermometer for corroboration. We've had one spell of hot
weather — temperature into the nineties, high humidity, bread
going moldy in a day, crackers limp as old lettuce — but that
was two weeks ago, and it has been cool since then, either rainy
and chill or bright and breezy and autumnal.

But the flowers keep their seasons. Our fields, especially the
poorer one that lies between the house and the river, are rich in
buttercup and vetch, lesser stitchwort, fragrant bedstraw, and
blue-eyed grass. From the standpoint of agriculture, these
plants are weeds, and therefore absolutely reliable. Cold, wet,
and drought do not deter them; the only way to thwart them is
by herbicide or fertilizer. The buttercups are long-stemmed and
grow in all but the lushest pastures. Vetch (called partridge-pea
in South Carolina) grows in little tangles of vine, like untrellised
morning glories, as do stitchwort and bedstraw, and so they fare
best in a thin, ledgy, or sandy soil, where the grass is meager.
On a moist, unsummery summer morning, these flowers make

soft clots and smears of color throughout the watery green of the pasture grasses. Thriving amid the adversities of soil and climate, their inconspicuous beauty seems reflective of rural New England, and it is pleasing to learn that people here once found more than aesthetic solace in them. Stitchwort was so named because it was thought to cure "stitches" — pains in the side, of the sort that runners get — while bedstraw was used to lie upon, back when a bed was a board, covered with straw, covered with a sheet. Fragrant bedstraw is quite odorless in life, but reputedly grows savory in death, when sufficiently dried.

Except for the vetch, we had nothing in South Carolina like these field flowers or the daisies and hawkweed that populate the road shoulders at this season of the year, and there is not a great deal in the Maine summer that particularly recalls the summers of my Southern boyhood. But that strange Wordsworthian hunger for landscape, growing out of an individual and cultural maturity, is complexly regressive and involves much attempted calling back of things that probably exist only in the echo of the caller's voice. Fewer and fewer of us have Wordsworth's privilege of inhabiting as adults the landscape we inhabited as children — and of learning to recognize in it what he called "the language of my former heart." Even if luck and resolution enable us eventually to live in places of great beauty and interest, there is some quality of internal exile that shadows our relation to them.

This is a particular problem if you are a non–New Englander who comes to live in New England. New England is an image ready-made for you, no matter where you come from. It has so defined the American conception of landscape, and of the ideal human response to landscape, that it is not easy to arrive at a direct relation to it. It's rather like being married to a celebrity — your own response responds to a simplified and magnified public perception, as well as to the thing itself. Or, as a friend of mine, a tough-minded New Yorker, observed to me one November day, while we sat in a skiff in Broad Cove, looking across blue water that glinted and sparkled as though it were already full of ice shards, through crystal air and toward the shore with its patchwork of fields, woodlots, and bleak, bone-white houses gleaming in the sun: "Who are they trying to kid? This is the most *derivative* goddamned landscape I've ever seen in my life."

Boyhood was once almost as distinct a part of the American terrain as New England is, and, like New England, it had its heyday in the nineteenth century, and continued to be valued because, until fairly recently, it went on evoking the life of that century. There is the image of a sandy or a dusty road, the feel of the road under the feet, the cane pole carried over the shoulder, the drone of cicadas, the hair warm from the sun: the barefoot boy with cheeks of tan, the etchings and engravings of Winslow Homer, and supremely and inevitably, *Tom Sawyer* and *Huckleberry Finn*. In contrast, *girlhood* does not seem to generate this mirage. It doesn't evoke the same semitribal life, the living in a world rather closer to the wordless world of smells, itches, and yapping contentions of the unregulated dogs of small-town America than to the world of adults, or even to the world of the sort of regimented, housebroken, neurotic, pedigreed canines that one finds in the houses of one's friends.

There is of course much compensatory distortion in this image of boyhood, but I do not think it is altogether false. The boredom was as thick as the heat in Conway, South Carolina, and one learned to relish both in the summers. In our neighborhood, which is now an attractive suburban network of streets overhung with water oaks and sycamores, the streets were not yet paved — there was still a lot of unpaved road in the South at that time — and that gave, in a small way, texture and variety to life. In rainy seasons, the roads were slick and the puddles would turn to bogs, rutted out and mucky; occasionally a car, ineptly driven by one of the ladies of the neighborhood, would get stuck. But by summer the sun would have baked the roads hard beneath the dust that powdered them, and boys wore shoes only under compulsion. That is not possible where the streets are asphalt, and the tar sticks to your feet like napalm. I think girls wore shoes more regularly, in the fashion of their sisters in cities, but many of my impressions of girlhood must have been taken from my own sister, who was four years older and that much more aware of the world beyond the doorstep. In any event, I tended to associate femininity with paved streets, and knew for a fact that it was the ladies of the neighborhood, my own mother not excepted, who were most insistent that the roads be paved, so that they would not get stuck in the rainy weather, or have their children tracking mud into the house or getting their feet full of ringworm. From listening to them, you would have thought that they were the Victorian wives of British colonials, suddenly finding themselves in the Burmese or Australian outback, amid conditions of an appalling primitiveness.

At that time, the paved road stopped at the railroad tracks, about a quarter mile from our house. Then one day my great friend Ricky McIver and I walked down to the railroad tracks, preparing to follow them (which we were forbidden to do) along the causeway that ran through the swamps and eventually reached the trestle over Kingston Lake. But there, where the pavement ended, was a roadblock and a detour sign, apologizing for the inconvenience and announcing that this section of the road was to be surfaced. It was the beginning of a lifetime of symbolic Luddite resistance. We pushed over the roadblock, which was no more than a sawhorse, and threw the sign into the ditch beside the road. To no avail, needless to say: the road got paved anyway. History does not leave the backwaters to boyhood alone, and Ricky would soon enough find himself personifying it to barefoot villagers, who liked it no better than he had, in dusty hamlets full of yapping dogs outside Da Nang.

We were not, of course, thinking of pavement in terms of abstractions like History or Progress. It might have crossed our minds that its coming would mean that we had to wear shoes — or that more dogs would be run over, because cars would travel so much faster on the asphalt, and the dogs, like the children, thought of the streets as places of concourse and recreation. But probably nothing even that theoretical occurred to us. I think it was that we were mostly considering the snapping turtles that would, some time in the middle of every summer, appear in the road — sturdy little fellows, their shells not much bigger than a silver dollar. Paving the road would be the end of them.

All these things came to mind on this Tuesday morning in Maine, with the fields full of flowers and late June imitating early May, because, as I started out down the gravel road that connects our house to the highway, and drew abreast of the little quarter-acre pond that sits to the left of the road, here was, large as life and squarely in my way, a big mama snapping turtle, excavating herself a hole to lay her eggs in. I was in no particular hurry, and so I stopped and got out to investigate. Snappers are the most widely distributed of North American turtles, and they are by no means uncommon in Maine, but they are normally reclusive, and when one makes a public appearance it is not an event to be passed over lightly. This particular one certainly had no intention of being passed over lightly: if she had intended to blockade the road, she couldn't have chosen a better spot.

Several things distinguish them from other freshwater turtles, most obviously their size. The one at my feet was about two feet long, from the tip of her snout to the tip of her tail. When I eventually picked her up by the tail (and that is another distinguishing feature of snapping turtles — you pick up an ordinary turtle by the rim of its shell, but a snapper's neck is remarkably long and flexible, so you grab the creature by the tail and hold it well out from your body), I guessed she weighed a good twenty pounds.

The general proportions of a snapping turtle are wrong. The head is far too big; the shell is too little. The plastron, or undershell, is ridiculously skimpy — it seems barely adequate for the purposes of decency, and as useless as a bikini would be as far as anatomical protection is concerned. Consequently a snapper cannot withdraw into itself as other turtles do. It retracts the head enough to shield its neck and doesn't even attempt to pull in its legs and feet. The legs and tail are large in relation to the body: when a snapper decides to walk it really *walks;* the bottom of the shell is a couple of inches off the ground, and, with its dorsally tuberculate tail, long claws, and wickedly hooked beak, it looks like a scaled-down stegosaur.

A snapper compensates for its inadequate armor in a variety of ways, the most immediately apparent of which is athletic ability combined with a very bad temper. It can whirl and lunge ferociously, and, if turned over on its back, can, with a thrust and twist of its mighty neck, be upright and ready for mayhem. If you approach one out of water, it opens its mouth and hisses; if you get closer, it lurches at you with such vehemence that it lifts itself off the ground, its jaws snapping savagely at empty air. Archie Carr, whose venerable *Handbook to Turtles* (1952) is the only authority on these matters I possess, states that the

disposition to strike is innate, and has been observed in hatchlings "not yet altogether free of their eggshells." An adult can
strike, he reports, "with the speed and power of a big rattle-
snake." Although Carr does not explicitly say so, the snapper
appears to be one of those animals, like the hognose snake, that
makes the most of its resemblance to a poisonous snake. Its pale
mouth gapes open like a moccasin's, and its aggressiveness involves a certain exaggerated and theatrical posturing. Its official
name specifically and subspecifically suggests the highly untur-
tlelike impression that this creates: *Chelydra serpentina serpentina*.
But the snapper, unlike the hognose, can back up its bluff. Its
first-strike capability isn't lethal, but it isn't trivial either. According to boyhood folklore, a snapper can bite a broomstick in two,
but I have seen the experiment conducted. It took a great deal
of goading to persuade the turtle to seize the broomstick at all
— it plainly would have preferred the hand that held it — but
it finally took it, held it, and crushed and pulped it. Mama's
broom handle came out looking like a piece of chewed-over
sugarcane. Putting your hand in range of a big snapper would
not be like putting it under a guillotine or ax; it would be more
like putting it under a bulldozer: a slow, complete crunching.

The shell and skin are a muddy gray; the eye, too, is of a
murky mud color. The pupil is black and shaped like a star or a
spoked wheel. Within the eye there is a strange yellowish glint,
as though you were looking down into turbid water and seeing,
in the depths of the water, light from a smoldering fire. It is one
of Nature's more nightmarish eyes. The eyes of dragonflies are
also nightmarish, but in a different way — they look inhuman,
like something out of science fiction. The same is true of the
eyes of sharks. The snapper's eye is dull, like a pig's, but inside
it there is this savage malevolence, something suggesting not
only an evil intention toward the world, but the torment of an
inner affliction. Had Milton seen one, he would have associated
it with the baleful eye of Satan, an eye reflecting some internal
hell of liquid fire — whether in Paradise or here on a soft June
day, with the bobolinks fluttering aloft and singing in the fields.
Snapping turtles did in fact once inhabit Europe, but they died
out by the end of the Pleistocene, and so were unknown to what
we think of as European history. But they look, nevertheless,

like something that Europeans had half-imagined or dimly remembered even before they came to the New World and saw
them for the first time: a snapper would do for a gargoyle, or a
grotesque parody of a knight on his horse, a thing of armored
evil.

Snappers feed on about anything, dead or alive: fish, flesh, or
fowl. The fish they catch by luring them into range with their
vermiform tongues, which may have something to do with the
role of trickster that they assume in the mythology of North
American Indians. But they can also be caught in a trap baited
with bananas. They are not fastidious: "Schmidt and Inger
(1957) tell the gruesome story of an elderly man who used a
tethered snapping turtle to recover the bodies of people who
had drowned."* We did not learn what this sinister gentleman
fed his useful pet to encourage its predilection for waterlogged
cadavers. I know on my own authority that snappers are death
on ducks, and will rise like a shadow from the oozy muck of the
bottom, under the jocund and unsuspecting drake as it briskly
preens and putters on the surface of the pond, lock sudden jaws
around one suspended leg, one webbed foot, and sink quietly
back to the depths, their weight too much for the duck to resist,
their jaws a functional illustration of necessity's sharp pinch.
There in the darkness the duck is ponderously mauled, mutilated, and eaten right down to the toenails. We watched a hen
mallard and a brood of ducklings disappear from the little pond
beside the road one summer — two or three inexplicable deduc-
tions per week — until at last only the very nervous hen and
one trusting little duckling remained. Then there was only the
duckling. It peeped and chirped and swam distractedly around
the pond in a most heart-rending fashion. I tried to trap it so
we could rear it in confinement and safety, but there was no
catching it, and the next day it was gone too.

The law of tooth and nail is all right with me when it involves
hawks and mice, or foxes and geese, or even sharks and swim-
mers — there is a redeeming elegance in most predators, a
breathtaking speed and agility. If I thought I could tempt an

* *Turtles: Perspectives and Research,* edited by M. Harless and H. Morlock (New
York: John Wiley and Sons, 1979), p. 289.

eagle to stoop, I'd gladly stake my best laying hen in the yard to see it happen. But a snapper is an ugly proposition, more like cancer than a crab is. If one grabs your finger, you do not get the finger back — that too is boyhood folklore, but I have never tested it. Some propositions call for implicit faith, even in these post-theological and deconstructing days.

Unlike most of the other freshwater turtles, snappers never emerge to bask on rocks or logs. They come out in late spring or early summer; their emergence here coincides with the vetch, the stitchwort, bedstraw, and hawkweed. They need sandy soil to lay their eggs in, and such soil isn't always close to the sorts of boggy, miry waters they inhabit. They will often go overland a surprising distance before finally deciding on a spot to dig. Roadbeds and railway embankments can provide good sites that are reasonably convenient to their usual habitats. Creatures of darkness, cursing the light, they lumber up from pond or river, and one morning you awake to the frantic yapping of dogs and go out, and there, foul and hissing, like some chieftain of the underworld at last summoned to justice and surrounded by reporters and cameras, stands a great gravid snapper. The flesh of her neck, legs, and tail — all the parts that ought to fit inside the shell but don't — has, on the underside, a grimy yellowish cast to it, is podgy, lewd, wrinkled, and soft. In Maine there will normally be one or two big leeches hanging on to the nether parts. These portions of the animal seem to have no proper covering — no scales, feathers, hair, or taut, smooth epidermis. It looks as though the internal anatomy had been extruded, or the whole animal plucked or flayed.

I'm not sure how much of this natural history Ricky McIver and I understood when we were nine or ten; we only knew that, trekking down a sandy road in midsummer, we would suddenly come upon a baby snapper, bustling along with remarkable purpose, as though on its way to catch a train. Of course we would catch the turtle, and one of us would take it home and put it in a dishpan with a little water and keep it under the bed, where all night long there would be the tinny scraping of little claws, as the turtle went round and round inside the pan. Sometimes one would escape, instigating a general panicky search of the room and the house. It would turn up far back under a sofa or cabinet, covered with dust and weakened by dehydration, but still able to muster a parched snap and hiss. Finally we would let it go into a drainage ditch. We never came upon a mother laying her eggs — given the heat, perhaps they did that at night down south. Up here I seem to come across one or two of them every year, and have learned to look for them along road shoulders in late June.

I backed the car up to the house to get Susan and Hannah — the older girls were still asleep — and our old pointer Jacob roused himself and walked down with us, conferring by his stiff-jointed, wheezing Nestorian solemnity an air of officialdom upon the occasion, as though we were a commission sent out to investigate an unregistered alien that had showed up in Bowdoinham. Hannah went along grudgingly, with a five-year-old's saving sense that any time the parents promised to show you something interesting, they probably had concealed motives of one sort or another. When we got to the turtle, Jacob hoisted his hackles, clapped his tail between his legs, and circled her a few times, then sat down and barked once. The turtle raised herself on her forelegs, head up, mouth agape; her hostility did not focus on any one of us so much as on the whole situation in which she found herself. Hannah looked at all of this and pronounced it boring; could she have a friend over to play? The dog seemed to feel that he had discharged his obligations by barking, and shambled over to the edge of the field, pawed fretfully at the ground, then settled himself, curled up, sighed, and went to sleep. The whole thing was beginning to take on the unpromising aspect of Nature Study, an ersatz experience.

We walked around behind the turtle, and there did make a discovery of sorts. Through all of the commotion that surrounded her anterior end, her hind legs were methodically digging. Their motion was impressively regular and mechanical — first one leg thrust down into the hole, then the other, smooth and steady as pistons. Whatever the snapper felt or thought about her situation plainly did not concern the legs, which were wholly intent on procreation. It seemed an awkward way to dig, the hind foot being a clumsy and inflexible instrument anyway, and having to carry on its operations huggermugger like that,

out of sight and out of mind too, if the turtle could be said to
have a mind. We could not see down into the hole, only the legs
alternately reaching down, and a rim of excavated sand that was
slowly growing up behind the rim of the turtle's shell. I was later
to learn that the digging action, once begun, is as involuntary as
the contractions of a mammal giving birth, and even a turtle
missing one hind leg will dig in the same fashion, thrusting
down first with the good leg, then with the amputated stump,
until the job is done.

Hannah, an aficionado of the sandbox, permitted herself a
cautious interest in this end of the turtle's operations, and
wanted to inspect her hole. I wasn't sure about the ethics of this.
It is a general law that you don't disturb nesting creatures; it
was, after all, no fault of the snapper's if she failed to excite in
us the veneration that generally attaches to scenes of maternity
and nativity. On the other hand, she had chosen a bad place. I
could see where my neighbor Gene Hamrick had carefully
driven around her, going well over onto the shoulder to do so.
Other neighbors might be less considerate, and the nest itself
would, in any event, be packed hard by the traffic in a few
weeks, rendering the future of the eggs and hatchlings highly
uncertain. So I grasped her tail and hoisted her up. Aloft, she
held herself rigidly spread-eagle, her head and neck parallel to
the earth, and hissed mightily as I took her over and put her in
the little ditch that drains the pond. Because of the recent rain,
the ditch was flowing, and as soon as her front feet touched the
water, all of her aggression ceased, and she seemed bent on
nothing but escape. She had surprising power as she scrabbled
at the banks and bottom of the ditch; it was like holding on to a
miniature bulldozer. I let her go and she surged off down the
ditch, head submerged and carapace just awash. She stopped
once and raised her head and fixed us with her evil eye; the
mouth dropped open in a last defiance. Then she lowered her
head again and waddled out of sight.

We examined the hole. It looked as though it had been dug
with a tablespoon — shapely and neat, a little wider at the bottom than at the top. There were no eggs. Hannah set methodically about refilling the hole, out of an instinct that seemed as
compelling as the one that dug it. As she disturbed the sand, I

caught a strong musky scent where the turtle had lain. That scent, which was also on my hand, recalled something that the sight of the turtle had not recalled, and that was a peculiar memory connected to the biggest snapping turtle I ever saw, or ever intend to see.

In my high school summers, I worked for the Burroughs Timber Company, which was owned by a group of my father's first cousins. My immediate boss was Mr. Henry Richards; the crew consisted of the two of us and two cousins, Billy and Wendell Watson. Mr. Richards was not an educated man, and had in his younger days been something of a drinker and a fighter, but he had straightened himself out and gotten some training in forestry. He was good at his job, as far as I could judge — his job largely consisting of cruising and marking timber, overseeing logging operations, and generally keeping track of the company's woodlands. These were mostly small tracts, seldom more than a few hundred acres, scattered from one end of Horry County to the other. Mr. Richards was handsome: lean and weathered, with dark wavy hair, sleepy eyes, and the sort of indolent rasping voice that conveyed the authority of someone who had not always been perfectly nice. He was in his forties. Billy and Wendell were younger by ten or fifteen years, and both were countrymen, from the vicinity of Crabtree Creek.

I am not sure what degree of cousinage joined Billy and Wendell. The Watsons, like the Burroughses and a great many other families in the country, were an extended and numerous clan, and such clans generally divided into what religion had taught us to regard as the children of promise and the children of perdition, or sheep and goats. The binary opposition would express itself in terms of whatever general station in life the family occupied. Thus my Burroughs cousins tended to be either sober, quietly respectable merchants and landowners concerned with tobacco and timber — or drunkards, wastrels, and womanizers, men notorious in Horry County for the frequency with which they married and divorced.

Wendell belonged to the reputable branch of the Watson family — small farmers who held on to their land and led hard, frugal lives. In town, such people were referred to, somewhat inscrutably, as the salt of the earth. Billy came from the other side — poachers, moonshiners, people likely to be handy with a straight razor, who kept six or eight gaunt and vicious hounds (half of them stolen and all of them wormy) chained in the yard, along with a few unfettered chickens and a ragged mule, but who could hardly be called farmers. Their style of life and economy had probably been formed by the county's long history as a demifrontier, and had changed only minimally to accommodate the twentieth century when it eventually arrived.

Wendell was one of those rare county people who, out of some reaction to the dirt and despair of agriculture, had a highly developed fastidiousness. His face was bony, angular, and prim around the mouth; he always wore a dapper straw hat instead of the usual cap, so that his brow was never browned or reddened by the sun. His work shirt and pants were neatly creased, and I never saw them stained with sweat. He would stop for a moment in the resinous, stifling heat of a pine wood, extract a red bandanna handkerchief from his pocket, unfold it, and delicately dab at his brow, removing his hat to do so. Then he would look at the moist handkerchief the way you might look at a small cut or blister, with a slight consternation and distaste, and then fold the handkerchief, first into halves, then into quarters, then into eighths, until it fit back into his hip pocket as neatly as a billfold.

He was lanky, with comically large feet and big, bony, lightly freckled hands and wrists, and you would have expected him to have no strength or stamina at all. But he could use any of the tools we used — bushax or machete or grubbing hoe — with no sign of strain or fatigue, all day long, holding the tool gingerly, so that you expected him to drop it at any moment, but keeping a pace that the rest of us could not sustain. He had a crooked, embarrassed grin and said little. In the midday heat, sometimes we would take our lunch to an abandoned tenant house, to eat on the porch and catch whatever breeze funneled through the doorway. Then three of us would stretch out on the warped floorboards, hats over our faces, and doze for half an hour. Wendell never did. He would sit with his back to one of the rough timbers that held up the porch, pull out his pocket knife, and set about pruning his fingernails; then he would stick the knife into a floorboard with an air of finality, lift his head and stare out over the fields with the intense, noncommittal scrutiny of a poker player examining his cards, or of what he was, a countryman watching the big banks of cumulus clouds pile up on a July afternoon. Or he might whittle himself a toothpick and ply it carefully between his teeth, or study a map of the tract we were to cruise in the afternoon. He always kept a watch over himself, as though he feared he might otherwise grow slack and slovenly. He did not own a car, and was permitted to use the company truck to go to and from his house, and to keep it over the weekend. On Monday mornings it would be all washed and cleaned; Mr. Richards would ask him whether he'd been courting in it or was he just planning to sell it. Wendell would only laugh awkwardly at himself, and at his inability to think of a smart retort.

Billy Watson, to hear him tell it, was chiefly proud of having spent six years in the fourth grade, at the end of which time he was sixteen and not legally obligated to go to school anymore. Mr. Richards could not get over it. "Damn, Billy," he said more than once, "don't seem like you're *that* stupid." He'd say it because he relished Billy's invariable answer, always delivered in the same tone of pious resignation, as though he were speaking of some cross that the Lord had, in His ungovernable wisdom, given him to bear: "Oh, I wa'n't stupid. Just ornery." He was a big man, about six foot three, with powerful, rounded shoulders. He had a peculiar sort of physical complacence with himself, was loose and supple as a cat, and could squat or hunker longer and more comfortably, it seemed, than the average man could sit in an armchair. His hair was lank and reddish brown, and was usually seconded by a four- or five-day growth of stubble beard, stained with tobacco juice at the lower right corner of the mouth. It was a big, misshapen mouth, distended by the pouch in one cheek that is the outcome of a lifetime of chewing tobacco — Day's Work or Sun Apple. His teeth were few and far between, worn and yellowed as an old mule's. He had certainly never been to a dentist in his life, and might have been surprised to learn that such a profession existed.

Billy was a river rat; if he could have, he would have lived by doing nothing but trapping and fishing. He sometimes fished

for sport: he could handle his stubby casting rod as though he
had a kind of intelligence in his hands, placing each cast, cast
after cast, far back under overhanging trees, with no pause, no
hesitation, no calculation of the risks of getting the plug hung
on a branch or snag. There was so much rhythm in it that you'd
find yourself patting your foot if you watched him long enough.
But he wasn't particular about how he caught fish or what fish
he caught: redbreast, bream, goggle-eye, stumpknocker, war-
mouth, bass, catfish, eel, mudfish, redfin, pike, shad, Virginia
perch — even the herring that ran upriver in the spring.

If early on a Saturday morning in the spring you happened
to be down by Mishoe's Fish Market, a little frame building
perched by the edge of Kingston Lake, you might see Billy
slipping easily along the near bank of the lake, in a ridiculously
undersized one-man paddling boat. He'd give you a look before
he drew up to the landing, ask you if there was anybody there.
You'd look around for only one thing, a yellow car with a long
antenna, because that might be someone from the state fish and
game department, which kept an eye on Mr. Mishoe, Not seeing
it, you'd say no, nobody here but old man Mishoe. There was a
strange, watery peace to it. All the drab, ordinary life of the
town was just a few hundred feet away, but here was Billy glid-
ing silently up to the landing, dropping the paddle with muffled
reverberation into the boat bottom, then stepping out, shackling
the little boat to a cypress, and bending over to lift from it two
moist croker sacks, each squirming with his night's work. You'd
want to follow him through the fish market to the back, where
Mr. Mishoe and one or two helpers would be cleaning and fil-
leting fish. They'd stop to watch Billy empty his sacks into a
cleaning sink — the secret, active ingredients of river and river
swamp, wriggling, flapping, and gasping there in the back room
of a store. The catfish, mudfish, eels, and shad were classified
as nongame species and could, within certain limits, be fished
and marketed commercially. The rest were pure contraband,
which presumably increased their market value. Whatever their
cash value was, Billy would receive it in a few greasy bills, walk
up to the drugstore on Main Street, and buy himself a cup of
coffee and a doughnut. Townspeople who did not know him
would edge away from the counter: he was a dirty, rough-look-

ing man, unlaced boots flapping open at his ankles. His eyes, which were small and deep-set, reflected light strangely; they were green and, in the strict sense of the word, *crazed*, as though the surface of the eye were webbed with minute cracks. You could not tell where they focused.

But Billy wasn't crazy or violent either, as far as I ever heard. Education is liberating in ways it does not always intend, and, by keeping Billy in the fourth grade, surrounded, year after year, by an unaging cohort of ten-year-olds, it liberated him from most notions of responsibility, foresight, or ambition. He had successfully learned how to avoid promotion, a lesson that ought to be learned and taught more often than it is. He had worked out at the plywood mill, upriver from Conway, and told me he had also done some house painting. But working for Mr. Richards and Burroughs Timber suited him best, and he was a valuable employee. He probably knew more about the company land than the company did, having hunted, fished, or trapped on most of it. When we would cruise timber, one of us would set the compass course for him, and then he could follow it, keeping careful count of his paces, marking each of the stations where we would stop and inventory all the timer in a quarter-acre plot, while Billy went ahead to the next station and marked the next plot. Often we would end the day on the back line of a tract, a long way from the truck. The logical thing in thick woods was to plot a course back to the truck and follow the compass out, but Billy would drop the compass into his pocket and strike off through the woods as nonchalantly as a man going across a parking lot. We'd follow. He did everything in such a headlong, unconsidering way that those of us who had gotten beyond the fourth grade could never bring ourselves to trust him entirely, and sooner or later somebody would call out: "Billy, you *sure* this is the right way?" "Time'll tell, boys; time'll tell," he'd call back. Time always did, and we would suddenly emerge from the woods, and there would be the road, and there would be the truck. Townspeople who knew Billy lost no occasion to point him out to you: "That's Billy Watson. Ain't got a lick of sense, but you won't find a better fisherman in this county."

*

We were working down toward the Pee Dee River, on a low, sandy ridge at the edge of the river swamp. The company had cleared the ridge two or three years earlier and planted it in pine seedlings, but now the hardwoods, regenerating from the stump, threatened to reclaim it for themselves. The smaller hardwoods we chopped down with machete or bushax; the larger ones we girdled — gouged a ring around the trunk, half an inch deep, which cut off the tree's supply of food and water, and left it to die on its feet. For this we had a machine called the Little Beaver. It consisted of a four-cycle Briggs and Stratton engine mounted on a pack frame, with a flexible hydraulic hose, at the end of which was a notched disk that did the girdling. The machine seemed to have no muffler at all — it was louder than a chainsaw, hot on the back, and the noise and vibration of it were stunning. It was late July, and that sandy patch of scrub oak and seedling pine afforded no protection from the sun. We would trade off the Little Beaver at thirty-minute intervals; not even Wendell volunteered to take any more of its hammering than that.

At noon, as was the custom, we knocked off. Mr. Richards drove out to the Georgetown highway. He knew of a country store across the river, over in Georgetown County, and proposed to take us there for lunch. It was owned by a man named Marlowe. I'd seen it often enough, the usual little mean, flat-topped cinder-block building, painted white, with a screened door for ventilation, within which you could expect to find the standard items: canned goods, bread, a bit of fishing tackle, and one or two coolers full of soft drinks and milk. As we drove, Mr. Richards talked about the Marlowes, and we learned that they were an infamous clan, divided into two subspecific groups which intermingled freely: the regular Marlowes and the murdering Marlowes. If you insulted a regular Marlowe — for example, by catching him stealing your boat — he would, within a week or ten days, set your woodlot on fire, slash your tires, or shoot your dog. But if you did the same thing to a murdering Marlowe, why then your troubles were over — instantly and permanently. That is what Mr. Richards said, but he was something of a talker and not above hyperbole. We didn't take it seriously and probably weren't meant to. Wendell didn't say much — he never did — but he had a tight little grin and plainly didn't believe what he was hearing. Billy was keeping his eye on the swamp and river as we crossed over them — the Pee Dee was outside his usual territory, and he'd been talking all morning about how he aimed to fish her this fall, from Gallivant's Ferry clear down to Yauhannah Bridge, where we were now. When we pulled off the highway and parked in the thin shade of an oak beside Marlowe's store, Mr. Richards said for us to remember to act polite; we didn't need any trouble with these folks, and neither did Burroughs Timber.

When you walk out of the dazzle of noon into a little roadside store like that, it is almost like walking into a movie theater, the darkness seems so great. By the door was a counter with a cash register on it and a man behind it, and there was a shadowy figure in the back of the store, who turned out to be a boy younger than myself, sweeping the single aisle between the shelves. And there was a figure seated to the left of the door as I came in, and on the floor, at my feet, there was a sudden lunging rush.

If you have gotten this far, you have the advantage of knowing that it was, of course, a snapping turtle, but I did not. In the South Carolina woods in the summertime, snakes are never far out of your mind, and, for the first hour of the day, you watch your step. Fatigue and distraction set in soon enough, and you forget about snakes, and you could easily go two weeks without having any particular reason to remember them. But sooner or later you would come upon one, usually a little copperhead, neatly coiled at your feet, and so perfectly merged with the shadow-dappled floor of the forest that you'd begin to worry about all the ones that you hadn't happened to see. So when I heard the hiss and the rush I jumped.

The man in the chair laughed: "Scared you, didden he? I be goddam if you didden *jump*, boy. Don't believe I ever knew a white boy to jump like that." By this time I could see what it was, a snapping turtle stretched out there on the cement floor. It was a huge one — the carapace was matted with dried algae; the head was about the size of a grapefruit. The whole creature could not have been fitted into a washtub. It looked, once I had calmed down enough to look at it, ancient and tired, as though oppressed by its own ponderous and ungainly bulk. The room was thick with a swampy, musky smell, which at the time I did not realize came from the turtle. When I smelled it again in Maine, it did not specifically recall the physical scene — the turtle, the Marlowes, the dark little store. Instead, it brought back directly a sensation of alarm, confusion, and disorientation, in about the same way that the smell of ether does not bring back the operating room so much as it brings back the vertiginous feeling of the self whirling away from itself.

The others came in right behind me. I was too mortified by my own embarrassment and disgrace to see how they reacted to the whole scene, but I think they must have enjoyed it. It had been a good joke, to place the turtle just inside the threshold like that; if it had been played on anyone else, I would have laughed myself. Billy looked down at the turtle and said he'd never seen one that big. In the corner of the evil mouth, which was gaping open, was a big hook, with a piece of heavy line attached to it. "Caught him on a trotline, I see," said Billy.

Trotlines — a short length of line tied to a branch that overhangs the water, so that the baited hook is just below the surface — were and are a common way of fishing, and they were perfectly legal for catching certain species of fish at certain times of year. But they were so widely used by poachers that to call a man a *trotliner* might, if the man were sufficiently thin-skinned, seem tantamount to an indictment. I don't know. I only know that when Billy said "trotline" the man in the chair gave him a sudden look and got up.

When he stood, he lurched and swayed, and we could see that he was ruinously drunk. He was wiry, short, and grizzled, wore knee-high rubber boots with the swamp mud still on them. He glared at Billy: "Your name ain't *McNair*, is it?" Billy said it wasn't and tried to ask the man if anything besides turtles had been biting that morning, but the man kept on: "You sure it ain't *McNair*? You sure you ain't some of them wildlife boys come down here? What you got that aerial on your truck for if you ain't?" He was right about at least that much. The company truck did have a two-way radio, and it was painted yellow, which gave it an official look, but it seemed not simply ridiculous but perverse for the man to take the four of us — hot, dirty, and dressed in ordinary work clothes — for some kind of under-cover squad from the Department of Fish and Wildlife.

The man behind the counter told him to shut up and sit down, but he spoke in a halfhearted way, as though he knew it was useless. The boy in the back of the store, where I'd gone to get some crackers, had stopped sweeping and gone up to the front to watch the fun. The drunk man was telling Billy exactly what he'd do to McNair if McNair ever stuck his nose in here; he got louder and louder, and seemed to be working himself into the conviction that Billy really was McNair. I got my crackers and came up to the counter. It did not occur to me that anything serious was going on, and even if it was, there was no reason to worry. The drunk man's head scarcely came to Billy's shoulder. It seemed that all of this might in some way still be part of the joke; if not, it would make a good joke to tell, how Billy Watson, of all people, had been mistaken for a game warden.

I was paying for my crackers when the man said: "Let McNair come in here and I'll show him *this*," and I looked up and he had a pistol in his hand. It came from under the counter, as I later learned — the drunk man had reached over and grabbed it when the man behind the counter had turned to the cash register.

It changed everything; the world began to slip away. I had no impulse to act, and did not exactly feel fear. It was more an instinct to call out to everybody, to say *Wait a minute; how did we get here? What's going on? Let's talk this over and see if we can't make sense of it.* Billy's back was to me. The pistol was a snub-nosed revolver — a heavy, ugly, blunt thing. It was as though I could see through Billy's eyes the rounded noses of the cartridges in the open ends of the cylinders. Everything was utterly distinct and utterly unreal: we were under water, or had fallen asleep and were dreaming and were struggling mightily to waken ourselves from the dream before it reached the point it was meant to reach. Nobody moved to interfere. The thing was going to take its course.

The drunk man had the pistol right in Billy's face, shaking it. His own face was white with rage. "I'd show him *this*," he said, "and *this* is what I'd do with it." He reached down so abruptly and savagely that I winced, and he snatched the turtle by the tail and dragged it out the door, onto the concrete pad beside the gas pumps. The weight of the turtle was great; the man straightened himself slowly, as though only his wrath had enabled him to haul it this far. The turtle seemed weary, deflated, too long out of water. The man nudged its head with his boot, and the turtle hissed and struck feebly toward him. The man glared down at it, letting his rage recover and build back in him. He looked like a diver, gathering to plunge. The turtle's mouth hung open; when it hissed again the man's arm suddenly jerked down with the pistol and he shot it, shattering the turtle's head. "That's what I'd do to that goddamned McNair."

The man came back in and sat down heavily, spent, and the world returned to its ordinary focus. Blood had spattered onto the man's boot and pant leg. By the time we finished buying lunch and were ready to leave, he was snoring easily. The man behind the cash register told the boy to tote that thing off into the bushes, and the boy did, dragging the turtle by the tail, the blood still welling from the smashed head. When we got back to the truck I glanced over there, not wanting to, and could see the head swarming with flies, the big feet limp in the sand.

As we were getting into the truck, Wendell (who seldom said anything) said, "Well." We looked at him. He elaborated, his face perfectly deadpan: "Well. Good thing none of them *bad* Marlowes happened to be in today."

Hannah finished filling the hole, tamped the sand smooth, and brushed her palms briskly against each other, signifying that the job was done. The dog roused himself and we all walked back up toward the house. A yellow warbler flew across in front of us — a quick flash of color — perched on a willow branch, sang its hurried, wheezy song, and dropped from sight. Birdsong lasts longer into the morning on these cool, overcast days. The bobolinks were still busy about it, a song that sounds something like an audiotape being rewound at high speed. A robin in a clump of sumacs sang its careful phrase, as though for the edification of less gifted birds, then listened to itself a moment, head cocked appreciatively, then sang the phrase again. A meadowlark whistled from a fencepost. New England seemed, as it often does, more perfect in the intensity of its seasonal moment, and in the whole seasonal cycle that can be felt within the moment, than any place has a right to be. I felt the fatal parental urge, wanting to point out to Hannah all the richness that surrounded her. But to Hannah such familiar sights and sounds were equivalent to presuppositions, invisible until disturbed.

Animals fit themselves enigmatically into the secondary ecology of human thinking. "They are all beasts of burden, in a sense," says Thoreau, "made to carry some portion of our thoughts." Turtles are especially burdened. In Hindu myth, Vishnu, floating on the cosmic sea, takes the form of a tortoise and sustains the world on his back. North American Indians, unacquainted with any sizable tortoises, nevertheless had the same myth of Turtle as Atlas. The Senecans told how the first people lived in the sky, until a woman, whose transgression involved a tree, was thrown out. Below her — very far below — there was only water. A few water birds were there, and these, seeing her descending, hurried to prepare a place for her. They dived to the bottom, found mud and a turtle, and persuaded the turtle to let them place mud on its back, and make a dry spot for her to land on. The woman landed; vegetation grew up out of the mud; and the familiar world we know came into being.

But the Indians weren't through with the turtle, or vice versa. Turtle turns trickster and, disguised as a young brave, seduces the daughter of the first woman. When the daughter realizes what her lover is, she dies, and from her body, as she prophesies in dying, grow the first stalks of corn and the equivocal blessings of agriculture. Among other tribes, in other myths, Turtle continues his depredations. Many tribes tell of his going on the warpath against the first people, who at last catch him and prepare his death. They threaten him with fire; he tells them that he loves fire. They threaten him with boiling water; he begs to be put immediately into the kettle, because he so relishes being boiled. They threaten to throw him into the river. "Anything but that," says Turtle, and so they throw him in. He sticks out his snout and laughs; they curse him and throw sticks, but he easily avoids them. And so Turtle takes up, one would surmise, the life of a snapper, coming ashore only briefly each year, seeming about as old as the earth, and spreading consternation. God knows what burden of thought the big snapper had borne for the drunk man at Yauhannah Bridge — he symbolized, I believe, a good deal more than the man's adversary, McNair.

I found myself wishing that Hannah had stumbled upon this morning's turtle herself and had confronted the potent oddity of the beast without having it all explained away for her. It might have stood a better chance then than it did now of becoming a fact in her imagination: something she would eventually remember and think about and think with from her days as a country girl. But what any child will think or remember is beyond anybody's knowing, including its own. The turtle had disappeared down the ditch; its hole had been filled. Meanwhile, Hannah let us know that we had on our hands a Tuesday morning in June, which was, with kindergarten over, a problem to be solved. Could she have a friend over? Could we go to town?

FRANK CONROY

Think About It

WHEN I WAS sixteen I worked selling hot dogs at a stand in the
Fourteenth Street subway station in New York City, one level
above the trains and one below the street, where the crowds
continually flowed back and forth. I worked with three Puerto
Rican men who could not speak English. I had no Spanish, and
although we understood each other well with regard to the tasks
at hand, sensing and adjusting to each other's body movements
in the extremely confined space in which we operated, I felt
isolated with no one to talk to. On my break I came out from
behind the counter and passed the time with two old black men
who ran a shoeshine stand in a dark corner of the corridor. It
was a poor location, half hidden by columns, and they didn't
have much business. I would sit with my back against the wall
while they stood or moved around their ancient elevated stand,
talking to each other or to me, but always staring into the distance as they did so.

As the weeks went by I realized that they never looked at
anything in their immediate vicinity — not at me or their stand
or anybody who might come within ten or fifteen feet. They did
not look at approaching customers once they were inside the
perimeter. Save for the instant it took to discern the color of the
shoes, they did not even look at what they were doing while they
worked, but rubbed in polish, brushed, and buffed by feel while
looking over their shoulders, into the distance, as if awaiting the
arrival of an important person. Of course there wasn't all that
much distance in the underground station, but their behavior

was so focused and consistent they seemed somehow to transcend the physical. A powerful mood was created, and I came almost to believe that these men could see through walls, through girders, and around corners to whatever hyperspace it was where whoever it was they were waiting and watching for would finally emerge. Their scattered talk was hip, elliptical, and hinted at mysteries beyond my white boy's ken, but it was the staring off, the long, steady staring off, that had me hypnotized. I left for a better job, with handshakes from both of them, without understanding what I had seen.

Perhaps ten years later, after playing jazz with black musicians in various Harlem clubs, hanging out uptown with a few young artists and intellectuals, I began to learn from them something of the extraordinarily varied and complex riffs and rituals embraced by different people to help themselves get through life in the ghetto. Fantasy of all kinds — from playful to dangerous — was in the very air of Harlem. It was the spice of uptown life.

Only then did I understand the two shoeshine men. They were trapped in a demeaning situation in a dark corner in an underground corridor in a filthy subway system. Their continuous staring off was a kind of statement, a kind of dance. Our bodies are here, went the statement, but our souls are receiving nourishment from distant sources only we can see. They were powerful magic dancers, sorcerers almost, and thirty-five years later I can still feel the pressure of their spell.

The light bulb may appear over your head, is what I'm saying, but it may be a while before it actually goes on. Early in my attempts to learn jazz piano, I used to listen to recordings of a fine player named Red Garland, whose music I admired. I couldn't quite figure out what he was doing with his left hand, however; the chords eluded me. I went uptown to an obscure club where he was playing with his trio, caught him on his break, and simply asked him. "Sixths," he said cheerfully. And then he went away.

I didn't know what to make of it. The basic jazz chord is the seventh, which comes in various configurations, but it is what it is. I was a self-taught pianist, pretty shaky on theory and harmony, and when he said sixths I kept trying to fit the information into what I already knew, and it didn't fit. But it stuck in my mind — a tantalizing mystery.

A couple of years later, when I began playing with a bass player, I discovered more or less by accident that if the bass played the root and I played a sixth based on the fifth note of the scale, a very interesting chord involving both instruments emerged. Ordinarily, I suppose I would have skipped over the matter and not paid much attention, but I remembered Garland's remark and so I stopped and spent a week or two working out the voicings, and greatly strengthened my foundations as a player. I had remembered what I hadn't understood, you might say, until my life caught up with the information and the light bulb went on.

I remember another, more complicated example from my sophomore year at the small liberal-arts college outside Philadelphia. I seemed never to be able to get up in time for breakfast in the dining hall. I would get coffee and a doughnut in the Coop instead — a basement area with about a dozen small tables where students could get something to eat at odd hours. Several mornings in a row I noticed a strange man sitting by himself with a cup of coffee. He was in his sixties, perhaps, and sat straight in his chair with very little extraneous movement. I guessed he was some sort of distinguished visitor to the college who had decided to put in some time at a student hangout. But no one ever sat with him. One morning I approached his table and asked if I could join him.

"Certainly," he said. "Please do." He had perhaps the clearest eyes I had ever seen, like blue ice, and to be held in their steady gaze was not, at first, an entirely comfortable experience. His eyes gave nothing away about himself while at the same time creating in me the eerie impression that he was looking directly into my soul. He asked a few quick questions, as if to put me at my ease, and we fell into conversation. He was William O. Douglas from the Supreme Court, and when he saw how startled I was he said, "Call me Bill. Now tell me what you're studying and why you get up so late in the morning." Thus began a series of talks that stretched over many weeks. The fact that I was an ignorant sophomore with literary pretensions who knew nothing about the law didn't seem to bother him. We talked about everything from Shakespeare to the possibility of life on other planets. One day I mentioned that I was going to have dinner with Judge Learned Hand. I explained that Hand was my girl-friend's grandfather. Douglas nodded, but I could tell he was surprised at the coincidence of my knowing the chief judge of the most important court in the country save the Supreme Court itself. After fifty years on the bench Judge Hand had beome a famous man, both in and out of legal circles — a living legend, to his own dismay. "Tell him hello and give him my best regards," Douglas said.

Learned Hand, in his eighties, was a short, barrel-chested man with a large, square head, huge, thick, bristling eyebrows, and soft brown eyes. He radiated energy and would sometimes bark out remarks or questions in the living room as if he were in court. His humor was sharp, but often leavened with a touch of self-mockery. When something caught his funny bone he would burst out with explosive laughter — the laughter of a man who enjoyed laughing. He had a large repertoire of dra-matic expressions involving the use of his eyebrows — very use-ful, he told me conspiratorially, when looking down on things from behind the bench. (The court stenographer could not rec-ord the movement of his eyebrows.) When I told him I'd been talking to William O. Douglas, they first shot up in exaggerated surprise, and then lowered and moved forward in a glower.

"*Justice* William O. Douglas, young man," he admonished. "Justice Douglas, if you please." About the Supreme Court in general, Hand insisted on a tone of profound respect. Little did I know that in private correspondence he had referred to the Court as "The Blessed Saints, Cherubim and Seraphim," "The Jolly Boys," "The Nine Tin Jesuses," "The Nine Blameless Ethi-opians," and my particular favorite, "The Nine Blessed Chalices of the Sacred Effluvium."

Hand was badly stooped and had a lot of pain in his lower back. Martinis helped, but his strict Yankee wife approved of only one before dinner. It was my job to make the second and somehow slip it to him. If the pain was particularly acute he would get out of his chair and lie flat on the rug, still talking, and finish his point without missing a beat. He flattered me by asking for my impression of Justice Douglas, instructed me to convey his warmest regards, and then began talking about the Dennis case, which he described as a particularly tricky and difficult case involving the prosecution of eleven leaders of the Communist party. He had just started in on the First Amendment and free speech when we were called in to dinner.

William O. Douglas loved the outdoors with a passion, and we fell into the habit of having coffee in the Coop and then strolling under the trees down toward the duck pond. About the Dennis case, he said something to this effect: "Eleven Communists arrested by the government. Up to no good, said the government; dangerous people, violent overthrow, etc. First Amendment, said the defense, freedom of speech, etc." Douglas stopped walking. "Clear and present danger."

"What?" I asked. He often talked in a telegraphic manner, and one was expected to keep up with him. It was sometimes like listening to a man thinking out loud.

"Clear and present danger," he said. "That was the issue. Did they constitute a clear and present danger? I don't think so. I think everybody took the language pretty far in Dennis." He began walking, striding along quickly. Again, one was expected to keep up with him. "The FBI was all over them. Phones tapped, constant surveillance. How could it be clear and present danger with the FBI watching every move they made? That's a ginkgo," he said suddenly, pointing at a tree. "A beauty. You don't see those every day. Ask Hand about clear and present danger."

I was in fact reluctant to do so. Douglas's argument seemed to me to be crushing — the last word, really — and I didn't want to embarrass Judge Hand. But back in the living room, on the second martini, the old man asked about Douglas. I sort of scratched my nose and recapitulated the conversation by the ginkgo tree.

"What?" Hand shouted. "Speak up, sir, for heaven's sake."

"He said the FBI was watching them all the time so there couldn't be a clear and present danger," I blurted out, blushing as I said it.

A terrible silence filled the room. Hand's eyebrows writhed on his face like two huge caterpillars. He leaned forward in the wing chair, his face settling, finally, into a grim expression. "I am astonished," he said softly, his eyes holding mine, "at Justice Douglas's newfound faith in the Federal Bureau of Investigation." His big, granite head moved even closer to mine, until I could smell the martini. "I had understood him to consider it a politically corrupt, incompetent organization, directed by a power-crazed lunatic." I realized I had been holding my breath throughout all of this, and as I relaxed, I saw the faintest trace of a smile cross Hand's face. Things are sometimes more complicated than they first appear, his smile seemed to say. The old man leaned back. "The proximity of the danger is something to think about. Ask him about that. See what he says."

I chewed the matter over as I returned to campus. Hand had pointed out some of Douglas's language about the FBI from other sources that seemed to bear out his point. I thought about the words "clear and present danger," and the fact that if you looked at them closely they might not be as simple as they had first appeared. What degree of danger? Did the word "present" allude to the proximity of the danger, or just the fact that the danger was there at all — that it wasn't an anticipated danger? Were there other hidden factors these great men were weighing of which I was unaware?

But Douglas was gone, back to Washington. (The writer in me is tempted to create a scene here — to invent one for dramatic purposes — but of course I can't do that.) My brief time as a messenger boy was over, and I felt a certain frustration, as if, with a few more exchanges, the matter of *Dennis* v. *United States* might have been resolved to my satisfaction. They'd left me high and dry. But, of course, it is precisely because the matter did not resolve that has caused me to think about it, off and on, all these years. "The Constitution," Hand used to say to me flatly, "is a piece of paper. The Bill of Rights is a piece of paper." It was many years before I understood what he meant. Documents alone do not keep democracy alive, nor maintain the state of law. There is no particular safety in them. Living men and women, generation after generation, must continually remake democracy and the law, and that involves an ongoing state of tension between the past and the present which will never completely resolve.

Education doesn't end until life ends, because you never know when you're going to understand something you hadn't understood before. For me, the magic dance of the shoeshine men was the kind of experience in which understanding came with a kind of click, a resolving kind of click. The same with the experience at the piano. What happened with Justice Douglas and Judge Hand was different, and makes the point that understanding does not always mean resolution. Indeed, in our intellectual lives, our creative lives, it is perhaps those problems that will never resolve that rightly claim the lion's share of our energies. The physical body exists in a constant state of tension as it maintains homeostasis, and so too does the active mind embrace the tension of never being certain, never being absolutely sure, never being done, as it engages the world. That is our special fate, our inexpressibly valuable condition.

JOAN DIDION

Insider Baseball

FROM THE NEW YORK REVIEW OF BOOKS

1

IT OCCURRED to me, in California in June and in Atlanta in July and in New Orleans in August, in the course of watching first the California primary and then the Democratic and Republican national conventions, that it had not been by accident that the people with whom I had preferred to spend time in high school had, on the whole, hung out in gas stations. They had not run for student body office. They had not gone on to Yale or Swarthmore or DePauw, nor had they even applied. They had gotten drafted, gone through basic at Fort Ord. They had knocked up girls, and married them, had begun what they called the first night of the rest of their lives with a midnight drive to Carson City and a five-dollar ceremony performed by a justice still in his pajamas. They got jobs at the places that had laid off their uncles. They paid their bills or did not pay their bills, made down payments on tract houses, led lives on that social and economic edge referred to, in Washington and among those whose preferred locus is Washington, as "out there." They were never destined to be, in other words, communicants in what we have come to call, when we want to indicate the traditional ways in which power is exchanged and the status quo maintained in the United States, "the process."

"The process today gives everyone a chance to participate," Tom Hayden, by way of explaining "the difference" between 1968 and 1988, said to Bryant Gumbel on NBC at 7:50 A.M. on the day after Jesse Jackson spoke at the Democratic convention in Atlanta. This statement was, at a convention which had as its controlling principle the notably nonparticipatory idea of "unity," demonstrably not true, but people inside the process, constituting as they do a self-created and self-referring class, a new kind of managerial elite, tend to speak of the world not necessarily as it is but as they want people out there to believe it is. They tend to prefer the theoretical to the observable, and to dismiss that which might be learned empirically as "anecdotal." They tend to speak a language common in Washington but not specifically shared by the rest of us. They talk about "programs," and "policy," and how to "implement" them or it, about "trade-offs" and constituencies and positioning the candidate and distancing the candidate, about the "story," and how it will "play." They speak of a candidate's performance, by which they usually mean his skill at circumventing questions, not as citizens but as professional insiders, attuned to signals pitched beyond the range of normal hearing: "I hear he did all right this afternoon," they were saying to one another in the press section of the Louisiana Superdome in New Orleans on the evening Dan Quayle was or was not to be nominated for the vice presidency. "I hear he did O.K. with Brinkley." By the time the balloons fell that night the narrative had changed: "Quayle, zip," the professionals were saying as they brushed the confetti off their laptops.

These are people who speak of the process as an end in itself, connected only nominally, and vestigially, to the electorate and its possible concerns. "She used to be an issues person but now she's involved in the process," a prominent conservative said to me in New Orleans, by way of suggesting why an acquaintance who believed Jack Kemp was "speaking directly to what people out there want" had nonetheless backed George Bush. "Anything that brings the process closer to the people is all to the good," George Bush declared in his 1987 autobiography, *Looking Forward*, accepting as given this relatively recent notion that the people and the process need not automatically be on convergent tracks.

When we talk about the process, then, we are talking, increasingly, not about "the democratic process," or the general mech-

anism affording the citizens of a state a voice in its affairs, but
the reverse: a mechanism seen as so specialized that access to it
is correctly limited to its own professionals, to those who manage
policy and those who report on it, to those who run the polls
and those who quote them, to those who ask and those who
answer the questions on the Sunday shows, to the media consul-
tants, to the columnists, to the issues advisers, to those who give
the off-the-record breakfasts and to those who attend them; to
that handful of insiders who invent, year in and year out, the
narrative of public life. "I didn't realize you were a political
junkie," Marty Kaplan, the former *Washington Post* reporter and
Mondale speechwriter who is now married to Susan Estrich, the
manager of the Dukakis campaign, said when I mentioned that
I planned to write about the campaign; the assumption here,
that the narrative should be not just written only by its own
specialists but also legible only to its own specialists, is why,
finally, an American presidential campaign raises questions that
go so vertiginously to the heart of the structure.

What strikes one most vividly about such a campaign is precisely
its remoteness from the actual life of the country. The figures
are well known, and suggest a national indifference usually construed, by those inside the process, as ignorance, or "apathy," in
any case a defect not in themselves but in the clay they have
been given to mold. Only slightly more than half of those eligi-
ble to vote in the United States did vote in the 1984 presidential
election. An average 18.5 percent of what Nielsen Media Research calls the "television households" in the United States
tuned in to network coverage of the 1988 Republican convention in New Orleans, meaning 81.5 percent did not. An average
20.2 percent of these "television households" tuned in to network coverage of the 1988 Democratic convention in Atlanta,
meaning 79.8 percent did not. The decision to tune in or out
ran along predictable lines: "The demography is good even if
the households are low," a programming executive at Bozell,
Jacobs, Kenyon & Eckhardt told the *New York Times* in July
about the agency's decision to buy "campaign event" time for
Merrill Lynch on both CBS and CNN. "The ratings are about 9
percent off 1984," an NBC marketing vice president allowed,

again to the *New York Times*, "but the upscale target audience is there."

When I read this piece I recalled standing, the day before the California primary, in a dusty central California schoolyard to which the surviving Democratic candidate had come to speak one more time about what kind of president he wanted to be. The crowd was listless, restless. There were gray thunderclouds overhead. A little rain fell. "We welcome you to Silicon Valley," an official had said by way of greeting the candidate, but this was not in fact Silicon Valley: this was San Jose, and a part of San Jose particularly untouched by technological prosperity, a neighborhood in which the lowering of two-toned Impalas remained a central activity.

"I want to be a candidate who brings people together," the candidate was saying at the exact moment a man began shouldering his way past me and through a group of women with children in their arms. This was not a solid citizen, not a member of the upscale target audience. This was a man wearing a down vest and a camouflage hat, a man with a definite little glitter in his eyes, a member not of the 18.5 percent and not of the 20.2 percent but of the 81.5 percent, the 79.8 percent. "I've got to see the next president," he muttered repeatedly. "I've got something to tell him."

". . . Because that's what this party is all about," the candidate said.

"Where is he?" the man said, confused. "Who is he?"

"Get lost," someone said.

". . . Because that's what this country is all about," the candidate said.

Here we had the last true conflict of cultures in America, that between the empirical and the theoretical. On the empirical evidence this country was about two-toned Impalas and people with camouflage hats and a little glitter in their eyes, but this had not been, among people inclined to the theoretical, the preferred assessment. Nor had it even been, despite the fact that we had all stood together on the same dusty asphalt, under the same plane trees, the general assessment: this was how Joe Klein, writing a few weeks later in *New York* magazine, had described those last days before the California primary:

Breezing across California on his way to the nomination last week, Michael Dukakis crossed a curious American threshold . . . The crowds were larger, more excited now; they seemed to be searching for reasons to love him. They cheered eagerly, almost without provocation. People reached out to touch him — not to shake hands, just to touch him . . . Dukakis seemed to be making an almost subliminal passage in the public mind: he was becoming presidential.

Those June days on which Michael Dukakis did or did not cross a curious American threshold had in fact been instructive. The day that ended in the schoolyard in San Jose had at first seemed, given that it was the eve of the California primary, underscheduled, pointless, three essentially meaningless events separated by plane flights. At Taft High School in Woodland Hills that morning there had been little girls waving red and gold pompoms in front of the cameras; "Hold That Tiger," the band had played. "Dream . . . maker," the choir had crooned. "Governor Dukakis . . . this is . . . Taft High," the student council president had said. "I understand this is the first time a presidential candidate has come to Taft High," Governor Dukakis had said. "Is there any doubt . . . under those circumstances . . . who you should support?"

"Jackson," a group of Chicano boys on the back sidewalk had shouted in unison.

"That's what it's all about," Governor Dukakis had said, and "health care," and "good teachers and good teaching."

This event had been abandoned, and another materialized: a lunchtime "rally" in a downtown San Diego office plaza through which many people were passing on their way to lunch, a borrowed crowd but a less than attentive one. The cameras focused on the balloons. The sound techs picked up "La Bamba." "We're going to take child-support enforcement seriously in this country," Governor Dukakis had said, and "tough drug enforcement here and abroad." "Tough choices," he had said, and "we're going to make teaching a valued profession in this country."

Nothing said in any venue that day had seemed to have much connection with anybody listening ("I want to work with you and with working people all over this country," the candidate had said in San Diego, but people who work in San Diego do not think of themselves as "working people"), and late that afternoon, on the bus to the San Jose airport, I had asked a reporter who had traveled through the spring with the various campaigns (among those who moved from plane to plane it was agreed, by June, that the Bush campaign had the worst access to the candidate and the best food, that the Dukakis plane had average access and average food, and that the Jackson plane had full access and no time to eat) if the candidate's appearances that day did not seem a little off the point.

"Not really," the reporter said. "He covered three major markets."

Among those who traveled regularly with the campaigns, in other words, it was taken for granted that these "events" they were covering, and on which they were in fact filing, were not merely meaningless but deliberately so: occasions on which film could be shot and no mistakes made ("They hope he won't make any big mistakes," the NBC correspondent covering George Bush kept saying the evening of the September 25 debate at Wake Forest University, and, an hour and a half later, "He didn't make any big mistakes"), events designed only to provide settings for those unpaid television spots which in this case were appearing, even as we spoke, on the local news in California's three major media markets. "On the fishing trip, there was no way for television crews to get videotapes out," the *Los Angeles Times* noted a few weeks later in a piece about how "poorly designed and executed" events had interfered with coverage of a Bush campaign "environmental" swing through the Pacific Northwest. "At the lumber mill, Bush's advance team arranged camera angles so poorly that in one setup only his legs could get on camera." A Bush adviser had been quoted: "There is no reason for camera angles not being provided for. We're going to sit down and talk about these things at length."

Any traveling campaign, then, was a set, moved at considerable expense from location to location. The employer of each reporter on the Dukakis plane the day before the California primary was billed, for a total flying time of under three hours, $1,129.51; the billing to each reporter who happened, on the morning during the Democratic convention when Michael Dukakis and Lloyd Bentsen met with Jesse Jackson, to ride along on the Dukakis bus from the Hyatt Regency to the World Congress Center, a distance of perhaps ten blocks, was $217.18. There was the hierarchy of the set: there were actors, there were directors, there were script supervisors, there were grips. There was the isolation of the set, and the arrogance, the contempt for outsiders. I recall pink-cheeked young aides on the Dukakis campaign referring to themselves, innocent of irony and therefore of history, as "the best and the brightest." On the morning after the September 25 debate, Michael Oreskes of the *New York Times* gave us this memorable account of Bush aides crossing the Wake Forest campus:

> The Bush campaign measured exactly how long it would take its spokesman to walk briskly from the room in which they were watching the debate to the center where reporters were filing their articles. The answer was three-and-a-half minutes — too long for Mr. Bush's strategists, Lee Atwater, Robert Teeter and Mr. Darman. They ran the course instead as young aides cleared students and other onlookers from their path.

There was the tedium of the set: the time spent waiting for the shots to be set up, the time spent waiting for the bus to join the motorcade, the time spent waiting for telephones on which to file, the time spent waiting for the Secret Service ("the agents," they were called on the traveling campaigns, never the Secret Service, just "the agents," or "this detail," or "this rotation") to sweep the plane.

It was a routine that encouraged a certain passivity. There was the plane, or the bus, and one got on it. There was the schedule, and one followed it. There was time to file, or there was not. "We should have had a page-one story," a *Boston Globe* reporter complained to the *Los Angeles Times* after the Bush campaign had failed to provide the advance text of a Seattle "environment" speech scheduled to end only twenty minutes before the departure of the plane for California. "There are times when you sit up and moan, 'Where is Michael Deaver when you need him,' " an ABC producer said to the *Times* on this point.

A final victory, for the staff and the press on a traveling campaign, would mean not a new production but only a new location: the particular setups and shots of the campaign day (the walk on the beach, the meet-and-greet at the housing project) would fade imperceptibly, the isolation and the arrogance and the tedium all intact, into the South Lawns, the Oval Office signings, the arrivals and departures of the administration day. There would still be the "young aides." There would still be "onlookers" to be cleared from the path. Another location, another standup: "We already shot a tarmac departure," they say on the campaign planes. "This schedule has two Rose Gardens," they say in the White House press room. Ronald Reagan, when asked by David Frost how his life in the Oval Office had differed from his expectations of it, said this: ". . . I was surprised at how familiar the whole routine was — the fact that the night before I would get a schedule telling me what I'm going to do all day the next day and so forth."

American reporters "like" covering a presidential campaign (it gets them out on the road, it has balloons, it has music, it is viewed as a big story, one that leads to the respect of one's peers, to the Sunday shows, to lecture fees, and often to Washington), which is one reason why there has developed among those who do it so arresting an enthusiasm for overlooking the contradictions inherent in reporting that which occurs only in order to be reported. They are willing, in exchange for "access," to transmit the images their sources wish transmitted. They are even willing, in exchange for certain colorful details around which a "reconstruction" can be built (the "kitchen table" at which the Dukakis campaign conferred on the night Lloyd Bentsen was added to the Democratic ticket, the "slips of paper" on which key members of the Bush campaign, aboard Air Force Two on their way to New Orleans, wrote down their own guesses for vice president), to present these images not as a story the campaign wants told but as fact. This was *Time*, reporting from New Orleans:

Bush never wavered in support of the man he had lifted so high. "How's Danny doing?" he asked several times. But the Vice President never felt the compulsion to question Quayle face to face [after Quayle ran into difficulties]. The awkward investigation was left to Baker. Around noon, Quayle grew restive about answering further questions. "Let's go," he urged, but Baker pressed to know more. By early afternoon, the mood began to brighten in the Bush bunker. There were no new revelations: the media hurricane had for the moment blown out to sea.

This was Sandy Grady, reporting from Atlanta:

> Ten minutes before he was to face the biggest audience of his life, Mike Dukakis got a hug from his 84-year-old mother, Euterpe, who chided him, "You'd better be good, Michael." Dukakis grinned and said, "I'll do my best, Ma."

"Appeal to the media by exposing the [Bush campaign's] heavy-handed spin-doctoring," William Safire advised the Dukakis campaign on September 8. "We hate to be seen being manipulated."

"Periodically," the *New York Times* reported last March, "Martin Plissner, the political editor of CBS News, and Susan Morrison, a television producer and former political aide, organize gatherings of the politically connected at their home in Washington. At such parties, they organize secret ballots asking the assembled experts who will win. . . . By November 1, 1987, the results of Mr. Dole's organizing failures were apparent in a new Plissner-Morrison poll. . . ." The symbiosis here was complete, and the only outsider was the increasingly hypothetical voter, who was seen as responsive not to actual issues but to their adroit presentation: "At the moment the Republican message is simpler and more clear than ours," the Democratic chairman for California, Peter Kelly, said to the *Los Angeles Times* on August 31, complaining, on the matter of what was called the Pledge of Allegiance issue, not that it was a false issue but that Bush had seized the initiative, or "the symbolism."

"BUSH GAINING IN BATTLE OF TV IMAGES," the *Washington Post* headlined a page-one story on September 10, and quoted Jeff Greenfield, now an ABC News political reporter: "George Bush is almost always outdoors, coatless, sometimes with his sleeves rolled up, and looks ebullient and Happy Warrior-ish. Mike Dukakis is almost always indoors, with his jacket on, and almost always behind a lectern." The Bush campaign, according to that week's issue of *Newsweek*, was, because it had the superior gift for getting film shot in "dramatic settings — like Boston Harbor," winning "the all-important battle of the backdrops." A CBS producer covering the Dukakis campaign was quoted, complaining about an occasion when Governor Dukakis, speaking to students on a California beach, had faced the students instead of the camera. "The only reason Dukakis was out there on the ocean was to get his picture taken," the producer had said. "So you might as well see his face." Pictures, *Newsweek* had concluded, "often speak louder than words."

This "battle of the backdrops" story appeared on page 24 of the issue dated September 12, 1988. On pages 22 and 23 of the same issue there appeared, as illustrations for the lead National Affairs story ("Getting Down and Dirty: As the mudslinging campaign moves into full gear, Bush stays on the offensive — and Dukakis calls back his main street-fighting man"), two half-page color photographs, one of each candidate, which seemed to address the very concerns expressed on page 24 and in the *Post*. The photograph of Vice President Bush showed him indoors, with his jacket on, and behind a lectern. That of Governor Dukakis showed him outdoors, coatless, with his sleeves rolled up, looking ebullient, about to throw a baseball on an airport tarmac: something had been learned from Jeff Greenfield, or something had been told to Jeff Greenfield. "We talk to the press, and things take on a life of their own," Mark Siegel, a Democratic political consultant, said recently to Elizabeth Drew.

About this baseball on the tarmac. On the day that Michael Dukakis appeared at the high school in Woodland Hills and at the rally in San Diego and in the schoolyard in San Jose, there was, although it did not appear on the schedule, a fourth event, what was referred to among the television crews as a "tarmac arrival with ball tossing." This event had taken place in late morning, on the tarmac at the San Diego airport, just after the chartered 737 had rolled to a stop and the candidate had emerged. There had been a moment of hesitation. Then baseball mitts had been produced, and Jack Weeks, the traveling press secretary, had tossed a ball to the candidate. The candidate had tossed the ball back. The rest of us had stood in the sun and given this our full attention, undeflected even by the arrival of an Alaska 767: some forty adults standing on a tarmac watching a diminutive figure in shirtsleeves and a red tie toss a ball to his press secretary.

"Just a regular guy," one of the cameramen had said, his inflection that of the union official who confided, in an early Dukakis commercial aimed at blue-collar voters, that he had known "Mike" a long time, and backed him despite his not being "your shot-and-beer kind of guy."

"I'd say he was a regular guy," another cameraman had said. "Definitely."

"I'd sit around with him," the first cameraman had said.

Kara Dukakis, one of the candidate's daughters, had at that moment emerged from the 737.

"You'd have a beer with him?"

Jack Weeks had tossed the ball to Kara Dukakis.

"I'd have a beer with him."

Kara Dukakis had tossed the ball to her father. Her father had caught the ball and tossed it back to her.

"O.K.," one of the cameramen had said. "We got the daughter. Nice. That's enough. Nice."

The CNN producer then on the Dukakis campaign told me, later in the day, that the first recorded ball tossing on the Dukakis campaign had been outside a bowling alley somewhere in Ohio. CNN had shot it. When the campaign realized that only one camera had it, they had restaged it.

"We have a lot of things like the ball tossing," the producer said. "We have the Greek dancing, for example."

I asked if she still bothered to shoot it.

"I get it," she said, "but I don't call in anymore and say, 'Hey, hold it, I've got him dancing.' "

This sounded about right (the candidate might, after all, bean a citizen during the ball tossing, and CNN would need film), and not until I read Joe Klein's version of these days in Califor-

nia did it occur to me that this eerily contrived moment on the
tarmac at San Diego could become, at least provisionally, history. "The Duke seemed downright jaunty," Joe Klein reported.
"He tossed a baseball with aides. He was flagrantly multilingual.
He danced Greek dances." In the July 25 issue of *U.S. News and
World Report,* Michael Kramer opened his cover story, "Is Dukakis Tough Enough?" with a more developed version of the
ball tossing:

> The thermometer read 101 degrees, but the locals guessed 115 on
> the broiling airport tarmac in Phoenix. After all, it was under a
> noonday sun in the desert that Michael Dukakis was indulging his
> truly favorite campaign ritual — a game of catch with his aide Jack
> Weeks. "These days," he had said, "throwing the ball around when
> we land somewhere is about the only exercise I get." For 16 minutes,
> Dukakis shagged flies and threw strikes. Halfway through, he rolled
> up his sleeves, but he never loosened his tie. Finally, mercifully, it
> was over and time to pitch the obvious tongue-in-cheek question:
> "Governor, what does throwing a ball around in this heat say about
> your mental stability?" Without missing a beat, and without a trace
> of a smile, Dukakis echoed a sentiment he has articulated repeatedly
> in recent months: "What it means is that I'm tough."

Nor was this the last word. On July 31 in the *Washington Post,*
David S. Broder, who had also been with the Dukakis campaign
in Phoenix, gave us a third, and, by virtue of his seniority in the
process, perhaps the official version of the ball tossing:

> Dukakis called out to Jack Weeks, the handsome, curly-haired Welsh-
> man who good-naturedly shepherds us wayward pressmen through
> the daily vagaries of the campaign schedule. Weeks dutifully pro-
> duced two gloves and a baseball, and there on the tarmac, with its
> surface temperature just below the boiling point, the governor loos-
> ened up his arm and got the kinks out of his back by tossing a couple
> hundred 90-foot pegs to Weeks.

What we had in the tarmac arrival with ball tossing, then, was
an understanding: a repeated moment witnessed by many people, all of whom believed it to be a setup and yet most of whom

believed that only an outsider, only someone too "naive" to
know the rules of the game, would so describe it.

2

The narrative is made up of many such understandings, tacit
agreements, small and large, to overlook the observable in the
interests of obtaining a dramatic story line. It was understood,
for example, that the first night of the Republican National
Convention in New Orleans should be for Ronald Reagan "the
last hurrah." "REAGAN ELECTRIFIES GOP" was the headline the
next morning on page one of *New York Newsday;* in fact the
Reagan appearance, which was rhetorically pitched not to a live
audience but to the more intimate demands of the camera, was,
inside the Superdome, barely registered. It was understood,
similarly, that Michael Dukakis's acceptance speech on the
last night of the Democratic National Convention in Atlanta
should be the occasion on which his "passion," or "leadership,"
emerged. "Could the no-nonsense nominee reach within himself to discover the language of leadership?" *Time* had asked.
"Could he go beyond the pedestrian promises of 'good jobs at
good wages' to give voice to a new Democratic vision?"

   The correct answer, since the forward flow of the narrative
here demanded the appearance of a genuine contender (a contender who could be seventeen points "up," so that George Bush
could be seventeen points "down," a position from which he
could rise to "claim" his own convention), was yes: "The best
speech of his life," David Broder reported. Sandy Grady found
it "superb," evoking "Kennedyesque echoes" and showing "unexpected craft and fire." *Newsweek* had witnessed Governor Dukakis "electrifying the convention with his intensely personal
acceptance speech." In fact the convention that evening had
been electrified, not by the speech, which was the same series of
nonsequential clauses Governor Dukakis had employed during
the primary campaign ("My friends . . . it's what the Democratic
party is all about"), but because the floor had been darkened,
swept with laser beams, and flooded with "Coming to America,"
played at concert volume with the bass turned up.

*

It is understood that this invented narrative will turn on certain familiar elements. There is the continuing story line of the "horse race," the reliable daily drama of one candidate falling behind as another pulls ahead. There is the surprise of the new poll, the glamour of the one-on-one colloquy on the midnight plane, a plot point (the nation sleeps while the candidate and his confidant hammer out its fate) pioneered by Theodore H. White. There is the abiding if unexamined faith in the campaign as personal odyssey, and in the spiritual benefits accruing to those who undertake it. There is, in the presented history of the candidate, the crucible event, the day that "changed the life."

Robert Dole's life was understood to have changed when he was injured in Italy in 1945. George Bush's life is understood to have changed when he and his wife decided to "get out and make it on our own" (his words, or rather the speechwriter Peggy Noonan's, from the "lived the dream" acceptance speech, suggesting action, shirtsleeves, privilege cast aside) in west Texas. For Bruce Babbitt, "the dam just kind of broke" during a student summer in Bolivia. For Michael Dukakis, the dam is understood to have broken not during his student summer in Peru but after his 1978 defeat in Massachusetts; his tragic flaw, we have read repeatedly, is neither his evident sulkiness at losing that election nor what many since have seen as a rather dissociated self-satisfaction ("We're two people very proud of what we've done," he said on NBC in Atlanta, falling into a favorite speech pattern, "very proud of each other, actually . . . and very proud that a couple of guys named Dukakis and Jackson have come this far"), but the more attractive "hubris."

The narrative requires broad strokes. Michael Dukakis was physically small and had associations with Harvard, which suggested that he might be an "intellectual"; the "immigrant factor," on the other hand, could make him tough (as in "What it means is that I'm tough"), a "streetfighter." "He's cool, shrewd and still trying to prove he's tough," the July 25 cover of *U.S. News and World Report* said about Dukakis. "Toughness is what it's all about," one of his advisers is quoted as having said in the cover story. "People need to feel that a candidate is tough enough to be president. It is the threshold perception."

George Bush had presented a more tortured narrative prob-

lem. The tellers of the story had not understood, or had not
responded, to the essential Bush style, which was complex,
ironic, the diffident edge of the northeastern elite. This was
what was at first identified as "the wimp factor," which was
replaced not by a more complicated view of the personality but
by its reverse: George Bush was by late August no longer a
"wimp" but someone who had "thrown it over," "struck out" to
make his own way: no longer a product of the effete Northeast
but someone who had thrived in Texas, and was therefore
"tough enough to be president."

That George Bush might have thrived in Texas not in spite
of but precisely because he was a member of the northeastern
elite was a shading which had no part in the narrative: "He was
considered back at the time one of the most charismatic people
ever elected to public office in the history of Texas," Congressman Bill Archer of Houston has said. "That charisma, people
talked about it over and over again." People talked about it,
probably, because Andover and Yale and the inheritable tax
avoidance they suggested were, during the years George Bush
lived in Texas, the exact ideals toward which the Houston and
Dallas establishment aspired, but the narrative called for a less
ambiguous version: "Lived in a little shotgun house, one room
for the three of us," as Bush, or Peggy Noonan, had put it in
the celebrated no-subject-pronoun cadences of the "lived the
dream" acceptance speech. "Worked in the oil business, started
my own . . . Moved from the shotgun to a duplex apartment to
a house. Lived the dream — high school football on Friday
night, Little League, neighborhood barbecue . . . pushing into
unknown territory with kids and a dog and a car."

All stories, of course, depend for their popular interest upon
the invention of personality, or "character," but in the political
narrative, designed as it is to maintain the illusion of "consensus" by obscuring rather than addressing actual issues, this invention served a further purpose. It was by 1988 generally, if
unspecifically, agreed that the United States faced certain social
and economic realities which, if not intractable, did not entirely
lend themselves to the kinds of policy fixes people who run for
elected office, on whatever ticket, were likely to undertake. We

had not yet accommodated the industrialization of parts of the third world. We had not yet adjusted to the economic realignment of a world in which the United States was no longer the principal catalyst for change. "We really are in an age of transition," Brent Scowcroft, Bush's leading foreign policy adviser, recently told Robert Scheer of the *Los Angeles Times,* "from a postwar world where the Soviets were the enemy, where the United States was a superpower and trying to build up both its allies and its former enemies and help the Third World transition to independence. That whole world and all of those things are coming to an end or have ended, and we are now entering a new and different world that will be complex and much less unambiguous than the old one."

What continued to dominate the rhetoric of the campaign, however, was not this awareness of a new and different world but nostalgia for an old one, and coded assurance that symptoms of ambiguity or change, of what George Bush called the "deterioration of values," would be summarily dealt with by increased social control. It was not by accident that the word "enforcement," devoid of any apparent awareness that it had been tried before, kept coming up in this campaign. A problem named seemed, for both campaigns, a problem solved. Michael Dukakis had promised, by way of achieving his goal of "no safe haven for dope dealers and drug profits anywhere on this earth," to "double the number" of Drug Enforcement Administration agents, not a promising approach. George Bush, for his part, had repeatedly promised the death penalty, and not only the Pledge of Allegiance but prayer, or "moments of silence," in the schools. "We have to change this whole culture," he said in the Wake Forest debate; the polls indicated that the electorate wanted "change," and this wish for change had been translated, by both campaigns, into the wish for a "change back," a change to that "gentler nation" of which Vice President Bush repeatedly spoke.

To the extent that there were differences between the candidates, these differences lay in just where on the time scale this gentler America could be found. The Dukakis campaign was oriented to "programs," and the programs it proposed were similar to those that had worked (the encouragement of private sector involvement in low-cost housing, say) in the boom years after World War II. The Bush campaign was oriented to "values," and the values to which it referred were not postwar but prewar. In neither case did "ideas" play a part: "This election isn't about ideology, it's about competence," Michael Dukakis had said in Atlanta. "First and foremost, it's a choice between two persons," one of his senior advisers, Thomas Kiley, had told the *Wall Street Journal.* "What it all comes down to, after all the shouting and the cheers, is the man at the desk," George Bush had said in New Orleans. In other words, what it was "about," what it came "down to," what was wrong or right with America, was not a historical shift largely unaffected by the actions of individual citizens but "character," and if "character" could be seen to count, then every citizen — since everyone was a judge of character, an expert in the field of personality — could be seen to count. This notion, that the citizen's choice among determinedly centrist candidates makes a "difference," is in fact the narrative's most central element, and also its most fictive.

3

The Democratic National Convention of 1968, during which the process was put to a popular vote on the streets of Chicago and after which it was decided that what had occurred could not be allowed to recur, is generally agreed to have prompted the multiplication of primaries, and the concomitant coverage of those primaries, which led to the end of the national party convention as a more than ceremonial occasion. A year and a half ago, as the primary campaigns got under way for the 1988 election, David S. Broder, in the *Washington Post,* offered this analysis of the power these "reforms" in the nominating procedure had vested not in the party leadership, which is where this power of choice ultimately resides, but in "the existing communications system," by which he meant the press, or the medium through which the party leadership sells its choice:

Once the campaign explodes to 18 states, as it will the day after New Hampshire, when the focus shifts to a super-primary across the nation, the existing communications system simply will not accommodate more than two or three candidates in each party. Neither the television networks, nor newspapers nor magazines, have the resources of people, space and time to describe and analyze the dynamics of two simultaneous half-national elections among Republicans and Democrats. That task is simply beyond us. Since we cannot reduce the number of states voting on Super Tuesday, we have to reduce the number of candidates treated as serious contenders. Those news judgments will be arbitrary — but not subject to appeal. Those who finish first or second in Iowa and New Hampshire will get tickets from the mass media to play in the next big round. Those who don't, won't. A minor exception may be made for the two reverends, Jesse L. Jackson and Marion G. (Pat) Robertson, who have their own church-based communications and support networks and are less dependent on mass-media attention. But no one else.

By the time the existing communications system set itself up in Atlanta and New Orleans the priorities were clear. "NOTICE NOTICE NOTICE," read the typed note given to some print reporters when they picked up their credentials in Atlanta. "Because the National Democratic Convention Committee permitted the electronic media to exceed specifications for their broadcast booths, your assigned seat's sightline to the podium and the convention floor was obliterated." The network skyboxes, in other words, had been built in front of the sections originally assigned to the periodical press. "This is a place that was chosen to be, for all intents and purposes, a large TV studio, to be able to project our message to the American people and a national audience," Paul Kirk, the chairman of the DNC, said by way of explaining why the podium and the skyboxes had so reduced the size of the Omni Coliseum in Atlanta that some thousand delegates and alternates and guests had been, on the evening Jesse Jackson spoke, locked out.

Mayor Andrew Young of Atlanta apologized for the lockout, but said that it would be the same on nights to follow: "The 150 million people in this country who are going to vote have got to be our major target." Still, convention delegates were seen to have a real role: "The folks in the hall are so important for how it looks," Lane Venardos, senior producer in charge of convention coverage for CBS News, said to the *New York Times* about the Republican convention. The delegates, in other words, could be seen as dress extras.

During those eight summer evenings this year, four in Atlanta and four in New Orleans, when roughly 80 percent of the television sets "out there" were tuned somewhere else, the entire attention of those inside the process was directed toward the invention of this story in which they themselves were the principal players, and for which they themselves were the principal audience. The great arenas in which the conventions were held became worlds all their own, constantly transmitting their own images back to themselves, connected by skywalks to interchangeable structures composed not of floors but of "levels," mysteriously separated by fountains and glass elevators and escalators that did not quite connect.

In the Louisiana Superdome in New Orleans as in the Omni Coliseum in Atlanta, the grids of lights blazed and dimmed hypnotically. Men with rifles patrolled the high catwalks. The nets packed with thousands of balloons swung gently overhead, poised for that instant known as the "money shot," the moment, or "window," when everything was working and no network had cut to a commercial. The minicams trawled the floor, fishing in Atlanta for Rob Lowe, in New Orleans for Donald Trump. In the NBC skybox Tom Brokaw floated over the floor, adjusting his tie, putting on his jacket, leaning to speak to John Chancellor. In the CNN skybox Mary Alice Williams sat bathed in white light, the blond madonna of the skyboxes. On the television screens in the press section the images reappeared, but from another angle: Tom Brokaw and Mary Alice Williams again, broadcasting not just above us but also to us, the circle closed.

At the end of prime time, when the skyboxes went dark, the action moved across the skywalks and into the levels, into the lobbies, into one or another Hyatt or Marriott or Hilton or Westin. In the portage from lobby to lobby, level to level, the same people kept materializing in slightly altered roles. On a level of the Hyatt in Atlanta I saw Ann Lewis in her role as a Jackson adviser. On a level of the Hyatt in New Orleans I saw Ann Lewis in her role as a correspondent for *Ms.* Some pictures

were vivid: "I've been around this process a while, and one thing
I've noticed, it's the people who write the checks who get treated
as if they have a certain amount of power," I recall Nadine
Hack, the chairman of Dukakis's New York Finance Council,
saying in a suite at the Hyatt in Atlanta: here was a willowy
woman with long blond hair who was standing barefoot on
a table and trying to explain how to buy into the action.
"The great thing about those evenings was you could even
see Michael Harrington there," I recall Richard Viguerie saying to me at a party in New Orleans: here was the man who
manages the action for the American right trying to explain the
early sixties, and evenings we had both spent on Washington
Square.

There was in Atlanta, according to the Democratic National
Committee, "twice the media presence" that there had been at
the 1984 convention. There were in New Orleans "media work-
spaces" assigned not only to 117 newspapers and news services
and to the American television and radio industry in full
strength but to 52 foreign networks. On every corner one
turned in New Orleans someone was doing a stand-up. There
were telephone numbers to be called for quotes: "Republican
State and Local Officials" or "Pat Robertson Campaign" or
"Richard Wirthlin, Reagan's Pollster." Newspapers came with
teams of thirty, forty, fifty. In every lobby there were stacks of
fresh newspapers, the *Atlanta Constitution,* the *New Orleans Times-
Picayune,* the *Washington Post,* the *Miami Herald,* the *Los Angeles
Times.* In Atlanta these papers were collected in bins and "recy-
cled": made into thirty thousand posters, which were in turn
distributed to the press in New Orleans.

This perfect recycling tended to present itself, in the narcosis
of the event, as a model for the rest: like American political life
itself, and like the printed and transmitted images on which that
life depended, this was a world with no half-life. It was understood that what was said here would go on the wire and vanish.
Garrison Keillor and his cute kids would vanish. Ann Richards
and her peppery ripostes would vanish. Phyllis Schlafly and
Olympia Snowe would vanish. All the opinions and all the rumors and all the housemaid Spanish spoken in both Atlanta and
New Orleans would vanish, all the quotes would vanish, and all

that would remain would be the huge arenas themselves, the arenas and the lobbies and levels and skywalks to which they connected, the incorporeal heart of the process itself, the agora, the symbolic marketplace in which the narrative was not only written but immediately, efficiently, entirely, consumed.

A certain time lag exists between this world of the arenas and the world as we know it. One evening in New York between the Democratic and Republican conventions I happened to go down to Lafayette Street, to the Public Theatre, to look at clips from documentaries on which the English-born filmmaker Richard Leacock had worked during his fifty years in America. We saw folk singers in Virginia in 1941 and oil riggers in Louisiana in 1946 (this was *Louisiana Story,* which Leacock had shot for Robert Flaherty) and tent performers in the corn belt in 1954; we saw Eddy Sachs preparing for the Indianapolis 500 in 1960 and Piri Thomas in Spanish Harlem in 1961. We saw parades, we saw baton twirlers. We saw quints in South Dakota in 1963.

There on the screen at the Public Theatre that evening were images and attitudes from an America that had largely vanished, and what was striking was this: these were the very images and attitudes on which "the campaign" of 1988 was predicated. That "unknown territory" into which George Bush had pushed "with the kids and a dog and a car" had existed in this vanished America, and long since been subdivided, cut up for those tract houses on which the people who were not part of the process had made down payments. Michael Dukakis's "snow blower," and both the amusing frugality and the admirable husbandry of resources it was meant to suggest, derived from some half-remembered idea of what citizens of this vanished America had laughed at and admired. "The Pledge" was an issue from that world. "A drug-free America" had perhaps seemed in that world an achievable ideal, as had "better schools."

I recall listening in Atlanta to Dukakis's foreign policy expert, Madeleine Albright, as she conjured up, in the course of arguing against a "no first use" minority plank in the Democratic platform, a scenario in which "Soviet forces overrun Europe" and the United States has, by promising no first use of nuclear weapons, crippled its ability to act: she was talking about a world

that had not turned since 1948. What was at work here seemed
on the one hand a grave, although in many ways a comfortable,
miscalculation of what people in America might have as their
deepest concerns in 1988; it seemed on the other hand just
another understanding, another of those agreements to overlook the observable.

4

It was into this sedative fantasy of a fixable imperial America
that Jesse Jackson rode, on a Trailways bus. "You've never
heard a sense of panic sweep the party as it has in the last few
days," David Garth had told the *New York Times* during those
perilous spring weeks when there seemed a real possibility that
a black candidate with no experience in elected office, a candidate believed to be so profoundly unelectable that he could take
the entire Democratic party down with him, might go to Atlanta
with more delegates than any other Democratic candidate. "The
party is up against an extraordinary end-game," the pollster
Paul Maslin had said. "I don't know where this leaves us," Robert S. Strauss had said. One superdelegate then still uncom-
mitted, the *New York Times* had reported, "said the Dukakis
campaign had changed its message since Mr. Dukakis lost the
Illinois primary. Mr. Dukakis is no longer the candidate of 'inev-
itability' but the candidate of order, he said. 'They're not doing
the train's leaving the station and you better be on it routine
anymore,' this official said. 'They're now saying that the station's
about to be blown up by terrorists and we're the only ones who
can defuse the bomb.' "

The threat, or the possibility, presented by Jesse Jackson, the
"historic" (as people liked to say after it became certain he would
not have the numbers) part of his candidacy, derived from
something other than the fact that he was black, a circumstance
which had before been and could be again compartmentalized.
For example: "Next week, when we launch our black radio buys,
when we start doing our black media stuff, Jesse Jackson needs
to be on the air in the black community on our behalf," Donna
Brazile of the Dukakis campaign said to the *New York Times* on

September 8, by way of emphasizing how much the Dukakis campaign "sought to make peace" with Jackson.

"Black," in other words, could be useful, and even a moral force, a way for white Americans to attain more perfect attitudes: "His color is an enormous plus. . . . How moving it is, and how important, to see a black candidate meet and overcome the racism that lurks in virtually all of us white Americans," Anthony Lewis had noted in a March column explaining why the notion that Jesse Jackson could win was nonetheless "a romantic delusion" of the kind that had "repeatedly undermined" the Democratic party. "You look at what Jesse Jackson has done, you have to wonder what a Tom Bradley of Los Angeles could have done, what an Andy Young of Atlanta could have done," I heard someone say on one of the Sunday shows after the Jackson campaign had entered its "historic" (or, in the candidate's word, its "endless") phase.

"Black," then, by itself and in the right context — the "right context" being a reasonable constituency composed exclusively of blacks and supportive liberal whites — could be accommodated by the process. Something less traditional, and also less manageable, was at work in the 1988 Jackson candidacy. I recall having dinner, the weekend before the California primary, at the Pebble Beach house of the chairman of a large American corporation. There were sixteen people at the table, all white, all well off, all well dressed, all well educated, and all socially conservative. During the course of the evening it came to my attention that six of the sixteen, or every one of the registered Democrats present, intended to vote on Tuesday for Jesse Jackson. Their reasons were unspecific, but definite. "I heard him, he didn't sound like a politician," one said. "He's talking about right now," another said. "You get outside the gate here, take a look around, you have to know we've got some problems, and he's talking about them."

What made the 1988 Jackson candidacy a bomb that had to be defused, then, was not that blacks were supporting a black candidate, but that significant numbers of whites were supporting — not only supporting but in many cases overcoming deep emotional and economic conflicts of their own in order to support

— a candidate who was attractive to them not because but in spite of the fact that he was black, a candidate whose most potent attraction was that he "didn't sound like a politician." "Character" seemed not to be, among these voters, the point-of-sale issue the narrative made it out to be: a number of white Jackson supporters to whom I talked would quite serenely describe their candidate as a "con man," or even as, in George Bush's word, a "hustler."

"And yet . . ." they would say. What "and yet" turned out to mean, almost without variation, was that they were willing to walk off the edge of the known political map for a candidate who was running against, as he repeatedly said, "politics as usual," against what he called "consensualist centrist politics"; against what had come to be the very premise of the process, the notion that the winning and the maintaining of public office warranted the invention of a public narrative based only tangentially on observable reality.

In other words they were not idealists, these white Jackson voters, but empiricists. By the time Jesse Jackson got to California, where he would eventually get 25 percent of the entire white vote and 49 percent of the total vote from voters between the demographically key ages of thirty to forty-four, the idealists had rallied behind the sole surviving alternative, who was, accordingly, just then being declared "presidential." In Los Angeles, during May and early June, those Democrats who had not fallen in line behind Dukakis were described as "self-indulgent," or as "immature"; they were even described, in a dispiriting phrase that prefigured the tenor of the campaign to come, as "issues wimps." I recall talking to a rich and politically well-connected Californian who had been, through the primary campaign there, virtually the only prominent Democrat on the famously liberal west side of Los Angeles who was backing Jackson. He said that he could afford "the luxury of being more interested in issues than in process," but that he would pay for it: "When I want something, I'll have a hard time getting people to pick up the phone. I recognize that. I made the choice."

On the June night in Los Angeles when Michael Dukakis was declared the winner of the California Democratic primary, and the bomb officially defused, there took place in the Crystal Room of the Biltmore Hotel a "victory party" that was less a celebration than a ratification by the professionals, a ritual convergence of those California Democrats for whom the phones would continue to get picked up. Charles Manatt was there. John Van de Kamp was there. Leo McCarthy was there. Robert Shrum was there. All the custom-made suits and monogrammed shirts in Los Angeles that night were there, met in the wide corridors of the Biltmore in order to murmur assurances to one another. The ballroom in fact had been cordoned as if to repel late invaders, roped off in such a way that once the Secret Service, the traveling press, the local press, the visiting national press, the staff, and the candidate had assembled, there would be room for only a controllable handful of celebrants, over whom the cameras would dutifully pan.

In fact the actual "celebrants" that evening were not at the Biltmore at all, but a few blocks away at the Los Angeles Hilton, dancing under the mirrored ceiling of the ballroom in which the Jackson campaign had gathered, its energy level in defeat notably higher than that of other campaigns in victory. Jackson parties tended to spill out of ballrooms onto several levels of whatever hotel they were in, and to last until three or four in the morning: anyone who wanted to be at a Jackson party was welcome at a Jackson party, which was unusual among the campaigns, and tended to reinforce the populist spirit that had given this one its extraordinary animation.

Of that evening at the Los Angeles Hilton I recall a pretty woman in a gold lamé dress, dancing with a baby in her arms. I recall empty beer bottles, Corona and Excalibur and Budweiser, sitting around the loops of television cables. I recall the candidate himself, dancing on the stage, and, on this June evening when the long shot had not come in, this evening when the campaign was effectively over, giving the women in the traveling press the little parody wave they liked to give him, "the press chicks' wave," the stiff-armed palm movement they called "the Nancy Reagan wave"; then taking off his tie and throwing it into the crowd, like a rock star. This was of course a narrative of its own, but a relatively current one, and one which had, because it seemed at some point grounded in the recognizable,

a powerful glamour for those estranged from the purposeful
nostalgia of the traditional narrative.

In the end the predictable decision was made to go with the
process, with predictable, if equivocal, results. On the last afternoon of the Republican convention in New Orleans I walked
from the hotel in the Quarter where I was staying over to look
at 544 Camp Street, a local point of interest not noted on the
points-of-interest maps distributed at the convention but one
that figures large in the literature of American conspiracy. "544
Camp Street" was the address stamped on the leaflets Lee
Harvey Oswald was distributing around New Orleans between
May and September of 1963, the "Fair Play for Cuba Committee" leaflets that, in the years after Lee Harvey Oswald assassinated John F. Kennedy, suggested to some that he had been
acting for Fidel Castro and to others that he had been set up to
appear to have been acting for Fidel Castro. Guy Banister had
his detective agency at 544 Camp. David Ferrie and Jack Martin
frequented the coffee shop on the ground floor at 544 Camp.
The Cuban Revolutionary Council rented an office at 544
Camp. People had taken the American political narrative seriously at 544 Camp. They had argued about it, fallen out over it,
had hit each other over the head with pistol butts over it.

When I went to look for 544 Camp that afternoon twenty-five
years later there was, it turned out, no more such address: the
small building had been bought and torn down in order to
construct a new federal courthouse. Across the street in Lafayette Square that day there had been a loudspeaker, and a young
man on a makeshift platform talking about abortion, and un-
wanted babies being put down the Disposall and "clogging the
main sewer drains of New Orleans," but no one had been there
to listen. "Satan — you're the liar," the young woman with him
on the platform had sung, lip-syncing a tape originally made,
she told me, by a woman who sings with an Alabama traveling
ministry, the Ministry of the Happy Hunters. "There's one
thing you can't deny . . . you're the father of every lie." The
young woman had been wearing a black cape, and was made up
to portray Satan, or Death, I was unclear which, and it had not
seemed a distinction worth pursuing.

Still, there were clouds off the Gulf that day and the air was wet and there was about the melancholy of Camp Street a certain sense of abandoned historic moment, heightened, quite soon, by something unusual: the New Orleans police began lining Camp Street, blocking every intersection from Canal Street south. I noticed a man in uniform on a roof. Before long there were Secret Service agents, with wires in their ears. The candidates, it seemed, would be traveling north on Camp Street on their way from the Republican National Committee Finance Committee Gala (Invitation Only) at the Convention Center to the Ohio Caucus Rally (Media Invited) at the Hilton. I stood for a while on Camp Street, on this corner which might be construed as one of those occasional accidental intersections where the remote narrative had collided with the actual life of the country, and waited until the motorcade itself, entirely and perfectly insulated, a mechanism dedicated like the process for which it stood only to the maintenance of itself, had passed, and then I walked to the Superdome. "I hear he did O.K. with Brinkley," they said that night in the Superdome, and then, as the confetti fell, "Quayle, zip."

ANNIE DILLARD

Schedules

FROM TIKKUN

> What if man could see Beauty Itself, pure, unalloyed, stripped of
> mortality and all its pollution, stains, and vanities, unchanging, di-
> vine, . . . the man becoming, in that communion, the friend of God,
> himself immortal; . . . would that be a life to disregard?
> — Plato

I HAVE BEEN looking into schedules. Even when we read physics,
we inquire of each least particle, "What then shall I do this
morning?" How we spend our days is, of course, how we spend
our lives. What we do with this hour, and that one, is what we
are doing. A schedule defends from chaos and whim. It is a net
for catching days. It is a scaffolding on which a worker can stand
and labor with both hands at sections of time. A schedule is a
mock-up of reason and order — willed, faked, and so brought
into being; it is a peace and a haven set into the wreck of time;
it is a lifeboat on which you find yourself, decades later, still
living. Each day is the same, so you remember the series afterward as a blurred idyll.

The most appealing daily schedule I know is that of a certain
turn-of-the-century Swedish aristocrat. He got up at four and
set out on foot to hunt black grouse, wood grouse, woodcock,
and snipe. At eleven he met his friends who had also been out
hunting alone all morning. They converged "at one of these
babbling brooks," he wrote. He outlined the rest of his schedule.
"Take a quick dip, relax with a schnapps and a sandwich, stretch
out, have a smoke, take a nap or just rest, and then sit around

and chat until three. Then I hunt some more until sundown, bathe again, put on white tie and tails to keep up appearances, eat a huge dinner, smoke a cigar and sleep like a log until the sun comes up again to redden the eastern sky. This is living. . . . Could it be more perfect?"

There is no shortage of good days. It is good lives that are hard to come by. A life of good days lived in the senses is not enough. The life of sensation is the life of greed; it requires more and more. The life of the spirit requires less and less; time is ample and its passage sweet. Who would call a day spent reading a good day? But a life spent reading — that is a good life. A day that closely resembles every other day for the past ten or twenty years does not suggest itself as a good one. But who would not call Pasteur's life a good one, or Thomas Mann's?

Wallace Stevens in his forties, living in Hartford, Connecticut, hewed to a productive routine. He rose at six, read for two hours, and walked another hour — three miles — to work. He dictated poems to his secretary. He ate no lunch; at noon he walked for another hour, often to an art gallery. He walked home from work — another hour. After dinner he retired to his study; he went to bed at nine. On Sundays, he walked in the park. I don't know what he did on Saturdays. Perhaps he exchanged a few words with his wife, who posed for the Liberty dime. (One would rather read these people, or lead their lives, than be their wives. When the Swedish aristocrat Wilhelm Dinesen shot birds all day, drank schnapps, napped, and dressed for dinner, he and his wife had three children under three. The middle one was Karen, later known as Isak Dinesen.)

Like Stevens, Osip Mandelstam composed poetry on the hoof. So did Dante. Nietzsche, like Emerson, took two long walks a day. "When my creative energy flowed most freely, my muscular activity was always greatest. . . . I might often have been seen dancing; I used to walk through the hills for seven or eight hours on end without a hint of fatigue; I slept well, laughed a good deal — I was perfectly vigorous and patient" (Nietzsche). On the other hand, A. E. Housman, almost predictably, maintained, "I have seldom written poetry unless I was rather out of health." This makes sense, too, because in writing a book you can be too well for your own good.

Jack London claimed to write twenty hours a day. Before he undertook to write, he obtained the University of California course list and all the syllabi; he spent a year reading the textbooks in philosophy and literature. In subsequent years, once he had a book of his own under way, he set his alarm to wake him after four hours of sleep. Often he slept through the alarm, so, by his own account, he rigged it to drop a weight on his head. I cannot say I believe this, though a novel like *The Sea-Wolf* is strong evidence that some sort of weight fell on his head with some sort of frequency — though you wouldn't think a man would claim credit for it. London maintained that every writer needed experience, a technique, and a philosophical position. Perhaps the position need not be an airtight one; London himself felt comfortable with a weird amalgam of Karl Marx and Herbert Spencer. (Marks & Sparks.)

I write these words in my most recent of many studies — a pine shed on Cape Cod. The pine lumber is unfinished inside the study; the pines outside are finished trees. I see the pines from my two windows. Nuthatches spiral around their long, coarse trunks. Sometimes in June a feeding colony of mixed warblers flies through the pines; the warblers make a racket that draws me out the door. The warblers drift loosely through the stiff pine branches, and I follow through the thin long grass between the trunks.

The study — sold as a prefabricated toolshed — is eight feet by ten feet. Like a plane's cockpit, it is crammed with high-tech equipment. There is no quill pen in sight. There is a computer, a printer, and a photocopying machine. My backless chair, a prie-dieu on which I kneel, slides under the desk; I give it a little kick when I leave. There is an air conditioner, a heater, and an electric kettle. There is a low-tech bookshelf, a shelf of gull and whale bones, and a bed. Under the bed I stow paints — a one-pint can of yellow to touch up the window's trim, and five or six tubes of artists' oils. The study affords ample room for one. One who is supposed to be writing books. You can read in the space of a coffin, and you can write in the space of a toolshed meant for mowers and spades.

I walk up here from the house every morning. The study and its pines, and the old summer cottages nearby, and the new farm just north of me, rise from an old sand dune high over a creeky salt marsh. From the bright lip of the dune I can see oyster farmers working their beds on the tidal flats and sailboats under way in the saltwater bay. After I have warmed myself standing at the crest of the dune, I return under the pines, enter the study, slam the door so the latch catches — and then I cannot see. The green spot in front of my eyes outshines everything in the shade. I lie on the bed and play with a bird bone until I can see it.

Appealing workplaces are to be avoided. One wants a room with no view, so imagination can dance with memory in the dark. When I furnished this study seven years ago, I pushed the long desk against a blank wall, so I could not see from either window. Once, fifteen years ago, I wrote in a cinder-block cell over a parking lot. It overlooked a tar-and-gravel roof. This pine shed under trees is not quite so good as the cinder-block study was, but it will do.

"The beginning of wisdom," according to a West African proverb, "is to get you a roof."

It was on summer nights in Roanoke, Virginia, that I wrote the second half of a book, *Pilgrim at Tinker Creek*. (I wrote the first half in the spring, at home.) Ruefully I noted then that I would possibly look back on those times as an idyll. I vowed to remember the difficulties. I have forgotten them now, however, and I do, in fact, look back on those times as an idyll.

I slept until noon, as did my husband, who was also writing. I wrote once in the afternoon, and once again after our early dinner and a walk. During those months, I subsisted on that dinner, coffee, Coke, chocolate milk, and Vantage cigarettes. I worked till midnight, one, or two. When I came home in the middle of the night I was tired; I longed for a tolerant giant, a person as big as a house, to hold me and rock me. In fact, an exhausted daydream — almost a hallucination — of being rocked and soothed sometimes forced itself upon me, and interrupted me even when I was talking or reading.

I had a room — a study carrel — in the Hollins College library, on the second floor. It was this room that overlooked a tar-and-gravel roof. A plate-glass window, beside me on the left, gave out on a number of objects: the roof, a parking lot, a distant portion of Carvin's Creek, some complicated Virginia sky, and a far hilltop where six cows grazed around a ruined foundation under red cedars.

From my desk I kept an eye out. Intriguing people, people I knew, pulled into the parking lot and climbed from their cars. The cows moved on the hilltop. (I drew the cows, for they were made interestingly; they hung in catenary curves from their skeletons, like two-man tents.) On the flat roof just outside the window, sparrows pecked gravel. One of the sparrows lacked a leg; one was missing a foot. If I stood and peered around, I could see a feeder creek running at the edge of a field. In the creek, even from that great distance, I could see muskrats and snapping turtles. If I saw a snapping turtle, I ran downstairs and out of the library to watch it or poke it.

One afternoon I made a pen drawing of the window and the landscape it framed. I drew the window's aluminum frame and steel hardware; I sketched in the clouds and the far hilltop with its ruined foundation and wandering cows. I outlined the parking lot and its tall row of mercury-vapor lights; I drew the cars, and the graveled rooftop foreground.

If I craned my head, I could see a grassy playing field below. One afternoon I peered around at that field and saw a softball game. Since I happened to have my fielder's glove with me in my study, I thought it would be the generous thing to join the game. On the field, I learned there was a music camp on campus for two weeks. The little boys playing softball were musical whizzes. They could not all play ball, but their patter was a treat. "All right, MacDonald," they jeered when one kid came to bat, "that pizzicato won't help you now." It was slightly better than no softball, so I played with them every day, second base, terrified that I would bust a prodigy's fingers on a throw to first or the plate.

I shut the blinds one day for good. I lowered the venetian blinds and flattened the slats. Then, by lamplight, I taped my drawing to the closed blind. There, on the drawing, was the window's view: cows, parking lot, hilltop, and sky. If I wanted a sense of the world, I could look at the stylized outline drawing.

If I had possessed the skill, I would have painted, directly on the slats of the lowered blind, in meticulous colors, a *trompe l'oeil* mural view of all that the blinds hid. Instead, I wrote it.

On the Fourth of July, my husband and our friends drove into the city, Roanoke, to see the fireworks. I begged off; I wanted to keep working. I was working hard, although of course it did not seem hard enough at the time — a finished chapter every few weeks. I castigated myself daily for writing too slowly. Even when passages seemed to come easily, as though I were copying from a folio held open by smiling angels, the manuscript revealed the usual signs of struggle — blood stains, teeth marks, gashes, and burns.

This night, as on most nights, I entered the library at dusk. The building was locked and dark. I had a key. Every night I let myself in, climbed the stairs, found my way between the tall stacks in the dark, located and unlocked my study's door, and turned on the light. I remembered how many stacks I had to hit with my hand in the dark before I turned down the row to my study. Even if I left only to get a drink of water, I felt and counted the stacks with my hand again to find my room. Once in daylight I glanced at a book on a stack's corner, a book I presumably touched every night with my hand. The book was *The World I Live In,* by Helen Keller. I read it at once: it surprised me by its strong and original prose.

When I flicked on my carrel light, there it all was: the bare room with yellow cinder-block walls; the big, flattened venetian blind and my drawing taped to it; two or three quotations taped up on index cards; and on a far table some books, the fielder's mitt, and a yellow bag of chocolate-covered peanuts. There was the long, blond desk and its chair, and on the desk a dozen different-colored pens, some big index cards in careful, splayed piles, and my messy yellow legal pads. As soon as I saw that desktop, I remembered the task: the chapter, its problems, its phrases, its points.

This night I was concentrating on the chapter. The horizon of my consciousness was the contracted circle of yellow light inside my study — the lone lamp in the enormous, dark library. I leaned over the desk. I worked by hand. I doodled deliriously

in the legal-pad margins. I fiddled with the index cards. I reread
a sentence maybe a hundred times, and if I kept it I changed it
seven or eight times, often substantially.

Now a June bug was knocking at my window. I was wrestling
inside a sentence. I must have heard it a dozen times before it
registered — before I noticed that I had been hearing a bug
knock for half an hour. It made a hollow, bonking sound. Some
people call the same fumbling, heavy insects "May beetles." It
must have been attracted to my light — what little came between
the slats of the blind. I dislike June bugs. Back to work. Knock
again, knock again, and finally, to learn what monster of a fat,
brown June bug could fly up to a second story and thump so
insistently at my window as though it wanted admittance — at
last, unthinkingly, I parted the venetian blind slats with my
fingers, to look out.

And there were the fireworks, far away. It was the Fourth of
July. I had forgotten. They were red and yellow, blue and green
and white; they blossomed high in the black sky many miles
away. The fireworks seemed as distant as the stars, but I could
hear the late banging their bursting made. The sound, those
bangs so muffled and out of synch, accompanied at random the
silent, far sprays of color widening and raining down. It was the
Fourth of July, and I had forgotten all of wide space and all of
historical time. I opened the blinds a crack like eyelids, and it
all came exploding in on me at once — oh yes, the world.

My working the graveyard shift in Virginia affected the book.
It was a nature book full of sunsets; it wholly lacked dawns, and
even mornings.

I was reading about Hassidism, among other things. If you
stay awake one hundred nights, you get the vision of Elijah. I
was not eager for it, although it seemed to be just around the
corner. I preferred this: "Rebbe Shmelke of Nickolsburg, it was
told, never really heard his teacher, the Maggid of Mezritch,
finish a thought because as soon as the latter would say 'and the
Lord spoke,' Shmelke would begin shouting in wonderment,
'The Lord spoke, the Lord spoke,' and continue shouting until
he had to be carried from the room."

*

The second floor of the library, where I worked every night, housed the rare book room. It was a wide, carpeted, well-furnished room. On an end table, as if for decoration, stood a wooden chess set.

One night, stuck on an intractable problem in the writing, I wandered the dark library looking for distraction. I flicked on the lights in the rare book room and looked at some of the books. I saw the chess set and moved white's king's pawn. I turned off the light and wandered back to my carrel.

A few nights later, I glanced into the rare book room and walked in, for black's queen's pawn had moved. I moved out my knight.

We were off and running. Every day, my unseen opponent moved. I moved. I never saw anyone anywhere near the rare book room. The college was not in session; almost no one was around. Late at night I heard the night watchmen clank around downstairs in the dark. The watchmen never came upstairs. There was no one upstairs but me.

When the chess game was ten days old, I entered the rare book room to find black's pieces coming toward me on the carpet. They seemed to be marching, in rows of two. I put them back as they had been and made my move. The next day, the pieces were all pied on the board. I put them back as they had been. The next day, black had moved, rather brilliantly.

Late one night, while all this had been going on, and while the library was dark and locked as it had been all summer and I had accustomed myself to the eeriness of it, I left my carrel to cross the darkness and get a drink of water. I saw a strange chunk of light on the floor between stacks. Passing the stacks, I saw the light spread across the hall. I held my breath. The light was coming from the rare book room; the door was open.

I approached quietly and looked in the room from an angle. There, at the chess table, stood a baby. The baby had blond curls and was wearing only a diaper.

I paused, considering that I had been playing a reasonable game of chess for two weeks with a naked baby. After a while I could make out the sound of voices; I moved closer to the doorway and peered in. There was the young head librarian and his wife, sitting on chairs. I pieced together the rest of it. The librarian stopped by to pick something up. Naturally, he had a key. The couple happened to have the baby along. The baby, just learning to walk, had cruised from the chairs to the table. The baby was holding on to the table, not studying the chess pieces' positions. I greeted the family and played with the baby until they left.

I never did learn who or what was playing chess with me. The game went on until my lunatic opponent scrambled the board so violently the game was over.

During that time, I let all the houseplants die. After the book was finished I noticed them; the plants hung completely black, dead in their pots in the bay window. For I had not only let them die, I had not moved them. During that time, I told all my out-of-town friends they could not visit for a while.

"I understand you're married," a man said to me at a formal lunch in New York that my publisher had arranged. "How do you have time to write a book?"

"Sir?"

"Well," he said, "you have to have a garden, for instance. You have to entertain." And I thought he was foolish, this man in his seventies, who had no idea what you must do. But the fanaticism of my twenties shocks me now. As I feared it would.

STANLEY ELKIN

The Muses Are Heard

FROM HARPER'S MAGAZINE

AND JESUS, I'm thinking at the time, this snob of geography, this longitude-latitude fop, it can't have been but three weeks ago I was living in a villa on Lake Como, taking the gelato, the customized pastas; servants were cutting my meat. And tucking in, too, feasting on the blood-oranges architecture folded into the terraced hillsides organic as agriculture, the lake's thin gray porridge and lumpy Chinese mists. Well maybe, I'm thinking at the time, in spite of Missouri is my hometown, distance is only a different time zone of the head. Because I recognize nothing here, all jet-lagged out in the van, two or so hours southwest of St. Louis on I-44 deep — I see by the recurring billboards that keep on coming, popping up at us like an infinite loop of highway in some redneck video game — in the walnut-bowl belt, in roadside zoo land, cavern and cave country. Among fireworks stands. Live bait mines. And there's a sense, God bite my highhat tongue, of something so un-gun-controlled out there we may have fallen, may my swank wither and drop off, among a race of Minutemen. There's billboards for the Passion Play, for Silver Dollar City, for rides on the Wet Willies.

This ain't any America of franchise and one size fits all; this is a time warp. Some live-by-the-tourist, die-by-the-tourist figment of the imaginary bygones and halcyons, of fiddles and corncobs and jugs. We are, I mean, deep, real deep, in a hanger-on economy, in some landscape of the novelties, and I ask Ross Winter, founder and artistic director of the Mid America Dance Company (MADCO), the man who leads our troupe of modern

dancers bound for Springfield, Missouri, where we're performing Friday and Saturday evening, what folks do hereabouts
when they're not minding the bait stores and walnut-bowl fac-
tories.

"Don't know," he said. "Perhaps they groom each other for
ticks." It's improbably close to what I've been thinking myself,
for we seem to be traversing tracts of the summer pests and
poisons, a vast American steppe of allergens and contact toxins,
of wicked itch banes in the woods and high grasses.

The van, something in a fourteen- or fifteen-passenger Ford,
has been rented for the four days it will be required. A second
vehicle, also rented, containing the dance company's props,
wardrobe trunk, special equipment (some of which is also
rented), and rolls of the vinyl theatrical flooring it has just acquired and which will have to be paid for by matching grants,
had set out earlier, is probably already in Springfield, setting
up.

The dancers, I think, are used to me by now. (We go back.)
We are practically colleagues, these toned, flexible, almost joint-
less young men and women in their twenties and the crippled-
up fifty-eight-year-old man who has to negotiate the high step
up into the van by means of a high step up onto a milk case, a
breathtaking piece of choreography in its own right, let me tell
you. They call me by my first name, something which normally
squeaks against my blackboard like chalk — I am, by ordinary,
when not playing *la strada*, a teacher — but which, here, in these
circumstances, oddly I do not mind at all, and even find flatter-
ing, though I must say it's a little difficult to keep *their* names
straight, wait for others to say them first, only gradually con-
structing a private mnemonics. Liz is the married one. Her husband, James, is part of the tech crew and has gone out with
David in the other van. Raeleen is the one with the close-
cropped hair. Ellen is the tall one, so Darla must be the one with
the reddish hair and the expressive face you associate with white
clown makeup and one dark apostrophe standing for a tear.
The men are a bit easier. Paul is driving, Michael is reading the
Stephen King. Jeffrey, unseen in the van's last row, is apparently sleeping.

No one calls me by my first name now, or says much of any-

thing really. Indeed, they seem a bit torpid for a group normally
so casual with gravity. Not like last time when they stretched out
on the long ride to Winfield, Kansas, by improvising themselves
into various riffs of position, a kind of jazz yoga. Not like last
time when they passed the time in the moving vehicle playing
board games without a board and counting cows and doing
license-plate poker. When they made up ideas for dances. Even
me. "You pass out these dinky cardboard glasses," I said. "You
give a pair to everyone in the audience. There's this green lolli-
pop cellophane over one eye, this red over the other."

"So?"

"So you tell them if they put on the glasses they can see the
dance in three-D."

"Right," Paul said, "then we chuck spears at them."

Not like last time when I smelled, I swear it, the lightly
scorched odor of composition-rubber gym shoe in the van's
closed air and browsed the curious sampler of upscale magazines, *Interview* and *Elle* and *M,* that the company favors, and
dipped at will into proffered community snacks, introduced for
the first time to the delicious sodium nitrites and scrumptious
carcinogens of beef jerky, on whose long, tough leather I
chewed with pleasure for half an hour, for if I am crippled up
and need assistance to get into a van, I have the jaws of a grown
man. Nature gives with the right hand, takes with the left.

Now we don't stop for gas, so forget beef jerky. Forget dinner,
too. Not like last time. (Place in Kansas? No fast-food joint or
truck stop or theme restaurant but the genuine article, the kind
of place you see on the network news when Tom Brokaw breaks
bread with vox pop — a banker, a farmer, the John Deere man.
And there are plaques for Rotary, Jaycees? And Angie — the
company's high school apprentice — asked what the Optimist
Club was, and Liz told her it was a support group for people
who are too happy.)

Hi-diddle-de-dee, the actor's life for me!

Only it isn't the boards I want to trod, it's the Road. Having
been born with this J. B. Priestley sense of good companionship,
some troupe notion of traveled kinship, a true believer — my
pop was a traveling salesman — in lobby encounters, this vet of
the shifting, shared geography, this heart's perpetual reunion-

ist, you see, this sucker for chums, this long-standing-enough guy on that pavement in Paris who eventually runs into everyone he's ever known — this, this *auld acquaintance*. Because it ain't really friendship I'm talking about, it's *Miller time!* And even today I imagine all sports announcers, men covering not only different teams but different games even, know each other, and are always bumping into one another in the best hotels in the different towns — though it's always Cincinnati — and going off together to the good restaurants to catch up, to do the divvied shop talk of their lives, speaking in a jargon so closed it's almost ethnic of the great patsies and fall guys — did you see *Broadway Danny Rose?* like that — doing the anecdotal schmooze and war stories, all high life's tallest tales.

Still, not like last time. Because we really do go back. Well, a couple and a half years anyway.

Ross Winter was born in Australia. He studied at the University of New South Wales and, though he took modern-dance classes while he was a student, he ultimately went for an architect. Emigrating in 1959, he was with a film company in Portugal for a year, moved to London and set up in the design and architecture trade. He choreographed dances for the London and Edinburgh festivals, married, started a family, came to America and moved to St. Louis, and in the early seventies went to work for the Wetterau Corporation, a wholesale-food-distribution company, where he was head of the design department. While at Wetterau he founded, in 1976, the Mid America Dance Company, a sidebar to his life. Then, in 1984, the company closed down Winter's department, and it was suddenly a compulsory hi-diddle-de-dee on him. Missouri, Illinois, Kansas, Nebraska, Oklahoma, Arkansas, Texas — this is the venue of MADCO's modern dance.

Winter looks, in profile, rather like some King George on currency and, like other educated Australians, talks a sort of soft-edged English Prim, the vaguely indeterminate accent of someone raised in a mother tongue but an alien in the land where he speaks it. It's an agreeable, even amiable sound, but you can't imagine anyone ever shouting in it and so it seems, well, vulnerable, the patient calm of a forced, stoic courtesy. *(Aw *geez, come off it. What are we talking about here? Some great Greek patsy fall guy? A few not-like-last-times, and we're into the tragics? As Georgie Jessel said about his chauffeur forced to stand outside the limo and wait for him in the rain, "Nobody told him to go into his profession.")* At fifty-two, Winter is slightly egg-shaped. "The irony about dancing," he says, "is that as a dancer gets better his body only gets worse." In any event he hung up the taps years ago, though he still performs in "The Madcracker," his parody of *The Nutcracker* and the company's most popular dance.

MADCO doesn't do badly. That is, it's a wash. The company takes in and disburses about $150,000 a year. Between $35,000 and $40,000, or about 28 percent of its income, comes from grants; touring brings in another 34 percent; fixed-fee performances in St. Louis, 8 percent; box-office sales, 14 percent; educational performances in schools, 11 percent; fund-raising, 3 percent; with a miscellaneous 2 percent coming in from classes and such. Salaries for the dancers range from $115 to $210 per week. Liz, who's been with MADCO eight years, gets $210 (for a thirty- to thirty-five-week season), but the mean salary for the dancers is $150. Ross allows himself $330 a week. David Kruger, the tech man and company manager, books the tours and works on commission.

I come into it in 1986, about.

Ross wanted to choreograph a dance to prose and asked me to write a story that I could read downstage left while the dancers carry on behind me. When "Notes Toward a Eulogy for Joan Cohen" is performed on Saturday night in Springfield it will be the fourth time, not counting rehearsals, we will have worked together. It's a long piece, about forty-five minutes, and although, owing to my location onstage, I've never seen all of it, the bits I have seen — in MADCO's rehearsal studio — have always seemed to me rather sexy. Well, all dance is about screwing, finally, even the barn dance, even the waltz, but we're talking leotards and leg warmers here, we're talking spandex and muscle. We're also talking, in the instance of "Joan Cohen," about a rabbi who officiates at the funeral of a woman with whom he's been carrying on an adulterous affair — talking porno movies in a Philadelphia hotel room, talking blow-job discussions. We are a distance from *Swan Lake*. And did I mention that Springfield is the world headquarters of the Assemblies of God? Not so much the people who gave you Jimmy Swaggart as the folks who took him away.

When we danced the dance in St. Louis those other three times there seemed to be a lot of enthusiasm for my cane, applause all around the minute they saw it when I limped in from the wings to take my seat behind the table where I do my stuff — all my plucky Look, Ma, I'm Dancin's and show-my-flags. Well, I'm known in St. Louis, a known cripple. When I stumble on in Springfield Saturday night and they *don't* applaud I will think, this is some tough audience! Well, I'm spoiled. (And why, incidentally, do top-hat, white-tie-and-tail types like Tommy Tune and Fred Astaire use canes in *their* acts?)

If the collective mood isn't like last time, maybe it's because these are the final performances of the season; and for Liz, married now and who, whither thou/thither me, will be leaving the company and moving to Arizona with James in a week or so, it's a last tango in Springfield altogether. And because Darla, she of the reddish hair and supple face, has been in severe pain for eight months now and has either torn ligaments in her hip or a ruptured disk in her back, maybe both, which isn't great for the leg extension and presents difficulty for her turnout, and has given her more downtime than a computer; and even if the company *is* family, unlike real families it's forced to function, is burdened always — unlike me with my merely hail-fellow, good-time-Charley, Miller-time intentions, all my visions of those sugarplums in a weightless world — and if that's the case, what alternative did she have except to ask Ross if he had a minute and then offer her resignation?

Only I don't know all this yet. I'm still sitting innocent next to the Stephen King–reading Mike, a few rows up from invisible Jeff, apparently sleeping. Passing with Ross the time of the day and, deep in my heart, wondering what the place will be like where we're going to stay.

Well, not much. It doesn't have a restaurant, it doesn't even have a coffee shop, let alone a lobby where one can transact old times with the other announcers. It's a hot day in the summer

of the great drought and though there's an air conditioner in
my room, it doesn't work. Oh, it has the *sound* of air-condition-
ing down, but no B.T.U.'s. And there are bugs squished against
the walls. But hi-diddle-de-dee anyway, because isn't this how
it's supposed to be? To all intents, ain't it a kind of vaudeville
we're doing, riding the tour van like a time machine, all symbolic
trains, rails and clickety-clack like a montage in movies, name,
pop, and elevation wig-wagging above the stations like the accepted synecdoche for distance itself? Ain't it? We're paying our
dues, man. Look, Ma, I'm playing Springfield! Ain't I? Ain't we?
We're *taking* this show on the road! Ross, me, and the mean-
average twenty-five-year-olds, those hundred-fifty-buck dancers. Hell, if we had any sense we'd go *all* the way, split the motel
altogether, maybe look for a boardinghouse maybe, some place
with just the one telephone next to the landlady's apartment in
the front hallway, or something *really* fleabag, a hotel with old
bus-station chairs and ripped-up green plastic cushions in the
lobby. And that's *one* muse. The Muse of Myth, of How It Was.
There were hobos in the earth in those days, a race of fry cooks,
of broke-mouthed old fellows, closed-jaw, and all wide, ear-to-
ear, turned-in lip like Popeye the Sailor. And you know what?
If you permit me to get ahead of myself, you know what? There
still are. I saw them.

Friday, breakfast morning of show time, a bunch of us were
sitting around Orville & Betty's Café — SERVING DOWNTOWN
SPRINGFIELD FOR OVER EIGHT YEARS — doing the large o.j.,
French toast, sausage, and coffee, $3.25, when this bo came up.
His hair was perfectly black but he was toothless. He was wearing a T-shirt, his exposed arms so covered with tattoos he looked
abstract, as closely decorated with geometry as a mosque. He
needed a light for his cigarette. Liz, or maybe Jeffrey, lit his
cigarette, and he asked if anyone happened to know the time.
It was ten-thirty, and Liz filled him in. "Thank you. Is that A.M.
or P.M.?" "A.M.," said Liz, "it's ten-thirty in the morning." "You
want to buy a floor lamp for two dollars?" There it was, in the
corner, this classic floor lamp with this classic lamp shade, this
classic wire, this classic plug. (And for my money, in my book,
right there's another muse — the Muse of the Bizarre Confrontation. The muses are singing today, I'm thinking. How it was is

how it is, and I should get out more.) Liz didn't live in Springfield, she'd have no way to get it home. "I can understand that," he said reasonably. "I'm not from here myself. You can have it for a dollar." Betty, at the cash register, beside a wall mounted with a half-dozen stuffed heroic silver bass, is watching closely. Liz just plain doesn't want the damn thing. "Take it off my hands," pleads the tattooed man. Who is difficult to look at, on whom time, booze, and circumstance have worked their magic and whose colors are running, who, like some ancient, benighted schoolboy, cannot seem to stay within his own lines. "Take it off my hands, take it for nothing." Betty shoos him, but before he goes he asks the time again, and once more needs to know if that's A.M. or P.M. (Later, Ross will mention he's seen him in the street, that he didn't have the floor lamp with him so must have gotten his price, better than his price. There were two bucks in his hands, and he was counting them out like some crazed miser, turning them over and over. "A dollar, and a dollar, and a dollar, and another dollar . . .")

There are several agendas.

Even if five of the eleven of us showed up for breakfast today, it isn't often we're in the same place at the same time. Michael likes to stay in the room when he's not working, though when he's with us I've noticed he's a superb mimic, a parrot of the zeitgeist. Of the male dancers, he is the most solidly built, the most powerful, though it's Paul, I think, who is probably the best athlete. It's surprising to see him at the motel pool. Dancing must be a sort of ultimate acting. In a bathing suit he's almost scrawny. He *is* scrawny, yet when he swims there's no wasted motion, no energy loss. A few strokes take him the length of the pool. The women are similarly deceptive. Except for Ellen they're all relatively short, yet on stage they appear tall. In one of the dances Liz moves across the stage, apparently without effort, with Paul on her back. *(What's going on? Are you funny, are you in one of the high-risk categories?* No, of course not. *Of course not? Michael's powerfully built, Paul's the best athlete, Liz plays horsey with him? Of course not?* Well, it's the fashions. *The fashions.* The way their clothes fit, all right? *Are you caught up yet?* The way their clothes fit, I tell you. My clothes never fit me like that.

You're fifty-eight years old. Don't make excuses for me, they *never* fit. *Whiner, you're in mourning for a wardrobe?* Yes, sure, why not? Only not for a wardrobe, just that accident in the genetics that skewed my architecture and made me silly in caps, jeans, in Jockey and boxer shorts either, in all the extraordinary accessories of the rakish, wind-blown young down to the beaches in boaters and scarves. The only equality is the equality of sexual style, the Me Tarzan's, You Jane's, all the level playing fields of dalliance. You bet your ass I'm in a high-risk category, the highest. I'm not cute! *The grass is always greener, eh?* Always. *All right, get on with it.*)

So there are different agendas. Raeleen is at the theater with Ross, holding up costumes so David and James — who wears clip-on suspenders with a length of Mickey Mouses attached to trousers so baggy (fashion) he could be that Dutch kid who saved Holland — can preset the proper cues on the lighting board. Darla and Ellen are sunning themselves. Michael relates the plot of his Stephen King, and Jeffrey retrieves tossed dimes before they sink to the bottom of the pool. I chaise lounge alongside. Paul is dressing. There's a technical rehearsal at one.

"Step leap step skip," Liz drill-sergeants in theory class in Richardson Auditorium the afternoon of the performance at Southwestern College in Winfield, Kansas. "Swing and up, left two three. Over right, two three up," she calls out, commanding mantras of the dance, square-dance calls.

"Oof."

"Shit."

"Find your center, you're not finding your center."

Ellen pushes up on her push-up sleeves. Angie, the apprentice, fixes the off-the-shoulder sweatshirt on her shoulders. Everyone wears leg warmers, even the men, who appear oddly old in them, as if their circulation were impaired. Liz, a cappella, continues to snap her fingers, never surrendering the beat while the troupe in its artfully ripped sweatshirts (fashion! *fashion!*) hunts its lost center. Difficult, I imagine, to find in the near dark they're working in, all the three-ring din of the crew's preparations — they're putting together a jungle-gym forest for the set of "Lemurs," they're testing the fog machine, adjusting sound

levels for the romantic, boozy music of "Silver" while a stagehand kneels in the dark and blows up props, two dozen silver
cushions. "Are you the curtain puller?" Ross asks a student.
"When you're closing you can always be a little faster than when
you're opening," he says to him. "He's a quick study," he tells
David as the curtains come smoothly together.

"Two, that's warm." David addresses a person or persons unknown in the booth. He speaks, like an air-traffic controller,
into a microphone cantilevered across his mouth like a pros-
thesis, some orthodontics of sound. "Two and a half, that's even
warmer. Two and a quarter. Okay, that's good."

Liz crickets away, the dancers swarm.

They are theoried, beliefed, suffused with us/them, farmer/
rancher, mountain/shore antipathies and yin/yangs. Well, they
have nothing against ballet dancers *personally* . . .

Ballet dancers are bun heads.

     "   "   " robots.

     "   "   " toy soldiers.

As ruled and rigid as ice skaters doing all the compulsories
and mandatories of their frozen art. Ballet a by-the-numbers
game, *tableau vivant,* not classic so much as stiff, dead to the arts
as Latin is to language. Modern dance is to ballet what jazz is to
golden oldies. (Though how much is terror I can't say. Much
would have to be, no? It stands to reason, doesn't it? Life up on
pointe? Or down in plié? Lowered in painful rice-paddy
mother-squat? Because all dance really *is* about screwing. Even
ballet.)

When we get to the motel Ross hands envelopes to each of us.
They are pay envelopes. Because I think the check for my fee
will be in it I am embarrassed to open mine in front of them. I
open it in the room. It isn't my fee. It's my per diem — a lump
sum $45. This is Thursday, we will be leaving Sunday. It will
have to last me. (But I come back with money to spare. I could
have lived a week and a half in Springfield.)

When I finally see it, the Landers Theatre gives me the hi-
diddle-de-dees altogether. It's the real thing. A classically legiti-

mate legitimate theater. A theater like the theaters there used to be a broken heart for every light on Broadway for.

Once, years ago, in Rome, dubbing a film into English (I was Sextus, son of Pompey) and asked "What hour is it?" I was supposed to answer, "It is a quarter past the hour of the second watch." I delivered the line not only without credibility or good evidence that I could even tell time, but without any clear understanding (me, Sextus, a grown co-conspirator) that it was the time I was being asked to tell. I worked almost the entire morning before being fired. The point isn't that I was fired. It's that once, years ago, in Rome, *I* dubbed a movie. Wait, I take it back. The point is also that once, in Rome years ago, I was fired. Legitimate legitimate theater.

And the Landers is it. Built in 1909, it has two balconies. Its seats are plush, ornate. Great fierce gilded masks — almost gelded masks, not asexual, but not Comedy, not Tragedy, only dramatic — with bulbs sitting on their tongues line the sides of the theater and the bottom of each balcony, perched like gargoyles on Architecture. The second balcony isn't used now, but, in its day, a full house would have been about a thousand people.

This is it, all right. By *God,* it is!

There's a kid, maybe he's eighteen, who volunteers his time as a stagehand at the Landers. He says his ambition is to *own* a place like this someday. Not an actor, mind, but an impresario. I don't know why this should move me but it does, as I am moved by the theater, as I am moved by the dancers, as one is always moved by odd, off-center hope, by people hanging in there and the persistence of the obsolete. (*You, crybaby! You're so moved, why didn't you buy the bum's floor lamp? Why didn't you take it off his hands for two dollars?* That's something else. *Something else. Ri-ight.* Well it is. *Sure.* All right, smartguy, I've reason to believe it may have been an ill-gotten floor lamp. *Oh, an ill-gotten floor lamp!* I was *too* moved, I was *too!* Sometimes you're moved, sometimes you're only embarrassed. *This is a postmodern thing, right?* I could ask the same of you.) Because there's something in the blood, I think, eager to hold the other guy's coat, to present his card, to serve as second. That admires a blacksmith in the late 1980s but wouldn't necessarily care to be one. (*Didn't you used to be Charles Kuralt?*)

In the event, I am delighted to be at the Landers, thrilled in fact. And I can say *exactly* what it was like. It was like turning sixteen and getting your driver's license, receiving, I mean, the high privilege of doing what *real* people do. Because the guy is right, the grass *is* greener, and I wish I had Ross Winter's guts, or his dancers' bodies, or Ross Winter's guts *in* his dancers' bodies. Having it all on the low mean average. Not to fuss. Because *I* don't know how they do it. Hi-diddle-de-dee or no hi-diddle-de-dee, it can't be much of a picnic to have to live in America the Third World life.

To live it on a lark, of course, is a different story. Though it's odd, I'm thinking at the time, that I don't much care for back-stage, that I find it oppressive, in fact. (David Kruger says the Landers's "stagehouse" — the term for the dressing rooms and work areas, everything not properly the auditorium — is badly in need of attention.) Indeed, the stagehouse is itself a sort of Third World, as cluttered and underdeveloped as a favela. Everywhere are cables, ladders, light trees, sets, wardrobe racks, sound equipment, props and gels and Styrofoam cups, all the detritus of fast-food lunch, all theatrical schmutz, all dramatical squalor.

But mine ain't the only game in town. The company will perform two different programs in Springfield — "Pretty Fooles and Peasantries," "Silver," "Hard Day," "Tango Freeze," "Continents," and "Lemurs" Friday; "Flashpoint," "Canon Studies," "Hidden Walls of Time," and "Joan Cohen" Saturday — and they're doing the techs, not run-throughs exactly so much as a fitful electronic blocking on the new stage, vetting the audio. The dancers, for all their flexibility, are hostage to equipment. If movies are, as they say, a director's medium, then movies are the exception, for all the other performing arts belong to the technicians.

Indeed, watching the rehearsals, one is reminded of the book on movie stars, all the rap about the downside of glamour. The cliché must be true about the poor dears bored in their trailers. It's like the army, or being on time for your doctor appointments, like hurry-up-and-wait enterprises everywhere. These folks are disciplined but, not like me out of harm's way on my chair on the stage — where the easel once stood that identified an act in old vaudeville days. First, I can't make out Ross and

David's soft conferences, David's mumbled relays to James in
the booth. I don't even understand Ross's minimalist comments
to his dancers, his remote-control ways, the data they seem to
store about stages everywhere in their collective show-biz unconscious, a stage's invisible cuts and primes and vectors, all its
unmarked markings paced off in their heads meticulously as
the universal weights and measures of duelists' strides. Ross
waves them over or calls them in. He moves them about like a
manager adjusting his fielders.

It's *very* technical.

And, that night, it's the technical side which blows, the equipment which fails.

I'm seated beneath the overhang of the first balcony near the
back of the house, in a good seat on a side aisle. I want to get a
feel for the demographics. Which are sparsish, a scant sparsish
of demographics. Better than a handful, oh *way* better, but
hardly the "pretty good house tonight" that the house manager
promised, driven, I think, by hi-diddle-de-dees of his own, as if
— Kansas, Springfield, St. Louis: I'm an old hand by now — the
body counts and reassurances were intended to dish the same
calming hush-hush politicals as government handouts in a war
zone, say. Only kindly meant, servicing, stroking some perceived need for the old there-theres, palpable in performers as
an open wound. Except I'm only crippled up, not blind. There
are, oh, perhaps 150 summery souls in the demographics tonight. In a theater built to hold 1,000. Of these the vast majority
are women. Plus, of course, a bun-head contingent of little girls
and their younger brothers. A smattering (maybe) of the under-
writers, patrons, benefactors, contributors, and sponsors of
Springfield Ballet listed in the program. Most in frocks, the
comfortable, neutral, down-home dowdy of people who have
nothing to prove.

And they are appreciative, generous. On our side, they laugh
in the right places, applaud with enthusiasm. Though they are
so thinly spread out, I doubt if the dancers receive their message. I've noticed an audience's sound is tricky to hear onstage,
as though acoustics were a one-way street, or the stage a trans-
mitter, the house a receiver. Though the observation must be
tempered. The dancers have told me they frequently speak to

each other on stage, not pepper talk but flashing the clipped, distant early warning of contingency, guiding each other through the lifts and all the double- and triple-time of their close-order drill arrangements. Close to them as I am when we do "Joan Cohen," I've never heard them. So that's another thing — dead spots like the lead opaques of Superman's vision, all the willed limits of transmission, all reined-in, shut-lipped, back-of-the-throat pronouncements, For Performers' Ears Only's like the cleric's promptings and inaudibles to the bride and groom at a wedding.

But something's up — or down — with the sound system. MADCO's tapes are incompatible with the Landers's sound equipment. There'd been trouble at the technical, some missing-nail thing in the tape deck in a for-want-of-a-nail sequence, temporarily papered over by a run out to Radio Shack by somebody in one of the crews. (The Landers has a crew of its own.) Tonight, when the curtain rises and the lights come on, the bouncy, lusty music for "Pretty Fooles and Peasantries" is neither bouncy nor lusty. Indeed, it is scarcely heard. Certainly the dancers, who must take their cues and rhythm from it, have trouble hearing it. (What happened was this: the papered-over part tears. David, backstage, stage-managing, sends an SOS. James leaves his post at the light board and rushes to the second balcony, where their guy is running the sound equipment. James punches up the sound levels, amplifies the amplification. It's like Scotty giving the *Enterprise* warp speed by rubbing two sticks together. Afterward their guys will say our guys had improperly plugged something or other into something or other. It's a their guys/our guys thing, an honest-to-God territorial dispute.)

After the intermission the sound is back where it should be, but it's too late. The dancers are in a foul mood, David and James furious, Ross depressed. Personally I don't see what's so terrible, and argue so. They were pretty good despite, I tell them after the show. But there'll be no hanging out tonight. Again.

I am dressed in my suit of lights — my Brooks Brothers Golden Fleece and special-ordered pants. And, give or take a row, pretty much in the same seat I'd occupied the previous night.

I'm not nervous so much (though I'm nervous) as apprehensive, and not so much apprehensive as a wee gone with guilt. More than a wee. Why am I here? *I* don't have Ross's mission. The Regional Arts Commission, Arts and Education Council of Greater St. Louis, and Missouri and Illinois arts councils don't fund *me* to build an audience for modern dance. *Build* an audience? If I had my way, I'd disassemble what's here.

Though it's hardly SRO, or even the mythic "pretty good house" of our comforter's reports and special pleading, it's up from last night. Maybe 250. Many are little girls, even more than on Friday. More homemakers, too. I'm thinking of what I heard two ladies say to each other after MADCO's performance in Winfield: "Pretty neat, wasn't it?" "Oh, I thought it was *real* good." This far south in Kansas, I remember thinking, people sound as if they're from Oklahoma. It could be, this grammar, this music, this language of placed persons, the true, sweet, inflected neighborlies of Prairie itself.

Because I know what's coming after intermission.

Me. Yours truly's coming, the larky, city-slicker Jew with his love rabbi and his love rabbi's blow-job conversations and his love rabbi's death jive. Right here in walnut-bowl country, deep in the cavern counties, hard by Orville & Betty's two-buck ham 'n' egg breakfasts. In Passion Play territory. Only it's not like it sounds. I swear it isn't. I'm *not* afraid of them. I'm not. I just don't want to upset anyone's apple cart or ruffle the feathers. I would leave everyone's dander down where I found it. I've no desire to build an audience, even my own.

Only it goes without a hitch. Technical *or* spiritual. The applause is even more generous than last night. There are curtain calls. I get roses.

It's Ross, ringing me in my room, can he come over.

He sits in one of those light, polypropylene, contoured shell chairs, universal as coat hangers. He's drinking a generic 1.75-liter bourbon with ginger ale. I'm dressed, sprawled on the bedspread. He drinks, I think, recalling "affairs," like a Jew.

"I thought show people," I tell him, "were supposed to be sentimental, ceremonial. Well, those awards shows, those Oscars and Tonys, that Lifetime Achievement crap. Well those curtain

calls, well those roses." We're really talking about Darla, who
drove off after the performance with her parents and boyfriend
and scarcely a word to anyone. "I'd expected a scene, *counted* on
a scene. At least toasts, at least hugs and handshakes and the
we'll-meet-agains people taking their leave owe each other out
of respect for endings, rites of passage. My turnout ain't any
better than Darla's."

"Well," says Ross, "maybe not everyone can throw herself on
the mercy of the court with your abandon."

Ross is in a mood. Not a *bad* mood. Actually he's rather
pleased with how things turned out. Especially after last night's
performance. He blames the dancers. "They should have gone
to their battle stations."

We're gossiping, getting *down*. I have to be careful what I ask
him. He won't duck a question. He tells me what he makes, he
gives the reasons he broke up with his wife.

"Do you ever think of leaving St. Louis?"

"I think of changing my life. I don't mind about the money.
You can decorate an apartment quite nicely with what people
throw away. I would have taken that floor lamp. I didn't because
it was ugly. Some street people have no taste at all."

And ah, I'm thinking, ah, the young 'uns out on the town, me
and Ross waiting up for them, bandying our eleventh-hour
truck-farm confessions and plans, talking all the high and dry,
buddy-stranded locutions of lull.

"Well," Ross said, "I don't socialize with them anyway. They're
my tribal family. I'm their elder. It's nothing personal. I guess
Liz was teacher's pet. If I had one. By dint of long tenure, her
right-hand-man manners. *Droit de* right-handedness."

"I have to laugh," I say. "You know what they said at the
reception? 'Springfield needed to hear that.' *Jesus!* Want some
gum? I chew lots of gum since I quit smoking."

"I don't chew gum. In Australia, during my formative gum-
chewing years, it was rationed. Now it's too frustrating. I feel I
should be able to break it down and eat it."

"I understand. I really do."

If the place had room service I'd have sent out long ago.
There's nothing to nosh but gum, but we're all over the board.
We could be in Cincinnati, I'm thinking.

"Liz used to be a mouse," Ross says. "She used to dance with her body screaming 'Don't look.' And it hasn't quite clicked with Ellen yet that she's there solely for the pleasure of the audience. She's too shy with her talents. She has to learn to throw them out into the house. An audience wants to be flashed."

Paul's too intense, Ross says. He's very smart but too intense. In a mood, Ross doodles his dancers. Of the women, Raeleen's the strongest. Jeff has the best stretch and turnout, the most extension. Michael is a teddy bear and could be a wonderful dancer. He watches too much TV.

"Too much TV?"

"Turnout, extension, strength, and stretch are important. Mind is a dancer's most important instrument."

Liz, James, Jeffrey, and David are at the door.

"Come in," I say, flattered, "come in. Come in."

"Is Ross around?"

"Come in."

Jeffrey, subdued, is already anxious to leave. After Friday's performance he went for a walk. He'd been thinking about his career. He didn't get back to the motel until 2 A.M. He was pretty tired, he said. He thought he'd better get going.

Ross is using my bathroom. Liz says, "He has to know."

"Tonight? Come on," David says, "tonight was terrific. Don't bother him tonight."

"He should know. I don't care, he should. David, James, I'm going to tell him."

"Jeffrey should tell him."

"He just told *us*." When Ross comes back Liz says, "Ross, that Saturday Jeffrey missed rehearsal? When he said he'd made plans? He was in Chicago auditioning with Shirley Mordine's company."

Ross didn't say anything for a while. I know that's what they all say, that they don't say anything for a while. Or that they blanch, go white as the unimpeachable testimony of Darla's clown-white pain, but that's what happened. Maybe there's a muse of the autonomic physiologicals for bad news, or when you've been let down, badly disappointed, some Muse of the Involuntary Facials, and a muse working, too, when he recovers, finally speaks. The Muse of At a Loss, Vamp 'til Ready.

"If he'd asked I'd have let him. I would. It's helpful for a young dancer to audition, to get someone else's opinion of what he does wrong. I'd have let him."

"Did he get the job?" I ask.

"He says he has a good feeling," Liz says.

"You know Jeffrey," David says, "he has a good feeling if the ketchup on his hamburger isn't green."

"I'm dissolving the company."

"Ross, you're upset." Liz is stroking his arm, giving out comfort like first aid.

"Darla's gone. Liz is moving with James to Arizona. Now Jeffrey? I'm dissolving MADCO. It's my company, I can do what I please."

"And put the others out of work?"

"Sleep on it, Ross," James advises. "You're upset. Don't make rash decisions when you're upset."

"I'm a grown man. I'll make rash decisions when I please. More than just wedding bells are breaking up that old gang of mine," he tells him. "I'll tell them tomorrow."

But he doesn't. The Muse of Second Thoughts.

When Ross sent Jeffrey's check he thanked him for his patience but told him he was not being asked back for next season due to his lack of professionalism and commitment to the company. The women have been replaced, but until he can find a replacement for Jeffrey, they'll be dancing with two men, not three; six dancers, not seven. They book programs in advance. "Continents" may have to be dropped from the repertoire, though Paul thinks that with a quick costume change either he or Michael ought to be able to double up on one of the parts. "Hidden Walls of Time" and "Pretty Fooles and Peasantries" are definitely out, as is, of course, "Notes Toward a Eulogy for Joan Cohen."

The irony muse which plucks my gig and leaves this crippled-up old soul hi-diddle-de-deeless. Until, at least, Life breathes on my life again, the all-embracing muse of lark and unexpected compensations.

JOSEPH EPSTEIN

Confessions of a Low Roller

FROM THE AMERICAN SCHOLAR

OURS HAS LONG been a distinguished publishing family, if you take the adjective "distinguished" in a loose sense and if you allow a definition of "publishing" broad enough to include bookmaking. I don't mean to brag about family lineage, but I had an uncle, dead some years now, who had fully two sobriquets: in some quarters he was known as Lefty and in others as Square Sam. All gamblers, it is often enough said, die broke, but my uncle, whom I scarcely knew, is reported to have left the planet with something on the order of twenty-five Ultrasuede jackets hanging in the closet of his home in Los Angeles. Beginning life as a professional gambler, he soon went into publishing (or bookmaking) and eventually owned a small piece of a large casino-hotel in Las Vegas. To place him for you socially, he was a man at whose granddaughter's wedding a guest was Frank Sinatra. Need I say more?

Although this uncle did not carry my family name, there was a prominent gambler who did. Some years ago I read a lengthy obituary in a Chicago newspaper about a man who carried my exact name, first and last, and who was described in the obit headline as "Joseph Epstein, Gentleman Big-Time Bookie, Dies at 75." My namesake — or am I his? — turns out to have run, in the words of the obituarist, "a large betting layoff operation from offices [that covered] wagers that bookies across the nation could not handle." The obituarist continued: "Although his associates were more often coarse, devious, violent men, [he] had the reputation of a bookmaker who kept his word and was mild-mannered in the extreme. He was well-read, fancied himself as a Talmudic scholar and was clearly the intellectual bookie of his time." It gets better. It seems that this man bearing my name also served as a Professor Henry Higgins to a gangland moll named Virginia Hill, who came to Chicago from Alabama at seventeen, whose great and good friend, as *Time* magazine used to put it, he was, though she finally left him for Benjamin (Bugsy) Siegel. "A non-smoker," the obituary notes, "he remained in robust health almost until his death by taking long, daily walks through the city [of Chicago] from his hotel on Ohio St."

The gentleman big-time bookie bearing my name died in Chicago in 1976, a fact that fills me with double regret, first for his death, for he appeared to have been a decent sort, and second because I wish I had had the chance to meet and talk with him. It is not about the Talmud that I wish I could have talked with "the intellectual bookie of his time," but about shop — specifically, about gambling. No photograph appeared with his obituary, but I imagine him to be a smallish man, silver-haired, expensively yet not gaudily dressed, good shoes well shined, nails manicured. We might have walked along Michigan Boulevard together on a late, lightly breezy afternoon in May, past Tiffany and Cartier and Saks Fifth Avenue and Neiman-Marcus, stopping off for an apéritif in the cool, wood-paneled Coq d'Or bar in the Drake Hotel. Seated at one of the small tables in the dark room where sound tends to be gently muffled, I would have encouraged him to recount anecdotes about noble behavior on the part of crooks, in exchange for which I would have supplied him with anecdotes about what crooks academics can be. We should, I do not doubt, have addressed each other as "Mister," with the charm of adding to it our selfsame last name.

If the mood were right, perhaps our talk might have ascended to philosophy, always within the confines of shop, of course. Why do men gamble? I might have asked him. Is gambling in the end always a ruinous diversion? Is there something masochistic about it? Was Malraux right when he called it, in connection with his character Clappique in *Man's Fate*, "suicide without death"? Is gambling not a metaphor but a metaphorical activity, since, as has been noted, life itself goes off at something

like 6–5 against, though some think these odds unduly generous? Why does gambling excite, exhilarate, and depress some
people while not arousing the least interest in others? What does
gambling do for those people who go in for it in a big way? For
those who enjoy it only occasionally? And, while I am at it, I
might just have lowered the tone of the conversation and inquired if I was a chump to agree to an arrangement whereby I
would have to pay 10 percent juice, or vigorish, on a $300 bet
on this past year's World Series.

Consider, please, that figure $300, or $330 if I lost. Something rather hopeless about those numbers, if you ask me, something neither here nor there. I had originally intended to bet
$1,000 ("a grand," in the grand old term), which is a good deal
more than I have ever bet on anything, and then I decided that
$500 was sufficient. But when I reached an old friend who has
a bookie — I bet much too infrequently to have my own — I
heard myself say $300. I don't mean to suggest that $300 is a
negligible sum; if one is down and out, it is a most impressive
sum. I am sure that someone reading this is ready to inform me,
in a properly moral tone, that a family of four could eat for a
month on $300. Nowadays, though, there are restaurants in
New York where one has to cut corners — go for the California
wine instead of the French — to get a full dinner for two for
less than $300. I myself consider it immoral to dine in such
places. "It is all," as Albert Einstein must at some time have said
to Max Planck, "relative."

If all this sounds a little goofy, it is merely because it is. No
activity has been more rationalized than gambling — odds figured, probabilities worked out, point spreads meticulously es-
tablished — and no activity, surely, is finally more irrational. In
this essentially irrational activity, the first item that must be
fixed, and with some precision, is the stake. Above all, it cannot
be too little; it must be enough to stimulate whatever those
spiritual glands are that gambling calls into action. The punish-
ment must fit the crime; the agony of losing must be roughly
equivalent to the ecstasy of winning. In this sense, it becomes
clear that no bet can ever be too large; and herein lies the
madness inherent in gambling, for the more you have, the more
you need to risk.

"Important money" is what professional gamblers used to call big bets, and such fabled gamblers as Pittsburgh Phil (a horseplayer), Nick the Greek (cards and dice), and Ray Ryan (gin rummy) never played for unimportant money. Nick the Greek, whose last name was Dandolos, claimed once to have bet $280,000 on a five coming up before a seven in a crap game. The same Mr. Dandolos is said to have lost $900,000 in a single night in New York on the eve of a holiday trip to Europe, which — surprise! surprise! — had to be canceled. Winning a bet, Nick Dandolos used to say, is man's greatest pleasure; the second greatest pleasure, he claimed, is losing a bet. In more than fifty years of serious gambling, something on the order of $50,000,000 is supposed to have trafficked in and out of his hands. Yet Nick the Greek was no money snob. The late Jimmy Cannon, the sportswriter, told the story of the Greek's playing twenty-four hours straight at Arnold Rothstein's crap table and, after the crap game broke up, sitting down to play casino for twenty-five cents a hand with one of Rothstein's stickmen. "Action is all he wants," Cannon concluded, "and he has lasted longer than any of them and held on to his dignity."

Some gamblers get a thrill out of the action itself, while others need to be in action at high prices. The greater the stakes, the greater the pressure, the greater the cool (or courage) required. Damon Runyon, a gambler all his life and a student of gamblers, maintained he knew "men who will beat far better card players at gin [rummy] if the stakes are high enough just on simple courage." A gambler is like an airplane in that at a certain altitude — for the gambler, at certain high sums — the controls start to shake. I earlier mentioned certain "spiritual glands" that needed to be stimulated by gambling, but anatomical ones are often also called into play, producing sweaty hands, dry mouth, inconvenient loss of the control of facial muscles. No, nothing quite relaxes a fella like an evening of gambling.

Growing up in Chicago, I had a friend whose father was reputed to have bet $100,000 on a baseball game — and lost. This was during the early 1940s, when $100,000 was extremely important money and not the annual salary of a utility infielder or a Marxist professor of English at Duke University. Inconveniently, my friend's father didn't have the money; conveniently, there was a war on. As the story goes, he showed up the next afternoon at the bookie's with a smile and in a set of U.S. Navy bell bottoms, having enlisted that morning. The uniform, supposedly, saved his life, for no one was about to kill a man in uniform during wartime, and he was able to arrange terms to pay off his debt.

What made him bet such a sum? He was living in Los Angeles at the time — always a hot gambling town, according to Damon Runyon — and must have waked one sunny weekday morning (I always imagine it to be a Tuesday) in an impatient mood. A voice within must have whispered, "Let 'er rip!" He did, and it nearly tore him in two. Almost all baseball games were played during the day at that time, so he must have known not much later than 2:30 P.M. Los Angeles time that he had made a serious mistake. I am pleased not to have been the one to serve him that evening's dinner, or to have to ask him if the lamb was properly underdone.

He died before I knew him, whether of heart attack, cancer, or stroke I cannot recall, but he couldn't have been more than in his early fifties. His wife and only son lived on after him in what I think of not as shabby gentility but elegant shabbility. They lived in a small one-bedroom apartment in a building with a doorman on a once posh but now fading Chicago street. Wife and son spoke of him with affection and awe, and in one corner of the small apartment were framed glossy signed photographs taken of him in the company of famous Jewish comedians and Italian singers — or was it Italian comedians and Jewish singers? Not a marathon man, he lived life at a sprint, going fast and dying young. Why is it that we look with wonder upon a man who one day bets $100,000 on the outcome of a game and loses yet feel no wonder whatsoever looking upon a man who works a lifetime to stow away a few million?

My own interest in gambling — and now we return to someone never likely to have the mad courage to bet $100,000 or the powers of concentration to earn a million — initially derived from the social atmosphere in which I came of age. By this I certainly don't mean my home. My father had not the least interest in cards, sports, or gambling generally, preferring situations, such as the one he had inserted himself into as the owner of a small business, in which as far as possible he could control his own destiny. Most of the men in the rising middle-class Jewish milieu that I grew up in felt much the same. They were physicians and lawyers and businessmen, and worked hard so that their children could have an easier life than they, as the sons of immigrants, had had. Some among them gambled — played a little gin rummy or in a small-stakes poker game, bet $50 on a prizefight — but clearly work was at the center of their lives. They believed in personal industry, in thrift, in saving for the future. Entrepreneurial in spirit, they also believed that only a fool works for someone else.

On the periphery, though, were a small number of men who lived and believed otherwise. Two boys among my school friends and acquaintances had fathers who were bookies, and rather big-time ones, judging by the scale on which they lived. Nothing back of the candy store or Broadway cigar stand about them; they were rather like the rest of our fathers, but home more often and with better tans and more telephones in the house. They lived on the edge of the criminal world. So, too, I gather did the father of a girl I knew in high school; he played golf from April until October and from October until April played high-stakes gin rummy at a place atop the Sheraton Hotel called The Town Club; the younger brother of a Capone lieutenant, he was rumored to collect a dollar a month on every jukebox installed in Chicago. The brother of a man I once worked for when I was in high school was said to be a full-time gambler, making his living (he was a bachelor) betting on sports events. In his forties then, he carried the nickname "Acey"; if he is still alive, he would now be in his seventies, which is a bit old to carry around such a nickname. I would often see him at baseball games on weekday afternoons, where, well groomed and well rested, he looked as if his personal motto, an edited version of my father's and my friends' fathers', might read: "Only a fool works."

When young, I felt a strong attraction to such men. The attraction was to their seemingly effortless access to what I then took to be the higher and finer things of life. Their connection to corruption also excited me. Corruption was endemic to Chicago, a city that prided itself on its gangsters the way that other cities were proud of their artists, and one had to be brought up in a glass bubble — make that an isinglass bubble — not to come in contact with it. Dickens, Dostoyevsky, Dreiser, and many a novelist since knew that corruption is more alluring, and more convincingly described, than goodness. Goodness, on first acquaintance, is a bit boring — and, when young, the only thing duller than goodness is common sense.

I had an acquaintance whose father became a very rich man in a very brief time through selling very ugly aluminum awnings. One Saturday afternoon I went with him to his father's small factory, where, among his father and his father's salesmen, each with a high stack of bills in front of him, a serious poker game was in progress. My own father often used the phrase "place of business" with something of the same reverence that some reserve for the phrase "place of worship," and the idea of a poker game on the site of his business would have appalled him. At the time, it rather thrilled me. But then it would be many years until I came round to my father's view, which was essentially the view set out by Henry James in a youthful letter to his friend Charles Eliot Norton: "I have in my own fashion learned the lesson that life is effort, unremittingly repeated. . . . I feel somehow as if the real pity was for those who had been beguiled into the perilous delusion that it isn't."

So beguiled, I spent much of my adolescence in imitation of what I took to be the model of the gambler. During our last year of grammar school, my friends and I met for penny poker games on Saturday afternoons before ballroom dancing lessons. There we sat, at thirteen years old, neckties loosened, jackets draped over the backs of chairs, cigarettes depending unsteadily from the sides of our mouths, smoke causing our eyes to water and squint, playing seven-card stud, deuces usually wild. Quite a scene. Each of us must have thought himself some variant of George Raft, James Cagney, Humphrey Bogart, or John Garfield, when Leo Gorcey and the Dead End Kids gone middle class was much more like it. "My pair of jacks sees your three cents, Ronald, and I bump you a nickel."

A misspent youth? I suppose it was, though I never thought of it as such. Perhaps this was owing to its being so immensely enjoyable. In high school, gambling went from an occasional to an almost incessant activity. Although we never shot dice, my friends and I played every variation of poker, blackjack, and gin rummy. From city newsstand vendors we acquired and bet football parlay cards. Every so often, on weekend nights, we would travel out of the city to the sulky races, or "the trotters" as we called them, at Maywood Park. Some unrecognized genius invented a game called "pot-luck," a combination of blackjack and in-between, which guaranteed that, no matter how minimal the stakes to begin with, one would soon be playing for more than one could afford. With its built-in escalation element, pot-luck was a game that produced high excitement, for it was not unusual for someone to walk away from these games a $200 winner. I won my share, but more vividly than any win do I remember one gray wintry afternoon when, between four and six o'clock, I lost $125 — this at a time when that figure might pay a month's rent on a two-bedroom apartment in a respectable middle-class neighborhood. If the end of the world had been announced on that evening's news, I, at seventeen, shouldn't in the least have minded. In fact, as I recall, I felt it already had.

Gambling, though scarcely a valuable education in itself, did teach a thing or two about one's own nature. I learned about the limits of my courage with money, for one thing; for another, I learned that, in gambling, as in life, you could figure the odds, the probabilities, the little and large likelihoods, and still, when lightning struck in the form of ill luck, logic was no help. I learned I had to put a good, and insofar as possible stylish, face on defeat, even though losing was very far from my idea of a nice time. If you were even mildly attentive, gambling revealed your character to you, showed it in operation under pressure, often taught you the worst about yourself. Some people wanted to win too sorely; they whined and moaned, banged the table and cursed the gods when they lost and seemed smug and self-justified in victory. Others sat grim and humorless over their cards, gloomy in defeat and always ready to settle for a small win. Still others exhibited, even at sixteen or seventeen, a certain largeness of spirit; they were ready to trust their luck; they had a feeling for the game, which I took to be a feeling for life itself, and were delighted to be in action.

"In action" is an old gambler's phrase; and "the action" used to refer to gambling generally. Yet, for all its insistence on action, gambling can be excruciatingly boring. During one stretch in the army, I played poker at Fort Chaffee, in Arkansas, almost nightly for roughly six weeks; I played less for the excitement of gambling than to combat the boredom of army life when one is confined to a post. It turned out to be boredom pitted against boredom. In a rather low-stakes game over this period I emerged roughly a $400 winner. Some of this money I sent to a friend to buy me books in Chicago. The rest I spent on a steak and champagne dinner in the town of Fort Smith, Arkansas, for eight or nine barracks mates. Doing this seemed to me at the time a gesture of magnificence befitting a gambling man.

I remember this especially because it is the only use to which I can ever remember putting any money that I have won gambling. I cannot otherwise recall buying with gambling winnings a sweater, a shirt, a sock, a Q-Tip. Such money has had a way of disappearing from me. Poof: not very easily come, altogether mysteriously gone. Which reminds me that gambling has never, for me, been primarily about money. I was fortunate, of course, in never having to gamble with money intended for rent or food, thereby, as a character in Pushkin's gambling story "Queen of Spades" puts it, risking "the necessary to win the superfluous." When the money wasn't there — when I was a young husband and father with no extra "tease," as the old horseplayers used to call money — I was easily enough able to refrain from gambling, which strengthens me in my cherished belief that as a gambler I am merely a dreamer and a fool and not an addict.

Gambling addicts are not on the whole an elegant sight. The crowds one encounters at a Nevada casino or at a sulky track on a wintry Wednesday night are quite as depressing as those at a national meeting of the Modern Language Association. Many years ago, in an effort to turn up a bit of tease without actually having to gamble for it, I wrote a piece of journalism on an outfit known as Gamblers Anonymous, which operates on the same principles — confession and comradeship in crisis — as Alcoholics Anonymous. At these meetings one hears an *Iliad* of woe, with enough material left over for an *Odyssey* of misery and an *Aeneid* of heartbreak: story after story of disappointed children, weeping wives, broken bones accompanying unpaid debts, busted-up homes destroyed by busted-out gamblers. On view here is the other side of gambling, the creepy and crummy side, where one hears a man recount how one morning, when his wife is out at the beauty shop, he sells off all the family furniture to get the money to support his hot hunches at the track that afternoon ("I figured I'd buy all new furniture with my winnings," he reports, "a nice surprise for the wife"), hunches that of course didn't work out; another man recounts how he broke into his son's silver dollar piggy bank for action money, then says nothing when his wife accuses his young son's best friend of taking the money; a man . . . but you get the general idea.

A more particular idea that attendance at these Gamblers Anonymous meetings conveys is the power that gambling can exert over those hooked on it. In its thrall, all other appetites tend to diminish. While one is gambling, food is of no interest, nor is alcohol. Gambling can also throw off one's interior clock, and while at it one is capable of prodigious wakefulness, so that, within limits, gambling can be said to triumph over time and fatigue. When serious gambling is going on, sex seems quite beside the point. At the compulsive level, gambling is all-consuming, and while it doesn't, like drugs or alcohol, fog the mind, it generally monopolizes it. When winning at gambling, one is in the country of the blue; when losing, the world seems mean and red and utterly hopeless. Gambling, one is either flying or crawling, elated or degraded. If any gambler was ever able to find the golden mean, he would probably bet it on the six horse in the fourth race at Pimlico.

As an activity that issues only in extreme states, gambling is of course a great Russian subject. Russians have gone in for gambling in a big way, both actually and literarily. Pushkin turned a card or two in his time, and his story "Queen of Spades" gives ample evidence of his knowing at first hand the desolation of a resounding defeat at the tables. The dissipated young Count Leo Tolstoy was passionate about cards, though not very good at them, even though he devised a system that he set down on paper under the title "Rules for Card-Playing"; like many another such system, it plunged its creator into great debt. A 3,000-ruble loss forced Tolstoy to put himself on a 10-ruble-a-month budget. After suffering gambling losses, the young count would proceed to flog himself — in his diary, of course. When his debts grew too great, he could always sell off a meadow or forest or horses from his estate. This is the stuff out of which nineteenth-century Russian novels are made. Tolstoy didn't simply make it all up.

Nor did Dostoyevsky, whose gambling problem ran deeper than Tolstoy's if only because he, not being an aristocrat, had no estate to sell off to clear his debts. Unlike Tolstoy, too, Dostoyevsky's gambling was not a form of dissipation. He gambled for the most commonsensical of reasons: he needed the money. The problem is that gambling — especially roulette, which was Dostoyevsky's game — may be the quickest but is clearly not the most efficient way of obtaining it. According to Joseph Frank, in his splendid biography of Dostoyevsky, the novelist was unfortunate in winning 11,000 francs in his first attempt at gambling. The hook was in. Yet Dostoyevsky, again according to Professor Frank, was not a pathological gambler but a fitful and sporadic one. He did suffer the inability that gamblers share with gluttons — that of not knowing when to leave the table. After each of his inevitably disastrous gambling episodes, Joseph Frank reports, "Dostoyevsky always returned to his writing desk with renewed vigor and a strong sense of deliverance." Dostoyevsky's losses, then, turned out to be world literature's gain. Fate sometimes uses a strange accounting system.

A highly superstitious man, ever on the lookout for omens and portents, Dostoyevsky had a theory about how to win at gambling that was utterly opposed to his own nature. Dostoyevsky's theory, or system, or secret called for mastery of the emotions while in action. "This secret," Dostoyevsky writes in a letter, "I really know it; it's terribly stupid and simple and consists in holding oneself in at every moment and not to get excited, no matter what the play. And that's all; it's then absolutely impossible to lose, and one is sure of winning." Tolstoy's system, too, called for control of the emotions and moderation — precisely the two things Tolstoy himself was incapable of achieving. "Those who are indifferent are those who are rewarded," wrote

Jack Richardson, formulating this view in a single, short, well-made sentence in *Memoir of a Gambler,* his elegant, amusing, and profound book that itself sadly came up snake eyes, double zero, and busto in the casino of American publishing when it first appeared in 1979. Richardson's view, like those of Dostoyevsky and Tolstoy, assumes that the gods who watch over gambling are themselves not indifferent or are likely to be fooled by men pretending to a coolness it is not theirs to control. That either assumption is correct is, at best, 9–2 against.

If gambling seems an activity well suited to the Russian temperament with its taste for provoking fate, it is, even though illegal in forty-eight of America's fifty states, very far from un-American. To have come to America in the first place was to take a serious gamble. To advance with the country's frontier was another gamble. When one says that Americans like to gamble, one is of course really saying that the people who have come to America like to gamble. Whenever I have been in a casino, I have noted what seemed to me a high percentage of Asians, most of them Chinese. Jimmy Cannon recalls the older Irishmen in Greenwich Village, where he grew up, disapproving of gambling unless a man was single. Blacks were big for the numbers game and are now, I observe, heavy players in state lotteries. Jews and Italians grow up in gambling cultures — or at least they did when I was a boy — and some among them cross to the other side of the table, becoming bookies or casino owners, donning the expressionless face and the Ultrasuede jacket, like my deceased uncle, squarest of Sams. Texans, to touch on what is almost another ethnic group, have been known to be most earnest about poker played for heart-attack stakes. All of these are what are known as risky generalizations, subject to vehement exceptions: a friend who grew up in a Jewish working-class neighborhood, for example, informs me that in his youth a gambler was considered lower even than a Rumanian. Various anti-defamation leagues — Chinese, Black, Jewish, Italian, Irish, Texan, Rumanian — wishing to protest this paragraph may reach me at my office, care of the director, Center for Advanced Ethnic Insensitivity.

Men seem to go in for gambling more than women because, as boys, they often play games and thus early acquire the habits of competition. (Competition among women, even as young girls, is subtler, having to do with refinement, sophistication, beauty, and generally less blatant things than strength, agility, and speed.) Games that absorb one's energies in the playing of them do not require gambling for enjoyment. This is true of football, basketball, and baseball — on which men do often bet to get their competitive juices flowing after they are no longer able to play the games themselves — as well as tennis, running, and gymnastics. It isn't true of golf, which needs the stimulus of little side bets to get one round the course, or billiards, every shot of which seems to cry out for a bet. Chess and bridge are games of sufficient intellectual intricacy to be played without gambling, even though I realize many people — Somerset Maugham among them — have played bridge for high stakes. Poker, blackjack, and gin rummy without money riding on the outcome are games suitable only for some knotty-pined recreation room in hell.

In bringing up boyhood with regard to gambling, I am, I fear, playing into the strong hand of the Freudians. This is a dangerous thing to do, for those guys will sandbag you and whipsaw you. They endlessly raise the stakes. If you open by allowing that gambling is connected with youth, they will call and raise you by saying that it is a neurosis. Bid that gambling can give pleasure, they return by saying — I quote Dr. Otto Fenichel in *The Psychoanalytic Theory of Neurosis* — that the passion for gambling "is a displaced expression of conflicts around infantile sexuality, aroused by the fear of losing necessary reassurance regarding anxiety or guilt feelings." Aver that gambling issues in excitement, they — I quote Dr. Fenichel again — will counter by asserting that "the unconscious 'masturbatory fantasies' of gambling often center around patricide." I realize that W. H. Auden once remarked that "the attitude of psychology should always be, 'Have you heard this one?'" but "masturbatory fantasies" and "patricide"? Is this what is truly going on when one gambles? I wouldn't bet on it.

Freud claimed that much of what he knew he learned from the poets, and I, for one, would rather consult the poets than the Freudians on the subject of gambling. Unfortunately, the poets — and writers generally — do not seem to have had all that much to say about it. Pushkin's story "Queen of Spades" is about a young officer who commits murder in the attempt to obtain a secret system for winning at cards, a murder that is revenged when the system betrays him and causes him to live out his days in madness. Pushkin's is a morality tale and is not quite up to the mark either in explaining or depicting the passion for gambling. Dostoyevsky's *The Gambler* is much more like it. The novella's scenes set in the casino are absolutely convincing, not only in detail but in the understanding behind them of the wild roller coaster the gambler travels from exhilaration ("I was only aware of an immense enjoyment — success, victory, power — I don't know how to describe it") to damnable despair expressed in "calm fury" at realizing that one is not "above all these stupid ups and downs of fate" but finally, like everyone else, their victim. *The Gambler* is not among Dostoyevsky's great works; with its characters' propensity for bizarre behavior and the many loose ends that never quite get tied up at the story's conclusion, it is perhaps rather too Dostoyevskian, but it does have the immense authority of a work written by a man who knew his subject from the inside.

For my money, though, the best literary work on the subject of gambling was written by an outsider. That story is "James Pethel," in the collection *Seven Men* by Max Beerbohm, who, so far as I know, had no interest whatsoever in gambling. The James Pethel of Beerbohm's story is known as an active taker of big risks and one who has had tremendous good luck: in stock-market speculation, at the baccarat tables at the casino at Dieppe, on wildly venturesome foreign investments. Beerbohm makes plain that the mere sight of habitual gamblers "always filled me with a depression bordering on disgust." Pethel, however, is no ordinary gambler. On the night that he and Beerbohm meet, after Beerbohm warns him that the water isn't safe to drink, Pethel is encouraged to order not one but two glasses of it, the risk of typhoid only making it more enticing. Casino gambling, one learns, is really only Pethel's way of keeping in trim for such ventures as swimming in dangerous waters, driving at maniacal speed (with his wife and daughter, whom he dearly loves, and Beerbohm in the car), and stunt flying. Pethel is, in short, a risk freak, the ultimate gambler who can finally be stimulated only by the ultimate gambles — those in which his own life and the lives of those he loves are on the line. The story is made all the more chilling when at the end we learn that Pethel has died of a heart attack after a flying session, with his daughter and her infant son aboard, and that he had been suffering from a bad heart condition for many years. Beerbohm, with consummate artistry, concludes: "Let not our hearts be vexed that his great luck was with him to the end."

Max Beerbohm despises James Pethel; adore Max Beerbohm though I do, I cannot come down so strongly on his creation, even though I recognize him for the monster he is. The reason I cannot is that through my veins run a few stray particles of the virulent virus that has him firmly in its grip. To the vast majority of people it never occurs to gamble — on anything. To others the possibility of gambling is scratched at the painful prospect of losing; Montaigne, interestingly, was among this group, for, though a card player and crap shooter in his youth, he gave up gambling for the reason that "however good a face I put upon my losses, I did not fail to feel stung by them within." A small group of us feel the same sting Montaigne did — with, I suspect, quite the same intensity — but persist. Why?

Why, I ask myself, do I, who am surely among the world's luckiest men (I touch wood as I write out that last clause), need to risk $330 on a series of baseball games, the outcome of which is otherwise of less than negligible interest to me? I think it has to do with the need I from time to time feel for venturing forth, for striking out against what has become the general quietude and orderliness of my life. As a boy, I never expected to live so calmly as I now do, with the risk of sending up my cholesterol count from eating an occasional steak being perhaps the biggest risk I take. I live, by a choice I do not quite recall having made, a quiet life, for the most part contemplating the world's foolishness instead of partaking in it directly. But when the quiet life grows too quiet, when it threatens to lapse into the most dread disease I know, which is fear of living, then I call on the antidote of gambling.

Perhaps there are quicker antidotes than a World Series bet on which the tension can be drawn out over more than a week's time. But this was the medicine nearest to hand, and I availed myself of it. Observing myself in action over the course of what turned out to be an extended gamble provided its own slightly tortured amusement. As the Series unfolded, I went from mild depression to measured hopefulness to dignified optimism to serene confidence. I passed a local jeweler's window and noted that he was running a sale of 40 percent off on Movado wristwatches. I already own a Movado watch, but I thought I might use my winnings to buy another. Then it occurred to me to begin a small gambling account, out of which I would begin betting more regularly than I do now. Grand plans were abuilding when — *wham!* — the St. Louis Cardinals, the team I had bet on, lost the last two games of the World Series, and I was seated at my desk writing out a check for $330.

The gods, it is pleasing to learn, are still watching over me.

RICHARD FORD

Accommodations

FROM BANANA REPUBLIC TRIPS

AND WHAT was it like to live there? From my childhood, this memory: I am in bed. It is one o'clock in the morning. I am eleven years old, and in a room inside my grandfather's hotel — the room connecting to his. I am awake, listening. This is what I hear. Someplace, through walls, an argument is going on. A man and a woman are arguing. I hear some dishes rattle and then break. The words "You don't care. No, you don't" spoken by a woman. How far away this goes on I can't tell. Rooms away is all. I heard a door open into the hall, and a voice that's louder — the man's — say, "Better you than me in this is what I know. You bet." I hear keys jingling, a door close softly, then footsteps over the carpeted hallway. And then a smell of sweet perfume in my room, an orchid smell, all around me where I'm alone and in the dark, lying still. I hear an elevator grate drawn back. A second woman's voice farther away, talking softly, then the door closes, and it's quiet again inside. I hear a bus hiss at the station across the city street. A car horn blows. Somewhere outside someone begins to laugh, the laughter coming up off the empty pavement and into the night. Then no more noises. The perfume drifts through my room, stays in the air. I hear my grandfather turn in his sleep and sigh. Then sleep comes back.

This was the fifties, and my grandfather ran the hotel where we lived — in Little Rock, a town neither exactly south nor exactly west, just as it still is. To live in a hotel promotes a cool two-mindedness: one is both steady and in a sea that passes with tides. Accommodation is what's wanted, a replenished idea of permanence and transience; familiarity overcoming the continual irregularity in things.

The hotel was named the Marion, and it was not a small place. Little Rock was a mealy, low-rise town on a slow river, and the hotel was the toniest, plushest place in it. And still it was blowsy, a hotel for conventioneers and pols, salesmen and late-night party givers. There was a curving marble fish pond in the lobby; a tranquil, banistered mezzanine with escritoires and soft lights; a jet marble front desk; long, green leather couches, green carpets, bellboys with green twill uniforms and short memories. It was a columned brownstone with a porte-cochère, built in the twenties, with seven stories, three hundred rooms. Ladies from the Delta stayed in on shopping trips. The Optimists and the Rotarians met. Assignations between state officials went on upstairs. Senator McClellan kept a room. Visiting famous people stayed, and my grandfather kept their pictures on his office wall — Rex Allen the cowboy, Jack Dempsey the boxing champion, June Allyson and Dick Powell, Harry Truman (whose photograph I have, still), Ricky Nelson, Chill Wills. Salesmen rented sample rooms, suicides took singles. There were hospitality suites, honeymoon suites, a Presidential, a Miss America, Murphy beds, silver service, Irish napkins. There was a bakery, a print shop, an upholsterer, ten rooms (the Rendezvous, the Continental) for intimate parties, six more for large, and a ballroom with a Hammond organ for banquets. There was a beer bar in the lower lobby, a two-chair barbershop, a cigar stand, a florist, a travel agent, a news agent, a garage where you parked for nothing while you stayed. There was a drummer's rate, a serviceman's rate, a monthly rate, a day rate, even an hourly rate if you knew my grandfather. Everything happened there, at all hours. Privacy had a high value. To live in a hotel as a boy knowing nothing was to see what adults did to each other and themselves when only adults were present.

My grandfather, Ben Shelley, was a man of strong appetites — food, but other things, too. The usual things. He was a fatty who played winter golf in pleated gabardines, shot pool and quail. He qualified as a sport, a Shriner, a wide, public man, a toddling character in a blue suit with change in his pockets and a money clip. To me, he was the exotic brought to common earth, and I loved him. "The latchstring is always on the outside" was his motto, and he winked at you when he said that, smiled between his thick amorous lips, as though his words meant something else, which they may have. I could think different of him now, see him through new eyes, revise history, take a narrower, latter-day view. But why?

He had been a boxer — a featherweight, a club fighter; worked dining cars on the Rock Island as far as Tucumcari, waited tables in El Reno, been a caterer's assistant at the famous Muehlebach in Kansas City. That was the way up in the hotel business, and such work was his by nature. Service. That word meant something it doesn't mean now.

What his skills were, his acumen, his genius that got him down to Little Rock and into a good job in 1947, I don't know. Loyalty and firmness, I imagine. Discretion, certainly. A lack of frankness. Gratitude. Still good qualities. People liked him, liked staying there — which were similar experiences. Everyone approached him smiling, as if he knew something private about them, which he undoubtedly did. They were in his house when they were in his hotel, and he spoke to them at close range, in cagey whispers, his big stomach touching them. He held their arm, cradled their elbow, spoke while he seemed to look away, smiling. He knew the joke, that was his business, exactly. Nothing in the private sector deserves privacy but sex. And that was in the air about him and the whole place. A hotel is for that as much as — maybe more than — anything. And he knew it mattered less what you did than whether someone knew about it.

Normal life, I know now, is life that can be explained in one sentence. No questions needed. And that, I lacked. "You live right here in the hotel?" is what I heard. Afterwards, a smile. These were Southerners, guests I met briefly. They wanted their own straight line on the eccentric, which is what I was to them; wanted as always to compare and contrast lives to their own. It is the Southerner's favorite habit. My story, though, took too long to get into, and I wouldn't: my father was sick; he traveled for a living; my mother drove him; I was from another city, not here; these were my grandparents; I liked it here. It was only that complicated, but I left it alone. Accommodating

your own small eccentricity to yourself is enough. And even that
moves you toward remoteness, toward affection for half-truths,
makes you conspiratorial, a secret-keeper.

Certain things *were* acknowledged lacking. Neighbors. There
were none of those. Only employees, guests, "the Permanents"
(old bachelors, old shopkeepers, old married couples in cheap
rooms with no better homes to hold on to), lobby lizards —
older men with baffling nicknames like Spider, Goldie, Ish —
men who lived out in town but showed up each day. These were
all. No one was my age ever. There was no neighborhood of
other houses, no normal views out windows, no normal quiets
or light. We were downtown, detached from normal residential
lives. Town — the real city, the coarse town mix — started just
outside the lobby door: a liquor store, two cheap movies, a pool
room, a less-good hotel with whores, the bus depot. Everything
was immediate. No delays. At night, out my window from floor
six, I could see the town signs with black sky behind, a green
beacon farther off, could hear the Trailways heave in and out.
I saw sailors, single women, older black couples standing down
on the pavement stretching, taking their look around at a
strange city, using the phone on the wall, the bathroom, staring
across Markham Street at the hotel where they weren't staying
the night. Then getting on the bus again for St. Louis or Texas
or Memphis. Then gone. Was it lonely for me? No. Never. It is
not bad or lonely to see that life goes on at all times, with you or
without you. Home is finally a variable concept.

Travelers — our guests — were people I did not know. They
appeared with bags, wives, and kids — their cars outside. They
looked around the lobby, glanced into the fish pond, sniffed
the air, checked in, *became* guests, walked toward the elevators
and disappeared. I almost never noticed them again, did not
even imagine them — their days, their houses in other states,
their fatigues, where they'd already been that day, where they
lunched, whether they'd argued or why, where they might go
next. I resisted them. It might have seemed a conversation
would take too long, go nowhere. I did not really like traveling,
I think now. Traveling and hotels reflected things different at
heart.

And, of course, we lived *in,* in an apartment with four rooms

where we did not own the furniture but where we liked it —
room and board the highly valued parts of our deal. We ate
where we pleased — in the big kitchen downstairs or in the
dining room — The Green Room — in our apartment. We ordered room service. Laundry was free. A lot was free. My
grandfather kept bird dogs in the basement. We had TV early,
our car had a good spot in the garage and got washed every
day. The sheets were always clean. We saw few visitors. Complete freedom within limits. But if my grandfather lost his job
— always the backstage scare story — we lost it all. How fast we
could be "put on the street" for some vague infraction observed
by the captious owner was a topic much reviewed by my grandmother, who had been poor, though not by my grandfather,
who had been poor, too, but couldn't imagine it anymore, and
who too much loved his work. Employment was undemocratic
then. It lacked the redress we take for granted now — the doctrine of fairness. Hotels were thought to run best as sufferance,
with things in limbo. And every morning in the dark before
work, my grandfather would sit in a chair in his underwear, just
before lacing his shoes, and pray out loud for his job, thank God
for loyal employees, for his good boss, and for the trust he felt
he had, pray for the future. I could hear this from my bed in
the next room. It seemed prudent to me, as it still does.

Whatever his duties — and they were not so clear-cut to me
— he was up at six to do them, gone down the elevator in his
loose blue suit to "put in an appearance." Mostly his job was
simply that. Being there and only there. A presence and con-
server to his employees, a welcoming man to guests. He "toured
the house," saw that operations were operating. That is how a
hotel was run. He signed checks. He hired people, fired them.
He ate *in* to prove his food was good, lived in for the same
reason. His prosperity (in conspicuous evidence, always) promised others the same. In this he was not an *hôtelier*, not an inn-
keeper, he was a hotelman. He would not have been happy to
manage something else — a store or a row of trailers. He did
not look forward to advancement, only to more of the same.
Time has gone when men inhabited their jobs in that way, when
occupation signaled that.

And what did I do? Little. I was there, too. I lived *inside* and did not think of outside. I took few duties. I stood, I watched things pass by me. I rode the elevators, I chatted up bellboys and waiters and room clerks. I slouched around, watched lights light up on the PBX, saw operations operating over and over. I fed the fish. I was prized for my manners, for my height, for the fact that my father was sick and I was here — bravely and indefinitely. I was thought to be interested in hotel work and said that I was. I was curious, unperplexed, un-self-centered, as useless as any boy who sees the surface of life close and reclose over facts that are often not easily simplifiable. We can become familiar with a great many things.

To make regular life seem regular need not always be to bleach the strong colors out. But just for a time it can help. When you look for what's unique and also true of life, you're lucky to find less than you imagined.

How permanent is real life? That's the question, isn't it? The one we both want and don't quite want to hear told. Queasy, melancholic, obvious answers are there. In the hotel there was no center to things, nor was I one. It was the floating life, days erasing other days almost completely, as should be. The place was a hollow place, like any home, in which things went on, a setting where situations developed and ended. And I simply stood alongside that for a while in my young life — neither behind the scenes nor in front. What I saw then — and I saw more than I can say, more than I remember — matters less than what I thought about it. And what I thought about it was this: this is the actual life now, not a stopover, a diversion, or an oddment in time, but the permanent life, the one that will provide history, memory, the one I'll be responsible for in the long run. Everything counts, after all. What else do you need to know?

ALBERT GOLDBARTH

Parade March from
"That Creaturely World"

FROM THE GEORGIA REVIEW

THE HALVED HAM, with its dipsy smile and majorette boots. The headdress-topped pineapple in its sleek-lined 1950s bowl like a chieftain in canoe. The dapper pepper mill. The jitterbugging celery and tomato . . .

I would keep my father company on weekends. Mr. Penny-Insurance-Peddler. Mr. Shlep-and-Sell. He schmoozed, but he was honest. "Albie, you'll see. I'll joke but I won't lie." Mostly I didn't see, I stayed in the car while he labored up four floors with his enormously heavy leatherette case of waiting dotted lines, his promo giveaway cookbooks. I didn't want to go partners in this. The year 1956 — I was eight, I was only eight, but already it was clear to me: the fiscal wasn't my world.

So I sprawled dreamy on the front seat with the reading at hand. It was there in the car when we all went on vacation every summer, and it was in the apartment like water or electricity, some natural phenomenon you didn't question: *The Metropolitan Life Insurance Cook Book*. There were days, I suppose, when I spent more time in its heavily stylized cosmos — with those leap-frogging muffins, barbershop-quartet condiment bottles, deckle-edged lettuces, troupes of onion acrobats — than I did with my neighborhood friends.

"Memory food" my mother called fish. Is that why the shad on page 11, his body so scaled it's artichokelike, looks doleful?

Would he like to forget? Carrots were "good for your eyes" — though even then, I think I sensed that these ridiculous penile guys moved through their proper earthy domain by touch alone. What stayed with me most accurately was the final parade at the top of page 60, a marching pie with a pennant, a pear who's pouring his full rotundity into a trumpet blast . . .

Once in a while I did go up. These were buildings scant blocks out of some ghetto, where a brief shot at a foreman's job meant cheap pink gingham–curtained windows that might have been simply newspapered one year back. These were families ready to think *insurance* — Greek, Italian, Polish versions of the Jewish home I'd waked in that morning. Walking up the hallway — always to something like "Apartment 4D" in a courtyard building done in the thirties, its bricks a liver color . . . The smells of other-ethnic simmers wooed and unsettled me. Moussaka. Duck-blood soup.

I remember now: Mrs. Poniewiecz didn't know how to say it, coughed politely, roved her eyes. And it was true: I was trying to leave with 40 cents of *her* polite negotiations in my fist. *He* was so flustered; there was no joke for this. He built a rococo architecture of foot shuffle and apology, and I was ashamed: for him, not for myself. To me, it hadn't really seemed thieving. Just as those cartoon foods were my natural environment — not the intricate, ordinary grown-ups' world of the kitchen — so, too, the winking small change making its way through the riffle of tens of dollars was *my* province. Anyway, it only happened the once; I wasn't inveterate.

Oh, but I could feel, I could *hear* him turning red with embarrassment. Maybe that's why, all these years, I'd "remembered" a crimson lobster topping one page, a lobster in some unexplained dismay, although when I chanced on the book last week at a flea market . . . there's no lobster at all.

One of the luckless in the D.C. drug-trade wars, age twenty, was thrown in a motel bathtub filling with scalding water. This you don't forget: "As his skin was peeling off, they took turns urinating on him."

How ashamed would I have to feel for thinking *lobster,* for the tic that starts a joke from this scenario? But I did think that.

I read the story in *Time* that same afternoon I excavated the cookbook from its clutterbox of spotted farmer's almanacs and fifties "humor magazines" with teasing swimsuit cuties and titles like *Wink* and *Wow*.

He must have given out a terrible sound — even if it were silent, even if it only shrieked on the level of where his cellular chemistry broke, then altered.

Two texts, and I couldn't help thinking what I thought. It's night. I'm walking under stars we like to believe are stories or beam down influence over our lives, but how much here is ever seen in a nebulous "there"? I know the lettuce on 3 is frilled like a petticoated belle, the chickpea leaps arms out with cockamamie grace, the small soup-carrot rides its spoon as if some mermaid-costumed carnival queen in a Mardi Gras float . . .

And these two disparate texts and their denizens are real and both exist in the same world. This can't be but is.

And it can't be I wasn't there to hear that sound he made, I remember it so distinctly.

And the sound my father made in Chicago when I was in Texas: an egg, a very tiny egg, of pain. Just the size of one period out of that cookbook. First he centered it on his tongue, in 1985, in the Edgewater Hospital cardiac ward, then swallowed until it filled him.

Is this a recipe?

I can taste it.

And I see now what I couldn't (maybe *looked at,* yes, but not with real *seeing*) in those lolling hours waiting for my father in the half-paid-for fedora-gray '48 Chevy: that some of the cookbook's normally up-tempo population exhibits . . . well, twistedness.

A bowl of whites is being whipped by one of those handheld egg beaters looking as spiked and aggressive as any medieval mace. Of course it's a humanoid bowl, with two google eyes near its rim peeking fearfully upward, and two spidery arms, the spidery hands of which fidget. Its brains, essentially, are being violently frothed. Its cranium is open to the skies while this crude instrument of torture whirs erratic, turbid circles through its silky insides.

Who drew a thing like that? Who gave the world page 37's
dearly ambulatory sardine can — yes, with arms and legs, its
oval lid keyed open, so we see its brains are three individual
chartreuse fishlings in heavy oil? Whoever he is or was, he made
certain the human condition was emblemized within an adequate range, some touch of its uttermost limits, before he drew
the rest of his festive, comforting crew: a momma teapot gaily
pouring into a row of progeny cups, a group of sausages horsing
around like the guys in the locker room, a single blissful layer
cake as corpulent and knowing as a buddha.

I grew up with these. Once, age thirty, I needed a word for a
poem, some part a tractor drags, and tried describing it to Tony
and Theo. "Draw it for us," Tony told me. It was natural, my
tractor and these headlight eyes and a smiling mechanical snout.
Theo laughed. But Tony, who knew me longer and better,
shook his head and said to her, "No, it's not that funny. You
don't understand: *he* REALLY *sees the world that way.*"

That angered me so much it had to be right. And it delighted
me as well, in a way. I felt I'd been true to that eight-year-old
boy and his beat, breadwinner father. I can see them, tired,
cross with each other, but bonded by being tired and cross,
driving home through five o'clock Saturday traffic. There's no
radio; the father sings some popular hit. He loves the boy, who
he hopes will join in. The boy knows it and won't. It's a ritual —
even this bonds them. Sweaty, lazy, they stop at a carhop shack,
it might be Buns & Suds, and bask as well as they can in the feel
of two giant root beers. Even the Chevy gets to bask, in the
shade of the corrugated tin. It sighs, I hear it sigh, and it dips
its overwrought grille to that shade and drinks deeply.

". . . we give a chair arms, legs, a seat and a back, a cup has its
lip / and a bottle its neck" — this from a poem by Marvin Bell.
Yes, and a potato its eyes. The mandrake we give an entire
human body; if you tugged one from the soil in the year of our
Lord 1500 it might squeal deafeningly, an infant being murdered. Just ask anyone.

In Elizabeth Bishop's persona monologue "Crusoe in England" the rescued speaker, old now, "bored too," back in a
realm of courtesies and teatime, considers the knife that for so

many years was his closest companion and (even following Friday's arrival) the fondled, talked-to, slept-with, absolutely unrelinquishable, major-causal object of his universe. It's a souvenir now. "The living soul has dribbled away."

That knife. The simple Mesopotamian oracle plate which held the watchful consciousness of a god in its glaze. Some thumb-long balsa doll a child has loved so nuzzlingly much the face is rubbed away inversely to the personality quickened inside it: "my Wubsie" (though why Wubsie, no one knows), you swear if you slipped that doll from her sleeping grip it would squeal like an infant being murdered . . .

These come from what David Jones calls, in the preface to his novel *In Parenthesis*, "that creaturely world inherited from our remote beginnings." He wonders (this is 1937) if we'll come to see "newfangled technicalities as true extensions of ourselves, that we may feel for them a native affection." Maybe. Ten years after, men were tightening the last of the nuts of the Chevy they'd premiere that fall and my father would buy a year later, and curse, and coddle-coo, and intimately discourse with in ways I wouldn't have with any woman for a long bleak while, not even a woman I'd claim I "loved."

And I've watched my father's mother hold such forthright conversation with her ancient foot-treadle sewing machine. The bobbin was all business, but, oh, the vines carved over the wooden side drawers on the body were like a factory worker's secret descending tattoos. She didn't know I was there. She stitched all night alone with it, and while I only heard *her* voice — a kind of singing, really — I have no reason to say a kind of dialogue wasn't taking place.

I've seen her singing to the soup, low and Yiddish-guttural, seen her sing to the chicken she disemboweled, until the face of the man I was named for must have risen visibly in the soup-steam for her. What came then was the everyday talking of woman to man. He was dead. She was holding the heart of a chicken. Now I know, thirty-two years later: if she whistled, an ancient Egyptian bowl would arrive to receive that slick purple thing, would walk in slightly tilted on its own two childlike feet.

The fries in their wire fryer, like goldfinches sleeking about a cage. The froufrou cabbage in her indigo *chanteuse* ruffles. All those frolicking cub-scout olives, deviled eggs, radish rosettes: the Appetizer Troop, out on maneuvers . . .

In the sixteenth century, somebody's grabbing a mandrake's gnarly top and yanking hard (her ears are beeswaxed closed to muffle its shrill of agony) . . . Somebody's curing a headache by smearing his scalp with a lard-based walnut paste; why? simple: the meat of the nut resembles the brain . . . "Matter," Morris Berman says in *The Reenchantment of the World,* "possessed consciousness." And then goes on, after detailing much of alchemical versus Newtonian cosmologies, to a "conclusion . . . that will probably strike most readers as radical in the extreme. . . . It is not merely the case that men conceived of matter as possessing mind in those days, but rather that in those days, matter *did* possess mind, 'actually' did so."

When I was eight, wedges of cheese ran races around the fondue tureen, a Spanish onion promenaded hand-in-hand with a steak sauce bottle whose black cap fit him snug as a derby . . .

Morris Berman: "The animism implicit in quantum mechanics has been explored mathematically by the physicist Evan Harris Walker, who argues that every particle in the universe possesses consciousness."

. . . the cherry tomato, sighing with love for the urbane, professorly roast.

And if they *are* a denatured version of such primacy? Still, they're a version.

Skyler and Babs collect lobsterania: ashtrays, serving platters, blotters, squeeze toys, stamps, you name it.

What a creature! From the major bones of dinosaur, or of Cro-Magnon man, we can, in a rational process of retroextrapolation, construct the whole. But who could guess *this* whisker-sprouting jointed castanet armory from its insides? When we eat one, overblooming its shell like a split couch pillow — all those buttersweet meat feathers!

Lobster postcards are a specialty subgenre of postcard collecting. One, in high demand, is a photograph of The Lobsterettes: a chorine line in life-sized lobster costumes.

In a "fifties shop" in Kansas City, Skyler and I found a set of lobster salt-and-pepper shakers. They're standing up and might be rhumba partners or pugilists. Rarefied *kitsch.* They were screamingly fireplug-red on a shelf of pastel celadon and egg-shell 1950s radios, whose round contours and unashamed dials and gawking or grinning station bands easily give them the spirit of human faces.

In an African market, Skyler and Bobby Sue picked two apiece from wooden buckets and lugged them home by their antennae, giant specimens, a foot and a half. "They were lovely in their buckets — so many greens! They were . . . *hazel.*" "Like eyes?" I ask her. "Yes, that many colors. Like hazel eyes."

Wasn't it Gérard de Nerval — some Symbolist poet — who in a fit of revel or breakdown walked a lobster on a leash?

And why am I doing this, talking around it? Here, let me say his name: *Patrick Monfiston.* Twenty years old, his skin heated past being skin, and the live piss eating him.

Babs owns an inflatable lobster and one that leaps when you press a small rubber bulb.

I know how comic they can be.

I know what salt means too. I can't play with that shaker and not hear contents shifting — even if the shaker's empty.

Every year at the Passover holiday Jews dip a token of what they're feasting on, into a basin of salt water. To remind them of suffering. Wine and honey and singing until the table is cleared. And that: to remind them of suffering.

I remember it this vividly: the dining room light of that small apartment breaking into splinters on the knobules of the *Kiddush* goblet. Passover, and my father conducting the ceremonial meal. Grandma Nettie (yes, alive then) with her hands still bright from the only emollient they ever knew, fresh chicken fat. Uncle Morrie (alive then) making subterfuge cracker boats in his soup while the service drones on around us in Hebrew — he winks at me, but slyly. My mother. Aunt Sally. My sister Livia. The carpet is the sickly color of moss from a tree's wrong side, and Cousin Beverly's overenthusiastic oil portrait of Tuffy the poodle is still on the wall. And my father is singing the High Tongue, my father is opening Time itself until the days of the Bible pull chairs up to the table, and goatstink and angel shadows attend us. My father, alive then. I remember: his voice a ladder to God.

I remember, he demystified the intricacy of a necktie. I remember, once, in search of some keys I lucked upon the girlie coin ("heads" / "tails") under his handkerchiefs — that ripe clef of the body thereon. I remember his passion for home-pickling cukes. I remember his arm when he slammed on the brakes of the Chevy, instinctively bolting me safe from the windshield — do I really see it? Every hair, the cuff the day's stained gray.

And I can hear each lousy penny of that forty cents — one for each year of my life now — dropping out of my fingers, down the Grand Canyon, measured by Galileo himself for velocity, hitting the tin plate at the centermost magma of Earth and melting there to forty damp grains of salt.

I remember because I found them, in their camouflage of yellowed gazettes and palmistry tracts, and they're bringing it with them, all of it, and all of them, parading: the various eggs in their top hats and bonnets are here, and the drum-beating gourd, and the bread with his slices inching him along like the ribs of a snake, and the goof-off kidney and lima and chili beans like Shriners and Masons and lodge brothers everywhere marching and cavorting, and the burger gals are here, and the pear, and the phalanx of clown-nosed cookies . . .

And my dear old friend, the melancholy fish of page 11, isn't eaten.

Of course. Mr. Memory Food. Mr. Memory Food. Over time he'll consume himself.

PAUL GRUCHOW

Bones

FROM MINNESOTA MONTHLY

I HAVE ALWAYS had an eye for bones. As a child, I collected
them, and labeled them, and arranged them from biggest to
littlest on a shelf in the hayloft of our barn. On rainy summer
afternoons and snowy winter days, I retired to my museum and
played with the bones — turning them over in my hands, examining them in the dim light that seeped through the cracks
in the walls of the barn, running my fingers over worn incisors,
feeling the bald smoothness of skull bones, admiring the way
femurs balanced in my hands, listening to the wind in the cu-
polas and to the cooing pigeons, hearing the music of raindrops
or ice crystals pattering against the shingles. The bones spoke
to me on those dank afternoons, but I was a long time in deci-
phering what they said.

Even from the beginning, I declined to collect some bones.
There was a sinkhole at the bottom of our pasture. A cow had
mired and died there years before I chanced upon the place. Its
flesh had long since rotted away, devoured by billions of mi-
crobes. Nothing remained but a few tufts of its brown hair, some
scraps of its leathery hide, and its bones. The bones, already
bleached, had begun to gray with age. They lay half buried in
the muck, contorted still in the last paroxysm of life. The cow's
skull had separated from the vertebrae of its neck; it rested
upwind from the rest of the skeleton, facing north into the bitter
winds.

I encountered it one cold November afternoon when the
leaves had fallen from the willows and the sedges had turned

russet and gold. A pheasant bolted from the meadow grasses underfoot, startling me, and when I looked up I was staring into the cow's vacant eye sockets. They seemed to be staring back at me.

My first impulse was to collect the bones of the mired cow. But I resisted it. Something in those bones — some integrity — restrained me, commanded my reverence. Everything else I had collected had appeared at random: a skull here, a rib cage there — leavings scattered by scavengers, by wind and water and frost. To pick up such a bone is to join the forces of dispersal at restless work in the world, to become part of its natural history. But the bones of the cow, for whatever reasons, had remained intact, held in the continuing entrapment of the sinkhole. The site harbored something more than a death. It seemed to me that the cow was entombed there, and my passion for bones did not extend to the robbery of graves.

I was only a boy, but I knew something of graves. I knew the scent of gladiolus and strong perfume in the parlor, where the embalmed body of my grandfather had been propped for viewing before the ritual of the grave, and I'd felt the strong, icy wind blowing across the open prairie cemetery on the brown day when his bones were buried, and I'd heard the cold clank of the pebble in the first shovelful of earth hurled upon his burnished bronze casket. I remembered, even then, nothing of my living grandfather, but the memory of his bones lingers still. And I knew the smell of urine and rubber in the sickroom of my grandmother — the same parlor that had held my dead grandfather. She had been laid out there to die in a rented hospital bed, insensible after a stroke. We watched as she shriveled up day by day into a sack of sharp-edged bones.

And I had dug my share of graves. One of them was for the cottontail rabbit I'd raised in a chicken-wire cage in the back yard. I'd found it abandoned as an infant and had tended it all summer, feeding it with an eyedropper until it could be weaned. I'd brought it fresh tidbits from the garden: young cabbages and carrots and leaves of lettuce — treating it as the younger brother I did not have.

"You have got to let that thing go," my father had been saying. "The sooner the better. It can't stay the winter in that pen. It won't survive."

"Yes," I said. "I'll do it. Tomorrow."

One admonishment led to another, one tomorrow to the next. There were many distractions, and I didn't want to relinquish the rabbit.

One morning late in September, I went out to greet it, barefoot and still in my pajamas, and I found it quivering in the corner of its box, bleeding thickly from several savage gashes, inflicted by some predator that had improbably spared it. I wept over it and treated its wounds, but it did not survive the school day. That evening, I buried it — my heart heavier for the conviction, no doubt vain, that it might have escaped had it not been penned. At that age, I still had faith in a benign and brotherly nature, and I felt personally betrayed when it answered me in the language of violence and death.

On another day, a hot one in July, I learned to speak the same language myself. I had a cat, for whom I had vowed responsibility; she had produced a litter of kittens. I had been told, emphatically, that I could not keep those kittens — and as desperately as I tried, I could find no one to adopt them. None of the farming folks I knew needed or wanted another cat. So one awful day, in a terrible heat, I took them into an abandoned henhouse and did what needed to be done. One by one I picked up the lovely, mewing kittens and held them at the bottom of a bucket of water. When they stopped struggling, I carried them into the grove to the place where the rabbit's bones rested, and made ten tiny graves for them, and buried them like pieces of my own flesh. I hated my own flesh then, hated the ruthless efficiency with which it could be made to do such dirty work, and would as soon have buried myself. But another part of me yearned to live as violently as those kittens did when they were suffocating in a water pail in the close heat of a July afternoon.

There were many kinds of bones in those days: the leg bone our big tomcat chewed off — his own — when it was snapped in a trap, and withered, and rotted; the bones of the family goats, caught in a fire I had carelessly set and stinking like old tires burning; the neck bones of chickens crunching under the blows of my ax on butchering days; the carcasses of the rodents

I trapped, skinned, and offered to my dog, Mitsy, as a sacrifice of love; the bones of the ground squirrels I drowned in their holes and sold to the county government for a bounty of ten cents a head; the bones I carried home from my wanderings in fields and meadows. My life in those days had more to do with bones than it does now. I live a more genteel life these days, and a life a lot further from nature.

The bones often told stories of cruelty — many of them cruelties of my own creation. What was I to make of this? The obvious thing, I suppose: that life is sometimes cruel. That is a fact more to be respected than explained — like the fact that when you press your tongue to a pump handle in the wintertime, it bonds to the metal and you cannot pry it loose without tearing away some skin. I couldn't explain cruelty, and I didn't try. When my father insisted that my sister wear skirts to the school-bus stop half a mile away in vicious midwinter because he had religious scruples against females in trousers, and when she froze her legs and whimpered all the way to school from the sting and itch of the thawing, I thought him cruel and stupid and pious to a horrible fault, but still I loved him, and so, in her own way, did she. It was a mystery, but when was life or love ever not a mystery?

I vowed at a fairly early age to give up voluntary cruelties. I stopped keeping wild pets. I quit hunting and trapping for sport. I practiced a boyish asceticism, finding myself irregularly but powerfully attracted to the most extravagant habits of the third- and fourth-century desert eremites. One saint, whose name I've forgotten, particularly enchanted me. I'd read that he once spent forty days and forty nights sitting motionless in a swamp, enduring impassively whatever abuses came his way, in penance for having swatted a mosquito — one of God's creatures. I did not dare to hope for such saintliness, but I did, for a time, passionately admire it.

Still, I remained cruel. In the winter, feeling neither gratitude nor regret, I ate the sheep that had pulled me around the yard in a cart all summer. I fished for northerns in the rapids above the dam on the river — not for food, but for the fun of it. I particularly enjoyed beheading grasshoppers, and spent many pleasant hours doing so in the grain wagons at harvest time. It

was a crooked world, running along an ambiguous path overgrown with many obstructions, and I could not see the straight
way through it.

I suffer over this with my own children. My daughter is sometimes sensitive beyond reason. Once, as we were sitting around
a campfire, I absentmindedly crushed a cricket that had crawled
near the flame. My daughter burst into tears. I did not know
what she was crying about, which made everything much worse.
I begged her to explain what was wrong.

"You murdered it!" she finally said, between her sobs.

"Murdered it! Murdered what?" I said.

She stopped crying, looked at me coldly. "I suppose you really
don't know," she said.

I looked blank.

"The cricket!" she said. "The poor helpless cricket! Why did
you have to go and do that? It wasn't hurting anything, was it?"

"No," I had to admit, "it wasn't." At the same time, I was
impatient and unrepenting. My God, I thought, I have raised
an eremite. I wanted to say: "Be reasonable." And: "You know,
there are greater tragedies in life than the wanton death of a
cricket." But I kept silent, out of confusion and embarrassment,
and because I did not want to endorse wantonness, however
trivial. In some moral sense, I suspected, she was right. That is
one of the troubles with morality: its indifference to distinctions
of degree; its impracticality.

My son, on the other hand, sees nature as many children do:
as something to pillage, to plunder, to maim, to shoot, to catch.
So far as he is concerned, every wild creature is meant to be
carried home on a stringer or carted home in a box or a glass
bottle.

We fished one night for bullheads — a sport in which I in-
dulge him, though I find it contemptible: for the ease with
which bullheads can be caught; for the execrable waters they
inhabit; for their slimy skins, which seem to get slimier as the
summer wears on; for the greedy way they swallow hooks; for
the grotesque belches they emit when you squeeze their air blad-
ders, as you must if you wish to avoid their painful barbs while
unhooking them. I am suspicious of all hierarchies, but there is
no doubt in my mind that any one bass or trout or walleye is
infinitely more desirable than any dumpster full of bullheads.

We caught a mess of bullheads that day — and because the two of us were on an indulgent father-and-son outing, I promised to cook them for breakfast. We stashed the fish in the minnow bucket, watched the fire burn down and the heavens come alive, and went to bed. An hour or two later, I was awakened by the clatter of dishes in the opened camping box. Peering out into the moonlit night, I saw a raccoon sitting next to the box on the picnic table, picking marshmallows daintily out of a bag and eating them one at a time, very noisily and with much smacking of lips.

A raccoon is an exceedingly handsome and beguiling creature. I rather regretted getting up out of habit and shooing it away. I stashed the marshmallows in the car and went back to bed. Fifteen minutes later, the raccoon was back. This time it took hold of the minnow bucket, dragged it a little way off, tipped it on its side, inserted one paw through the trap door to hold it open, fished a bullhead out of the bucket, and ate it, smacking its lips even more loudly, obviously having a wonderful time. And so it went — bullhead after bullhead after bullhead. It was clear from the aplomb with which the raccoon executed this banquet that he was a grizzled veteran of the minnow-bucket circuit.

I made no attempt to stop him. The raccoon's gain was all the more mine. In my mind, I substituted pancakes for bullheads at breakfast — and fell contentedly, even joyfully, to sleep. In the morning, I put on a sad face and announced the tragedy to my son. I expected him to be heartbroken. He wasn't — not in the least. He immediately saw the germ of a grand new opportunity.

"I know what!" he said. "Let's go catch some more bullheads, and then we can use them for bait and catch that old raccoon!"

"But why would you want to do that?" I said, and then, looking into his face and seeing the futility in such a question, I lied. "We'll see," I said, knowing that I was seeming to acquiesce in a scheme that I had no intention of carrying forward.

I want to find, for myself, some middle ground between my daughter's naïve reverence for nature and my son's view of nature as a sport. Once, I think, I found it, but as my life grew more complicated, I lost it. I am thinking of that brief time when, as a country boy, I lived in the out-of-doors essentially as one might occupy a living room. I didn't make distinctions then that I routinely make now, because those distinctions — between inside and outside, between wild and domestic, between house and home — did not, for practical purposes, exist.

As a child in Chippewa County, Minnesota, I was never confined to any space so constricted as a house. Our family had a house, of course — a succession of houses: first a cement-block basement house; then a balloon-frame shack; finally an honest, full-fledged farmhouse with rooms and staircases and a real basement and rag rugs on the linoleum floors. But none of those houses fully contained the place in which I lived. Partly this was a matter of definition: in the country, one lives not in a house but on a farm, and one thinks of the space one occupies as including everything within the farm's fence lines. But for me, something else was at work. In our little country church, I heard often the promise of heaven. I visualized it not as cloudy and ethereal but as a concrete place, according to the words of Jesus: "In my father's house are many mansions." I thought of my own home as a smaller version of heaven — as a house of many mansions. There was the wooden frame house with the green mansard roof where I slept and ate and joined the life of the family. But it was only one of many mansions in which I lived contemporaneously.

I lived in the hayloft, where I stored my collection of bones. When it was too stormy to be outside, I was likely to spend the day there, swinging on the ropes and standing in the crow's nest at the peak of the gables, where I could see out across the river valley through a little round window. I kept company with the pigeons, read books, napped in a bed of hay, teased spiders out of their chambers, daydreamed.

And I lived in the limbs of an enormous black walnut tree at the far end of the pasture, in the company of squirrels and pale little tree frogs. It was always shady there, and even in the stillest and hottest weather, a fresh breeze always seemed to be blowing around it. Its limbs were broad enough to lie down upon, and I often did just that, listening to the lazy music of summer afternoons: the buzzing of flies, the droning of bumblebees, the singing of birds. Near the black walnut tree were the hollow of a pioneer's sod hut and a sweetwater spring that ran all winter long; hundreds of times I imagined that the sod house was mine in the making, that the spring had drawn me there, and that I would live forever in the shadow of the wide arms of the walnut tree.

And I lived along the shores of the pasture pond, where the pussy willows swelled in the springtime; where blackbirds wheezed and wheedled in the cattails; where muskrats swam in the musty, warm waters of summer, green with algae and duckweed. I lived among the arrowroots and jewelweeds, among the strawberries hiding in the cordgrass, in the company of minks and weasels and fat skunks. Water striders and boatmen and pill bugs squatted in my front yard, righthanded pond snails and leopard frogs in my back yard, dragonflies and damselflies in the fetid air overhead. I passed many happy hours in the upper reaches of a black willow tree, monitoring the progress of life in the fecund chambers of my pond mansion.

And I lived by the blue light of the moon along country lanes so quiet I could hear the traffic in the town, miles away, visible only as a burst of mysterious light on the distant horizon. Fireflies flashed in the ditches, and the long leaves of the corn sighed in the evening breezes. Here and there a dog barked in a farmyard. The sound of dogs barking in the night, echoing across the vast, empty countryside, was the surfacing sound of the wildness in them. I could hear in their voices the ancient cries of gray wolves, echoing from the days when great herds of bison roamed the plains and the moonlight danced in the endless waves of grass. I could feel, then, the wildness in my *own* bones.

And I lived in a woodpile, in a plum thicket, in the striped shade of a sweltering August cornfield where whirlwinds raced, showering dust like rain. I lived in a prairie meadow, among overgrazed river bluffs, on a granite island in a widening of the river, along a grassy fenceline where a lone green ash grew.

I lived along the banks of the river — where beaver built their dams; where mud turtles sunned on half-submerged logs; where bullheads and northern pike, saugers and buffalo fish swam the murky waters; where white-tailed deer came down to drink; where the tracks of mink mingled in the shoreline mud with the remains of the clams that raccoons had fished from the shallows. But mainly I dwelled along the river under the spell of its mysterious waters, running into the Minnesota River, and then into the Mississippi, and then down the central nervous cord of the continent, over the plains of Iowa, through the hills of Missouri and Arkansas, across the bayous of Louisiana, and into the Gulf of Mexico.

In my house were many mansions.

When I sat on the overhanging limb of the willow tree and dangled my bare feet into the brown waters of the Chippewa River and felt the slow, steady tug of its unfailing current against my toes, I connected myself to the great body of the continent. I was linked not merely with a small river in western Minnesota, but swept up into the gigantic stream of life. I lived then in the piney waters of the North Woods, in the thundering waters of St. Anthony Falls, in the icy rush of mountain streams, in the stagnant backwaters of Southern marshes, in the oceanic brine. I shared my mansion with little bullheads, yes, but also with ancient paddlefishes and cutthroat trout and sharks and catfishes as big as logs. I lived then among bald eagles and alligators and panthers. I lived where it always snows and where it never snows, high in the mountains and at the edge of the sea.

As a high school biology student, I once traced the cardiovascular system of a domestic cat whose blood vessels had been injected with a rubbery substance — blue for the veins, red for the arteries. Beginning at the heart, I traced the vessels up into its skull and down into its toes and out along its tail, following them as they branched into smaller and smaller streams. It was an ecstatic experience; I carried my half-excavated specimen home on the bus in a clear plastic bag, unable to bear the suspense of waiting until the next day's class to discover where all the vessels ran. No one would sit next to me. Everyone else on the bus found the smell of the preservative nauseating, the sight of the opened carcass disgusting, my enthusiasm for the project weird, sick. But I was too excited to mind. Here, in the body of the cat, lay a map of the world as I perceived it from my vantage point along the Chippewa River. I might be one red corpuscle swimming in the slenderest of the tail arteries, but I was an undeniable part of something big and alive, a constituent particle of the whole animal. I had seen the universe in a two-dollar laboratory specimen.

Now I live in a single house of eight rooms, from which I venture forth into nature as a tourist. Most mornings, I walk from my house around a shallow prairie lake to the two-room office in which I spend my days pacing, writing, reading, and staring out of the second-story windows into the canopy of a black walnut tree. It buds. It leaves. It flowers. It bears nuts. The yellow-green nuts turn brown and fall; the green leaves turn yellow and flutter to earth. In the winter I watch frozen pieces of the tree break off in the wind and scatter to the earth. In the spring, the tree buds again. Some would call this a cycle — the eternal cycle of nature — and find comfort in it. I don't. The tree is a little less young each spring, and so am I. Our time is running out. For the tree, as for me, the path is linear, not cyclical — and the end of the line is death. The best that can be said, in the meantime, is that neither of us has moved.

The skies beyond the tree change. One day dawns clear; the next, cloudy. Some days rain patters against the window glass. Some mornings the branches of the walnut are white with rime frost; others, with new snow. The wind blows, or doesn't. In the heated and air conditioned solitude of my study, it is all the same.

One summer afternoon a couple of years ago, the sky suddenly turned as black as ink. The streetlights switched on. A stillness fell, so deafening that it intruded even into my already silent rooms. Rain began to pour in torrents, as it does in a tropical forest, but the downpour was swept and swirled by violent winds that howled in the corners of the building. As suddenly as the rain came, so came the hail, thundering down upon the rooftop and smashing against the windows. One by one, the panes of glass shattered as I cowered in the middle of the outer room, paralyzed with awe and fear. Then, as suddenly as it had arrived, the storm cloud passed. The branches of the walnut tree hung in tatters, and icy water puddled on the windowsills where the rain had been driven through the cracks in the glass. In the streets, mist had already begun to rise from the hail drifts dissipating in the blazing heat of the sun. Ten million

dollars' damage in ten minutes in one small prairie town. I
thought of an outburst of John Berryman's I'd witnessed on
another summer day. Suddenly, while walking to the auditorium's center stage to deliver a lecture on James Joyce, he had
smashed a chair into the orchestra pit and bellowed incoher-
ently against janitors. "It was good for them," he later wrote of
us, his bewildered students. "A Zen touch: action in the midst
of thought."

But most days are not graced with such drama. They come to
a close, and I walk home — noticing, perhaps, whether it is hot
or cold, windy or calm; passing through a landscape so familiar
that I have ceased to see it; ready to take up residence for the
night in the only house I now know: a gray one of eight rooms,
a tight fortress against the world beyond its windows. I take the
telephone off the hook, throw the junk mail unopened into the
wastebasket, and sit in my brown chair, in the yellow light of a
lamp, listening to piano music arranged on a compact disc in
the order that someone else has determined would please me.
There are rooms in the house that I seldom visit, and, so far as
I am concerned, there are no other houses anywhere else in the
wide world.

When I want to visit the world in which I once lived, I consult
my maps, arrange my schedule, embark on an expedition to the
local stores for perishable supplies, pack the car, and set out
from my house — fearful sometimes, but full of new energy too,
as a tourist always is at the beginning of a journey. And when I
arrive, and set out on foot into some untamed place, I come
sooner or later to a bone or a shell, and often I pick it up
and carry it home with me. I keep my souvenirs here in my
office with me and on the mantel of the fireplace in my house:
the tooth of a bison washed out of the mud of a Nebraska
streambed; the carapace of a horseshoe crab picked up in a
Florida mangrove swamp; a bowlful of fossil shark teeth collected on a Gulf Coast beach; the shell of a land snail found in
the sandy soil of an arroyo in the Baja desert; the jaw bone of a
cow from the Great Basin of Wyoming; the antler of a white-
tailed deer, shed in the North Woods; the skull of a mule deer
attacked by coyotes on Montana's Front Range. Every bone re-

minds me of many others that I left uncollected somewhere when I was out hunting for lost mansions. Like the prophet, I have walked in a valley full of bones.

But the remarkable thing, in fact, is that one finds so few bones. Millions of creatures die every day. Where are their remains? Where have they all gone? And as for the creatures dying but not yet dead — where are they? You can walk for a thousand miles and never once see a creature dying. Death is nothing if not discreet.

The bones, every one, are miracles — the alms nature offers to life. We do not easily accept miracles; they seem to fall beyond the boundaries of cause and effect. But a miracle is nothing more than a story that begins after the cause and ends before the effect. It is the mysterious void at the heart of the story: the space between the particles of an atom that makes the substance of things possible. The miracle of a bone is that it is a moment frozen. A bone is the evidence of a life — a life unique, unprecedented, and never to be repeated, which, though it has vanished, nevertheless endures in the bone: a faint white glimmering, in some offhand place, of life everlasting.

CHRISTOPHER HITCHENS

On Not Knowing the Half of It: Homage to Telegraphist Jacobs

FROM GRAND STREET

IN THE EARLY DAYS of the December that my father was to die, my younger brother brought me the news that I was a Jew. I was then a transplanted Englishman in America, married, with one son and, though unconsoled by any religion, a nonbelieving member of two Christian churches. On hearing the tidings, I was pleased to find that I was pleased.

One of the things about being English, born and bred, is the blessed lack of introspection that it can confer. An interest in genealogy is an admitted national quirk, but where this is not merely snobbish or mercenary, it indulges our splendid and unique privilege of traceable, stable continuity. Englishmen do not have much time for angst about their "roots," or much of an inclination to the identity crisis. My paternal grandfather had a favorite joke, about a Wessex tenant in dispute with his squire. "I hope you realize," says the squire, "that my ancestors came with William the Conqueror." "Yes," returns the yeoman. "We were waiting for you." It was from this millennial loam that, as far as I knew, I had sprung. I had long since lapsed my interest in family history as being unlikely to prove any connection to title or fortune. For something to say, I would occasionally dilate on the pure Cornish origins of the name Hitchens, which had once been explained to me by A. L. Rowse in the course of a stuporous dinner at Oxford. The Celtic strain seemed worth mentioning, as representing a sort of romantic, insurgent leaven in the Anglo-Saxon lump. But having married a Greek (accepting confirmation in the Orthodox Church with about as much emotion as I had declined it in the Anglican one) and left England, I never expected any but routine news from the family quarter.

My brother's account was simple but very surprising. Our mother had died tragically and young in 1973, but her mother still lived, enjoying a very spry tenth decade. When my brother had married, he had taken his wife to be presented to her. The old lady had later complimented him on his choice, adding rather alarmingly, "She's Jewish, isn't she?" Peter, who had not said as much, agreed rather guardedly that this was so. "Well," said the woman we had known all our lives as "Dodo," "I've got something to tell you. So are you."

My initial reaction, apart from pleasure and interest, was the faint but definite feeling that I had somehow known all along. Well used to being taken for English wherever I went, I had once or twice been addressed in Hebrew by older women in Jerusalem (where, presumably, people are looking for, or perhaps noticing, other characteristics). And, though some of my worst political enemies were Jewish, in America it seemed that almost all my best personal friends were. This kind of speculation could, I knew, be misleading to the point of treachery, but there it was. Then, most provoking and beguiling of all, there was the dream. Nothing bores me more than dream stories, so I had kept this one to myself. But it was the only one that counted as recurrent and I had also experienced it as a waking fantasy. In this reverie, I am aboard a ship. A small group is on the other side of the deck, huddled in talk but in some way noticing me. After a while a member of the group crosses the deck. He explains that he and his fellows are one short of a quorum for prayer. Will I make up the number for a *minyan?* Smiling generously, and swallowing my secular convictions in a likable and tolerant manner, I agree to make up the number and stroll across the deck.

I hesitate to include this rather narcissistic recollection, but an account of my reactions would be incomplete without it, and I had had the dream recently enough to tell my brother about it. He went on to tell me that our grandmother had enjoined us to silence. We were not to tell our father, who, we knew, was extremely unwell. He had not known that he had a Jewish wife, any more than we had known we had a Jewish mother. It would not be fair to tell him, at the close of his life, that he had been kept in the dark. I felt confident that he would not have minded learning the family secret, but it was not a secret I had long to keep. My father died a matter of weeks after I learned it myself.

The day after his funeral, which was held in wintry splendor at the D-day Chapel overlooking our native Portsmouth, whence he had often set sail to do the King's enemies a bit of no good, I took a train to see my grandmother. I suppose that in childhood I had noticed her slightly exotic looks, but when she opened the door to me I was struck very immediately by my amazing want of perception. Did she look Jewish? She most certainly did. Had I ever noticed it? If so, it must have been a very subliminal recognition. And in England, at any rate in the milieu in which I had been brought up, Jew-consciousness had not been a major social or personal consideration.

We had family grief to discuss and I was uncertain how to raise the other matter that was uppermost in my mind. She relieved me of the necessity. We were discussing my father's last illness and she inquired his doctor's name. "Dr. Livingstone," I replied. "Oh, a Jewish doctor," she said. (I had thought Livingstone a quintessentially English or Scots name, but I've found since that it's a favorite of the assimilated.) At once, we were in the midst of a topic that was so familiar to her and so new and strange to me. Where, for a start, were we *from?*

Breslau. The home of B. Traven and the site of a notorious camp during the *endgültige Lösung.* Now transferred to Poland and renamed Wroclaw. A certain Mr. Blumenthal had quit this place of ill omen in the late nineteenth century and settled in the English Midlands. In Leicester, he had fathered thirteen children and raised them in a scrupulously orthodox fashion. In 1893, one of his daughters had married Lionel Levin, of Liverpool. My maternal grandmother, Dorothy Levin, had been born three years later.

It appeared that my great-grandparents had removed to Oxford, where they and their successors pursued the professions of dentistry and millinery. Having spent years of my life in that town as schoolboy and undergraduate and resident, I can readily imagine its smugness and frigidity in the early part of the century. Easy to visualize the retarding influence of the Rotary Club, and perhaps Freemasonry and the golf club, on the aspirations of the Jewish dentist or hatter. By the time of the Kaiser, the Levins had become Lynn and the Blumenthals Dale. But I was glad to learn that, while they sought to assimilate, they did not renounce. Of a Friday evening, with drawn curtains, they would produce the menorah. The children were brought up to be unobtrusively observant. How, then, could such a seemingly innocuous and familiar tale come to me as a secret? A secret which, if it were not for the chance of my grandmother outliving both my parents, I might never have learned?

Dodo told me the occluded history of my family. "Oxford," she said, materializing my suspicions, "was a very bad place to be Jewish in those days." She herself had kept all the Jewish feasts and fasts, but I was slightly relieved to find that, aged ninety-two, she was staunchly proof against the claims of religion. "Have any of your friends ever mentioned Passover to you?" she inquired touchingly. I was able to say yes to that, and to show some knowledge of Yom Kippur and Chanukah, too. This seemed to please her, though she did add that as a girl she had fasted on Yom Kippur chiefly to stay thin.

The moment had arrived to ask why this moment had arrived. Why had I had to bury my father to get this far? On the mantelpiece was a photograph of my mother, looking more beautiful than ever, though not as beautiful as in the photograph I possessed, which showed her in the uniform of the Royal Navy, in which she had met my father. I had been interrogating this photograph. It showed a young, blond woman who could have been English or (my fancy when a child) French. Neither in profile nor in curls did it disclose what Gentiles are commonly supposed to "notice."

"Your mother didn't much want to be a Jew," said Dodo, "and I didn't think your father's family would have liked the idea. So we just decided to keep it to ourselves." I had to contend with a sudden access of hitherto buried memories. Had my father shown the least sign of any prejudice? Emphatically not; he had been nostalgic for Empire and bleakly severe about the consequences of losing it, but he had never said anything ugly. He had been a stout patriot, but not a flag waver, and would have found racism (I find I can't quite add "and chauvinism") to be an affront to the intelligence. His lifetime of naval service had taken him to Palestine in the 1930s (and had involved him in helping to put down a revolt in my wife's neighboring country of Cyprus in 1932), but he never droned on about lesser breeds as some of his friends had done in my hearing when the gin bottle was getting low. If he had ever sneered at anyone, it had been Nasser (one of our few quarrels).

But I could recall a bizarre lecture from my paternal grandfather. It was delivered as a sort of grand remonstrance when I joined the Labour party in the mid-1960s. *"Labour,"* my working-class ancestor had said with biting scorn, "just look at them. Silverman, Mendelson, Driberg, Mikardo . . ." and he had told off the names of the leading leftists of the party at that period. At the time, I had wondered if he was objecting to *German* names (that *had* been a continuous theme of my upbringing) and only later acquired enough grounding in the tones of the British right to realize what he had meant. Imagining the first meeting between him and my maternal grandmother, as they discussed the betrothal, I could see that she might not have been paranoid in believing her hereditary apprehensions to be realized.

And then came another thought, unbidden. Oxford may have been a tough place to be a Jew, but in the European scale it did not rank with Mannheim or Salonika. Yet my parents had been married in April 1945, the month before the final liberation of Germany. It was the moment when the world first became generally aware of the Final Solution. How galling it must have been, in that month, to keep watch over one's emotions, and to subsume the thought of the Breslau camp in the purely patriotic rejoicing at the defeat of the archenemy.

"Well, you know," said Dodo, "we've never been liked. Look at how the press treats the Israelites. They don't like us. I know I shouldn't say it, but I think it's because they're jealous." The "they" here clearly meant more than the press. I sat through it feeling rather reticent. In January of 1988, the long-delayed revolt in Gaza had electrified Fleet Street, more because some ambitious Thatcherite junior minister had got himself caught up in it than for any reason of principle. The following Sunday, I knew, the *Observer* was to publish a review of *Blaming the Victims*, a collection of essays edited by Edward Said and me. This book argued correctly that the bias was mostly the other way; even if, as Edward had once put it so finely in a public dialogue with Salman Rushdie, this was partly because the Palestinians were "the victims of the victims." I didn't know how to engage with my grandmother's quite differently staged conviction. But when I offered that the state she called "Israelite" had been soliciting trouble by its treatment of the Palestinians, she didn't demur. She just reiterated her view that this wasn't always the real reason for the dislike they — "we" — attracted.

Well, I knew *that* already. The Harold Abrahams character in *Chariots of Fire* says rather acutely of English anti-Semitism that "you catch it on the edge of a remark." Whether or not this is more maddening than a direct insult I could not say from experience, but early in life I learned to distrust those who said, "Fine old Anglo-Saxon name," when, say, a Mr. Rubinstein had been mentioned. "Lots of time to spare on Sundays" was another thoughtless, irritating standby. This was not exactly *Der Sturmer*, but I began to ask myself: had I ever let any of it go by? Had I ever helped it on its way with a smart remark? Had I ever told a joke that a Jew would not have told? (Plenty of latitude there, but everybody "knows" where it stops.) In this mood I bid farewell to my grandmother and, leaving her at her gate, rather awkwardly said, *"Shalom!"* She replied, *"Shalom, shalom,"* as cheerfully and readily as if it had been our greeting and parting since my infancy. I turned and trudged off to the station in the light, continuous rain that was also my birthright.

Enough of this, I suddenly thought. A hidden Jewish parentage was not exactly the moral equivalent of Anne Frank, after all. Anti-Jewish propaganda was the common enemy of humanity, and one had always regarded it as such; as much by instinct as by education. To claim a personal interest in opposing it seemed, especially at this late stage, a distinct cheapening of the commitment. As the makers of Levy's rye bread had once so famously said, "You don't have to be Jewish." You don't have to be Jewish to find a personal enemy in the Jew baiter. You don't have to be a Palestinian to take a principled position on the West Bank. So what's new? By a celebrated and practiced flick of the lever, your enemies can transfer you from the "anti" column to the "self-hating." A big deal it isn't.

Well, then, why had my first reaction to the news been one of pleasure? Examining my responses and looking for a trigger, I turned back to *Daniel Deronda*, which I had thought when I first read it to be a novel superior even to *Middlemarch*:

> "Then I *am* a Jew?" Deronda burst out with a deep-voiced energy that made his mother shrink a little backward against her cushions. ... "I am glad of it," said Deronda, impetuously, in the veiled voice of passion.

This didn't at all meet my case. It was far too overwrought. For one thing, I had never had the opportunity to question my mother. For another, I had not (absent the teasing of the dream) had Deronda's premonitions. My moment in the Jerusalem bookshop, accosted by a matronly woman, did not compare with his *rencontre* in the Frankfurt synagogue. On the other hand, the response of Deronda's mother did seem to hit a chord:

> "Why do you say you are glad? You are an English gentleman. I secured you that."

Another memory. I am sitting on the stairs in my pajamas, monitoring a parental dispute. The subject is me, the place is on the edge of Dartmoor and the year must be 1956 or so, because the topic is my future education. My father is arguing reasonably that private schooling is too expensive. My mother, in tones that I can still recall, is saying that money can be found. "If there is going to be an upper class in this country," she says forcefully, "then Christopher is going to be in it." My ideas about the ruling class are drawn from Arthurian legend at this point, but I like the sound of her reasoning. In any case, I yearn for boarding school and the adventure of quitting home. She must have had her way, as she customarily did, because a few months later I was outfitted for prep school and spent the next decade or so among playing fields, psalms, honors boards and the rest of it. I thus became the first Hitchens ever to go to a "public" school; to have what is still called (because it applies to about 1 percent of the population) a "conventional" education, and to go to Oxford.

Until very recently, I had thought of this parental sacrifice — I was ever aware that the costs were debilitating to the family budget — as the special certificate of social mobility. My father had come from a poor area of Portsmouth, was raised as a Baptist, and had made his way by dint of scholarships and the chance provided by the navy. My mother — well, now I saw why questions about her background had been quieted by solemn references to Dodo's early bereavement. And now I wish I could ask my mother — was all this effort expended, not just to make me a gentleman, but to make me an Englishman? An odd question to be asking myself, at my age, in a new country where most of my friends thought of me as "a Brit." But an attractive reflection, too, when I thought of the Jewish majority among my circle, and the special place of the Jews in the internationalist tradition I most admired. It counted as plus and minus that I had not had to sacrifice anything to join up. No struggle or formative drama, true, but no bullying at school, no taunting, not the least temptation to dissemble or to wish otherwise. In its review at the time, *The Tablet* (what a name!) had complained of *Daniel Deronda* that George Eliot committed "a literary error when she makes Deronda abandon, on learning the fact of his Jewish birth, all that a modern English education weaves of Christianity and the results of Christianity into an English gentleman's life." Nobody would now speak with such presumption and certainly about "the results of Christianity," but insofar as this abandonment would not be an act of supererogation on my part, it was by now impossible in any case. In other words, the discovery came to me like a gift. Like Jonathan Miller in his famous writhe in *Beyond the Fringe*, I could choose to be "not a Jew, but Jew-*ish*."

Or could it be that easy? I had two further visitations of memory to cogitate. At the age of about five, when the family lived in Scotland, I had heard my mother use the term "anti-Semitism." As with one or two other words in very early life, as soon as I heard this one I immediately, in some indefinable way, *knew what it meant.* I also knew that it was one of those cold, sibilant, sinister-sounding words, innately repugnant in its implications. I had always found anti-Jewish sentiment to be disgusting, in the same way as all such prejudices, but also in a different way, and somehow more so. To hear some ignorant person denouncing Pakistani or Jamaican immigrants to Britain was one thing — there would be foul-mouthed complaints about cooking smells, about body odors and occasionally about sexual habits. This was the sort of plebeian bigotry that one had to learn to combat, in early days as an apprentice canvasser, as a sort of Tory secret weapon in the ranks of the Labour vote. But anti-Semitic propaganda was something else. More rarely encountered, it was a sort of theory; both pseudo- and anti-intellectual. It partook of a little learning about blood, soil, money, conspiracy. It had a fetidly religious and furtively superstitious feel to it. (Nobody accuses the blacks of trying to take over international finance, if only because the racists don't believe them capable of mounting the conspiracy.) When I came across Yevtushenko's poem "Babi Yar" at the age of sixteen, I realized that he had seized the essence of the horror I felt; the backwardness and cunning that could be mobilized. I memorized the poem for a public reading that my school organized for the Venice in Peril Fund, and can remember some lines even now without taking down the Peter Levi translation:

> No Jewish blood runs among my blood
> But I am as bitterly and as hardly hated
> By every anti-Semite
> As if I were a Jew.

That seemed to me a fine ambition, even if easily affected at a civilized English boys' school. I know that it was at about that time that I noticed, in my early efforts at leftist propaganda, that among the few reliable allies in a fairly self-satisfied school were the boys with what I gradually understood were Jewish names. There was occasional nudging and smirking in chapel when we sang the line "Ye seeds of Israel's chosen race" in the anthem "Crown Him." What did it mean, "chosen"? Could it be serious? I hadn't then read *Daniel Deronda,* but would have

shared his stiff and correct attitude (antedating his discovery)
that:

> Of learned and accomplished Jews he took it for granted that they
> had dropped their religion, and wished to be merged in the people
> of their native lands. Scorn flung at a Jew as such would have roused
> all his sympathy in grief of inheritance; but the indiscriminate scorn
> of a race will often strike a specimen who has well-earned it on his
> own account.

Oh, I was fair-minded all right. But strict fair-mindedness
would suggest the conclusion that it didn't *matter* who was
Jewish. And to say that it didn't matter seemed rather point-
missing.

The second memory was more tormenting. Shortly before
her death, and in what was to be our last telephone conversation, my mother had suddenly announced that she wanted to
move to Israel. This came to me as a complete surprise. (My
grandmother, when I told her fifteen years later, was likewise
unprepared for the revelation.) Now I ransacked that last exchange for any significance it might retrospectively possess.
Having separated from my father and approaching middle life,
my mother was urgently seeking to make up for time lost and
spoke of all manner of fresh starts. Her praise for Israel was of
the sort — "It's a new country. It's young. They work hard.
They made the desert bloom" — that one read in the Gentile as
well as the Jewish press. The year was 1973 and the time was
just after the Yom Kippur war, and in trying to moderate her
enthusiasm I spoke of the precariousness of the situation. This
was slightly dishonest of me, because I didn't doubt Israel's
ability to outfight its neighbors. But I suspected that any
mention of the Palestinians would be a pointless expense of
breath. Besides, I wasn't entirely sure myself how I stood on
that question.

In June 1967 I had sympathized instinctively with the Jewish
state, though I remember noting with interest and foreboding a
report from Paris which said that triumphalist demonstrators
on the Champs-Elysées had honked their car horns — *Isra-el
vain-cra!* — to the same beat as the OAS's *Algé-rie Fran-çaise!* My
evolution since then had been like thousands of other radicals:

misery at the rise of the Israeli right and enhanced appreciation of the plight of the Palestinians, whether in exile or under occupation. Several visits to the region meant that I had met the Palestinians and seen conclusively through those who had argued that they did not "really" exist. By the time I moved to the United States, the left and even the liberals were thrown on the defensive. In America at least, a major part of the ideological cement for the Reagan-Thatcher epoch was being laid on by the neoconservative school, which was heavily influenced by the Middle East debate and which did not scruple to accuse its critics of anti-Semitism. My baptism of fire with this group came with the Timerman affair, which has been unjustly forgotten in the record of those years.

Even though Jacobo Timerman had been incarcerated and tortured *as a Jew*, his Argentine fascist tormentors were nonetheless felt, by the Reagan administration and by the pre-Falklands Thatcherites, to be fundamentally on our side. (This in spite of the horridly warm relations between the Buenos Aires junta and the Soviet Union.) They did not count, in the new *Kulturkampf*, as a tyranny within the meaning of the act. As a result, Jacobo Timerman had to be defamed.

He was accused of making up his story. He was reviled in an attack that presaged a later hot favorite term, of covert sympathy for "terrorism" in Argentina. He was arraigned for making life harder, by his denunciation, for Argentina's peaceable Jewish community. (This charge was given a specially ironic tone by the accusation, made in parallel, that he had overstated the extend of anti-Semitism in that country.) Although some of this slander came from the Francoist right, who were later to appear in their true colors under the banner of General Singlaub and Colonel North, the bulk of the calumny was provided by neoconservative Jewish columnists and publications. I shall never forget Irving Kristol telling a dinner table at the Lehrman Institute that he did not believe Timerman had been tortured in the first place.

I was very much affected by Timerman's book *Prisoner Without a Name, Cell Without a Number,* partly because I had once spent a few rather terrifying days in Buenos Aires, trying to get news of him while he was incommunicado. Not even the most pessimistic person had appreciated quite what he was actually

going through. As I read the account of his torture, at the hands
of the people who were later picked by Reagan and Casey to
begin the training of the contras, I was struck by one page in
particular. An ideologue of the junta is speaking:

> Argentina has three main enemies: Karl Marx, because he tried to
> destroy the Christian concept of society; Sigmund Freud, because he
> tried to destroy the Christian concept of the family; and Albert Ein-
> stein, because he tried to destroy the Christian concept of time and
> space.

Here was the foe in plain view. As that pure Austrian Ernst
Fischer puts it so pungently in his memoir, *An Opposing Man:*
"The degree of a society's culture can be measured against its
attitude towards the Jews. All forms of anti-Semitism are evidence of a reversion to barbarism. Any system which persecutes
the Jews, on whatever pretext, has forfeited all right to be regarded as progressive."

Here were all my adopted godfathers in plain view as well;
the three great anchors of the modern, revolutionary intelligence. It was for this reason that, on the few occasions on which
I had been asked if I was Jewish, I had been sad to say no, and
even perhaps slightly jealous. On the other hand, when in early
1988 I told an editor friend my news, her response was sweet
but rather shocking. "That should make your life easier," she
said. "Jewish people are *allowed* to criticize Israel." I felt a surge
of annoyance. Was that the use I was supposed to make of it?
And did that response, typical as I was to find it, suggest the
level to which the debate had fallen? It seemed to me that since
the Middle East was becoming nuclearized, and since the United
States was a principal armorer and paymaster, it was more in
the nature of a civic responsibility to take a critical interest. If
Zionism was going to try to exploit Gentile reticence in the post-
Holocaust era, it might do so successfully for a time. But it
would never be able to negate the tradition of reason and skepticism inaugurated by the real Jewish founding fathers. And
one had not acquired that tradition by means of the genes.

As I was preparing for my father's funeral, and readying a short
address I planned to give to the mourners, I scanned through a
wartime novel in which he had featured as a character. Warren

Tute was an author of the *Cruel Sea* school, and had acquired a
certain following by his meticulous depiction of life in the Royal
Navy. His best known book, *The Cruiser*, had my father in the
character of Lieutenant Hale. I didn't find anything in the narrative that would be appropriate for my eulogy. But I did find
an internal monologue, conducted by the Master at Arms as he
mentally reviewed the ship's complement of HMS *Antigone*. The
Master at Arms dealt in stereotypes:

> He knew that Stoker First Class Danny Evans would be likely to
> celebrate his draft by going on the beer for a week in Tonypandy
> and then spending the next three months in the Second Class for
> Leave. He knew that Blacksmith First Class Rogers would try and
> smuggle service provisions ashore for his mother and that Tele-
> graphist Jacobs was a sea lawyer who kept a copy of Karl Marx in his
> kitbag.

Good old Telegraphist Jacobs! I could see him now, huddled
defensively in his radio shack. Probably teased a bit for his bookishness ("a copy" of Marx, indeed); perhaps called "Four Eyes"
for his glasses and accused of "swallowing the dictionary" if he
ever employed a long word. On shore leave at colonial ports,
sticking up for the natives while his hearty shipmates rolled the
taxi drivers and the whores. Perhaps enduring a certain amount
of ragging at church parade or "divisions" (though perhaps not;
the British lower deck is, if anything, overly respectful of "a
man's religion"). Resorted to by his comrades in the mess when
there was a dispute over King's Regulations or the pay slips.
Indefinitely relegated when promotion was discussed — a Captain Jacobs R.N. would have been more surprising than an Ad-
miral Rickover. In those terrible days of war and blockade,
where the air is full of bombast about fighting the Hun, or just
fighting, Telegraphist Jacobs argues hoarsely that the enemy is
fascism. Probably he has rattled a tin for Spain; collected ban-
dages in the East End for the boys of the International Brigade
(whose first British volunteers were two Jewish garment workers). When the wireless begins to use the weird and frightening
new term "total war," Telegraphist Jacobs already knows what
it means. The rest of the time, he overhears the word "trouble-
maker" and privately considers it to be no insult.

My father never knew that he had a potential Telegraphist Jacobs for a son, but he hardly ever complained at what he did get, and I salute him for that. I also think with pleasure and pride of him and Jacobs, their vessel battered by the Atlantic and the Third Reich, as they sailed through six years of hell together to total victory. Commander Hitchens, I know, would never have turned a Nelson eye to any bullying. They were, much as the navy dislikes the expression, in the same boat.

As I believe is common with elder sons, I feel more and more deprived, as the days pass, by the thought of conversations that never took place and now never will. In this case, having had the Joycean experience of finding myself an orphan and a Jew more or less simultaneously, I had at least the consolation of curiosity and interest. A week or so after returning from the funeral in England, I telephoned the only rabbi I knew personally and asked for a meeting. Rabbi Robert Goldburg is a most learned and dignified man, who had once invited me to address his Reform congregation in New Haven. He had married Arthur Miller to Marilyn Monroe (converting the latter to Judaism), but resisted the temptation to go on about it too much. After some initial banter about my disclosure ("Aren't you ashamed? Did you see Rabin saying to *break their bones?*") he appointed a time and place. I wanted to ask him what I had been missing.

It may be a bit early to say what I learned from our discussion. The course of reading that was suggested is one I have not yet completed. No frontal challenge to my atheism was presented, though I was counseled to reexamine the "crude, Robert Ingersoll, nineteenth-century" profession of unbelief. Ever since Maimonides wrote of the Messiah that "he may tarry," Judaism seems to have rubbed along with a relaxed attitude to the personal savior question, and a frankly skeptical one about questions of wish-thinking such as the afterlife. A. J. Ayer once pointed out that Voltaire was anti-Semitic because he blamed the Jews for Christianity, "and I'm very much afraid to say that he was quite right. It *is* a Jewish heresy." When I had first heard him say that, I thought he might be being flippant. But as I talked more with Rabbi Goldburg, I thought that Judaism might turn out to be the most ethically sophisticated tributary of humanism. Einstein, who was urged on me as an alternative to

Ingersoll, had allowed himself to speak of "The Old One," despite refusing allegiance to the god of Moses. He had also said that the old one "does not play dice with the universe." Certainly it was from Jews like him that I had learned to hate the humans who thought themselves fit to roll the dice at any time.

Rabbi Goldburg's congregation is well-to-do, and when I visited them as a speaker I had been very impressed by the apparent contrast between their life style, for want of a better term, and their attitudes. I say "apparent contrast" because it is of course merely philistine to assume that people "vote their pocketbook" all the time, or that such voting behavior is hardheaded realism instead of the fatuity it so often is. The well-known Jewish pseudo-intellectual who had so sweetly observed that American Jews have the income profile of Episcopalians and the voting habits of Puerto Ricans was an example of Reaganism, of what Saul Bellow once called "the mental rabble of the wised-up world."

Anyway, what struck me when I addressed this highly educated and professional group was the same as what had struck me when I had once talked to a gathering of Armenians in a leafy suburb in California. They did not scoff or recoil, even when they might disagree, as I droned on about the iniquity and brutality, the greed and myopia that marked Reagan's low tide. They did not rise to suggest that the truth lay somewhere in between, or that moderation was the essential virtue, or that politics was the art of the possible. They seemed to lack that overlay of Panglossian emollience that had descended over the media and the Congress and, it sometimes seemed, over every damn thing. Over drinks afterwards I suddenly thought: Of course. These people already know. They aren't to be fooled by bubbles of prosperity and surges of good feeling. *They know the worst can happen.* It may not be in the genes, but it's in the collective memory and in many individual ones too.

Was this perhaps why I had sometimes "felt" Jewish? As I look back over possible premonitions, echoes from early life, promptings of memory, I have to suspect my own motives. I am uneasy because to think in this way is, in Kipling's frightening phrase, "to think with the blood." Jews may think with the blood if they choose; it must be difficult not to do so. But they — we

— must also hope that thinking with the blood does not become general. This irony, too, must help impart and keep alive a sense of preparedness for the worst.

Under the Nuremberg laws, I would have been counted a Blumenthal or Breslau and the denial of that will stop with me. Under the Law of Return I can supposedly redeem myself by moving into the Jerusalem home from which my friend Edward Said has been evicted. We must be able to do better than that. We still live in the prehistory of the human race, where no tribalism can be much better than another and where humanism and internationalism, so much derided and betrayed, need an unsentimental and decisive restatement.

EDWARD HOAGLAND

Heaven and Nature

FROM HARPER'S MAGAZINE

A FRIEND OF MINE, a peaceable soul who has been riding the New York subways for thirty years, finds himself stepping back from the tracks once in a while and closing his eyes as the train rolls in. This, he says, is not only to suppress an urge to throw himself in front of it but because every couple of weeks an impulse rises in him to push a stranger onto the tracks, any stranger, thus ending his own life too. He blames this partly on apartment living, "pigeonholes without being able to fly."

It is profoundly startling not to trust oneself after decades of doing so. I don't dare keep ammunition in my country house for a small rifle I bought secondhand two decades ago. The gun had sat in a cupboard in the back room with the original box of .22 bullets under the muzzle all that time, seldom fired except at a few apples hanging in a tree every fall to remind me of my army training near the era of the Korean War, when I'd been considered quite a marksman. When I bought the gun I didn't trust either my professional competence as a writer or my competence as a father as much as I came to, but certainly believed I could keep myself alive. I bought it for protection, and the idea that someday I might be afraid of shooting myself with the gun would have seemed inconceivable — laughable.

One's fifties can be giddy years, as anybody fifty knows. Chest pains, back pains, cancer scares, menopausal or prostate complications are not the least of it, and the fidelities of a lifetime, both personal and professional, may be called into question. Was it a mistake to have stuck so long with one's marriage, and to have stayed with a lackluster well-paying job? (Or *not* to have stayed and stuck?) People not only lose faith in their talents and their dreams or values; some simply tire of them. Grow tired, too, of the smell of fried-chicken grease, once such a delight, and the cold glutinosity of ice cream, the boredom of beer, the stop-go of travel, the hiccups of laughter, and of two rush hours a day, then the languor of weekends, of athletes as well as accountants, and even the frantic birdsong of spring — red-eyed vireos that have been clocked singing twenty-two thousand times in a day. Life is a matter of cultivating the six senses, and an equilibrium with nature and what I think of as its subdivision, human nature, trusting no one completely but almost everyone at least a little; but this is easier said than done.

More than thirty thousand Americans took their own lives last year, men mostly, with the highest rate being among those older than sixty-five. When I asked a friend why three times as many men kill themselves as members of her own sex, she replied with sudden anger, "I'm not going to go into the self-indulgence of men." They won't bend to failure, she said, and want to make themselves memorable. Suicide is an exasperating act as often as it is pitiable. "Committing" suicide is in bad odor in our culture even among those who don't believe that to cash in your chips ahead of time and hand back to God his gifts to you is a blasphemous sin. We the living, in any case, are likely to feel accused by this person who "voted with his feet." It appears to cast a subversive judgment upon the social polity as a whole that what was supposed to work in life — religion, family, friendship, commerce, and industry — did not, and furthermore it frightens the horses in the street, as Shaw's friend Mrs. Patrick Campbell once defined wrongful behavior.

Many suicides inflict outrageous trauma, burning permanent injuries in the minds of their children, though they may have joked beforehand only of "taking a dive." And sometimes the gesture has a peevish or cowardly aspect, or seems to have been senselessly shortsighted as far as an outside observer can tell. There are desperate suicides and crafty suicides, people who do it to cause others trouble and people who do it to save others trouble, deranged exhibitionists who yell from a building ledge and close-mouthed, secretive souls who swim out into the ocean's anonymity. Suicide may in fact be an attempt to escape death, shortcut the dreadful deteriorating processes, abort one's natural trajectory, elude "the ruffian on the stairs," in A. E. Housman's phrase for a cruelly painful, anarchic death — make it neat and not messy. The deed can be grandiose or self-abnegating, vindictive or drably mousy, rationally plotted or plainly insane. People sidle toward death, intent upon outwitting their own bodies' defenses, or they may dramatize the chance to make one last, unambiguous, irrevocable decision, like a captain scuttling his ship — death before dishonor — leaping toward oblivion through a curtain of pain, like a frog going down the throat of a snake. One man I knew hosted a quietly affectionate evening with several unknowing friends on the night before he swallowed too many pills. Another waved an apologetic goodbye to a bystander on a bridge. Seldom shy ordinarily, and rarely considerate, he turned shy and apologetic in the last moment of life. Never physically inclined, he made a great vault toward the ice on the Mississippi.

In the army, we wore dog tags with a notch at one end by which these numbered pieces of metal could be jammed between our teeth, if we lay dead and nameless on a battlefield, for later sorting. As "servicemen" our job would be to kill people who were pointed out to us as enemies, or make "the supreme sacrifice" for a higher good than enjoying the rest of our lives. Life was very much a possession, in other words — not only God's, but the soldier's own to dispose of. Working in an army hospital, I frequently did handle dead bodies, but this never made me feel I would refuse to kill another man whose uniform was pointed out to me as being inimical, or value my life more tremulously and vigilantly. The notion of dying for my country never appealed to me as much as dying free-lance for my ideas (in the unlikely event that I *could* do that), but I was ready. People were taught during the 1940s and 1950s that one should be ready to die for one's beliefs. Heroes were revered because they had deliberately chosen to give up their lives. Life would not be worth living under the tyranny of an invader and Nathan Hale apparently hadn't paused to wonder whether God might not have other uses for him besides being hung. Nor did the pilot Colin Kelly hesitate before plunging his plane into a Japanese battleship, becoming America's first well-publicized hero in World War II.

I've sometimes wondered why people who know that they are terminally ill, or who are headed for suicide, so very seldom have paused to take a bad guy along with them. It is lawless to consider an act of assassination, yet hardly more so, really, than suicide is regarded in some quarters (or death itself, in others). Government bureaucracies, including our own, in their majesty and as the executors of laws, regularly weigh the pros and cons of murdering foreign antagonists. Of course the answer is that most individuals are fortunately more timid as well as humbler in their judgment than government officialdom, but beyond that, when dying or suicidal, they no longer care enough to devote their final energies to doing good works of any kind — Hitler himself in their gunsights they would have passed up. Some suicides become so crushed and despairing that they can't recognize the consequences of anything they do, and it's not primarily vindictiveness that wreaks such havoc upon their survivors but their derangement from ordinary life.

Courting the idea is different from the real impulse. "When he begged for help, we took him and locked him up," another friend of mine says, speaking of her husband. "Not till then. Wishing to be out of the situation you are in — feeling helpless and unable to cope — is not the same as wishing to be dead. If I actually wished to be dead, even my children's welfare would have no meaning."

You might think the ready option of divorce available lately would have cut suicide rates, offering an escape to battered wives, lovelorn husbands, and other people in despair. But it doesn't work that way. When the number of choices people have increases, an entire range of possibilities opens up. Suicide among teenagers has almost quadrupled since 1950, although the standard of comfort that their families enjoy is up. Black Americans, less affluent than white Americans, have had less of a rise in suicides, and the rate among them remains about half of that for whites.

Still, if a fiftyish fellow with fine teeth and a foolproof pension plan, a cottage at the beach and the Fourth of July weekend coming up, kills himself, it seems truculent. We would look at

him bafflingly if he told us he no longer likes the Sturm und
Drang of banging fireworks.

Then stay at your hideaway! we'd argue with him.

"Big mouths eat little mouths. Nature isn't 'timeless.' Whole
lives are squeezed into three months or three days."

What about your marriage?

"She's become more mannish than me. I loved women. I don't
believe in marriage between men."

Remarry, then!

"I've gone impotent, and besides, when I see somebody young
and pretty I guess I feel like dandling her on my knee."

Marriage is friendship. You can find someone your own age.

"I'm tired of it."

*But how about your company? — a widows-and-orphans stock that's
on the cutting edge of the silicon frontier? That's interesting.*

"I know what wins. It's less and less appetizing."

You're not scared of death anymore?

"It interests me less than it did."

What are you so sick of? The rest of us keep going.

"I'm tired of weathermen and sportscasters on the screen. Of
being patient and also of impatience. I'm tired of the president,
whoever the president happens to be, and sleeping badly, with
forty-eight half-hours in the day — of breaking two eggs every
morning and putting sugar on something. I'm tired of the
drone of my own voice, but also of us jabbering like parrots at
each other — of all our stumpy ways of doing everything."

You're bored with yourself?

"That's an understatement. I'm maybe the least interesting
person I know."

But to kill yourself?

"You know, it's a tradition, too," he remarks quietly, not making so bold as to suggest that the tradition is an honorable one,
though his tone of voice might be imagined to imply this. "I
guess I've always been a latent maverick."

Except in circumstances which are themselves a matter of life
and death, I'm reluctant to agree with the idea that suicide is
not the result of mental illness. No matter how reasonably the
person appears to have examined his options, it goes against the

grain of nature for him to destroy himself. And any illness that threatens his life changes a person. Suicidal thinking, if serious, can be a kind of death scare, comparable to suffering a heart attack or undergoing a cancer operation. One survives such a phase both warier and chastened. When — two years ago — I emerged from a bad dip into suicidal speculation, I felt utterly exhausted and yet quite fearless of ordinary dangers, vastly afraid of myself but much less scared of extraneous eventualities. The fact of death may not be tragic; many people die with a bit of a smile that captures their mouths at the last instant, and most people who are revived after a deadly accident are reluctant to be brought to life, resisting resuscitation, and carrying back confusing, beamish, or ecstatic memories. But the same impetuosity that made him throw himself out of the window might have enabled the person to love life all the more if he'd been calibrated somewhat differently at the time of the emergency. Death's edge is so abrupt and near that many people who expect a short and momentary dive may be astounded to find that it is bottomless and change their minds and start to scream when they are only halfway down.

Although my fright at my mind's anarchy superseded my fear of death in the conventional guise of automobile or airplane crashes, heart seizures, and so on, nightmares are more primitive and in my dreams I continued to be scared of a death not sought after — dying from driving too fast and losing control of the car, breaking through thin ice while skating and drowning in the cold, or falling off a cliff. When I am tense and sleeping raggedly, my worst nightmare isn't drawn from anxious prep school memories or my stint in the army or the bad spells of my marriages or any other of adulthood's vicissitudes. Nothing else from the past half century has the staying power in my mind of the elevated-train rides that my father and I used to take down Third Avenue to the Battery in New York City on Sunday afternoon when I was three or four or five so I could see the fish at the aquarium. We were probably pretty good companions in those years, but the wooden platforms forty feet up shook terribly as trains from both directions pulled in and out. To me they seemed worse than rickety — ready to topple. And the roar was fearful, and the railings left large gaps for a child to fall through, after the steep climb up the slat-sided, windy, shaking stairway from street level. It's a rare dream, but several times a year I still find myself on such a perch, without his company or anybody else's, on a boyish or a grown-up's mission, when the elevated platform begins to rattle desperately, seesaw, heel over, and finally come apart, disintegrate, while I cling to struts and trusses.

My father, as he lay dying at home of bowel cancer, used to enjoy watching Tarzan reruns on the children's hour of television. Like a strong green vine, they swung him far away from his deathbed to a world of skinny-dipping and friendly animals and scenic beauty linked to the lost realities of his adolescence in Kansas City. Earlier, when he had still been able to walk without much pain, he'd paced the house for several hours at night, contemplating suicide, I expect, along with other anguishing thoughts, regrets, remembrances, and yearnings, while the rest of us slept. But he decided to lie down and die the slower way. I don't know how much of that decision was for the sake of his wife and children, how much was because he didn't want to be a "quitter," as he sometimes put it, and how much was due to his believing that life belongs to God (which I'm not even sure he did). He was not a churchgoer after his thirties. He had belonged to J. P. Morgan's church, St. George's, on Stuyvesant Square — Morgan was a hero of his — but when things went a little wrong for him at the Wall Street law firm he worked for and he changed jobs and moved out to the suburbs, he became a skeptic on religious matters, and gradually, in the absence of faith of that previous kind, he adhered to a determined allegiance to the social order. Wendell Willkie or Dwight D. Eisenhower instead of J. P. Morgan became the sort of hero he admired, and suicide would have seemed an act of insurrection against the laws and conventions of the society, internationalist-Republican, that he believed in.

I was never particularly afraid that I might plan a suicide, swallowing a bunch of pills and keeping them down — only of what I think of as being Anna Karenina's kind of death. This most plausible self-killing in all of literature is frightening because it was unwilled, regretted at midpoint, and came as a complete surprise to Anna herself. After rushing impulsively, in great misery, to the Moscow railway station to catch a train, she ended up underneath another one, dismayed, astonished, and trying to climb out from under the wheels even as they crushed her. Many people who briefly verge on suicide undergo a mental somersault for a terrifying interval during which they're upside down, their perspective topsy-turvy, skidding, churning; and this is why I got rid of the bullets for my .22.

Nobody expects to trust his body overmuch after the age of fifty. Incipient cataracts or arthritis, outlandish snores, tooth-grinding, ankles that threaten to turn, are part of the game. But not to trust one's *mind?* That's a surprise. The single attribute that older people were sure to have (we thought as boys) was a stodgy dependability, a steady temperance or caution. Adults might be vain, unimaginative, pompous, and callous, but they did have their affairs tightly in hand. It was not till my thirties that I began to know friends who were in their fifties on equal terms, and I remember being amused, piqued, irritated, and slightly bewildered to learn that some of them still felt as marginal or rebellious or in a quandary about what to do with themselves for the next dozen years as my contemporaries were likely to. That close to retirement, some of them harbored a deep-seated contempt for the organizations they had been working for, ready to walk away from almost everybody they had known and the efforts and expertise of whole decades with very little sentiment. Nor did twenty years of marriage necessarily mean more than two or three — they might be just as ready to walk away from that also, and didn't really register it as twenty years at all. Rather, life could be about to begin all over again. "Bummish" was how one man described himself, with a raffish smile — "Lucky to have a roof over my head" — though he'd just put a child through Yale. He was quitting his job and claimed with exasperation that his wife still cried for her mother in her sleep, as if they'd never been married.

The great English traveler Richard Burton quoted an Arab proverb that speaks for many middle-aged men of the old-fashioned variety: "Conceal thy Tenets, thy Treasure, and thy Traveling." These are serious matters, in other words. People didn't conceal their tenets in order to betray them, but to fight for them more opportunely. And except for kings and princelings, concealing whatever treasure one had went almost without saying. As for travel, a man's travels were also a matter of gravity. Travel was knowledge, ambiguity, dalliances or misalliances, divided loyalty, forbidden thinking; and besides, someday he might need to make a run for it and go to ground someplace where he had made some secret friends. Friends of mine whose husbands or whose wives have died have been quite startled afterward to discover caches of money or traveler's checks concealed around the house, or a bundle of cash in a safe deposit box.

Burton, like any other desert adage-spinner and most individuals over fifty, would have agreed to an addition so obvious that it wasn't included to begin with: "Conceal thy Illnesses." I can remember how urgently my father worried that word would get out, after a preliminary operation for his cancer. He didn't want to be written off, counted out of the running at the corporation he worked for and in other enclaves of competition. Men often compete with one another until the day they die; comradeship consists of rubbing shoulders jocularly with a competitor. As breadwinners, they must be considered fit and sound by friend as well as foe, and so there's lots of truth to the most common answer I heard when asking why three times as many men as women kill themselves: "They keep their troubles to themselves"; "They don't know how to ask for help." Men greet each other with a sock on the arm, women with a hug, and the hug wears better in the long run.

I'm not entirely like that, and I discovered that when I confided something of my perturbation to a woman friend she was likely to keep telephoning me or mailing cheery postcards, whereas a man would usually listen with concern, communicate his sympathy, and maybe intimate that he had pondered the same drastic course of action himself a few years back and would end up respecting my decision either way. Open-mindedness seems an important attribute to a good many men, who pride themselves on being objective, hearing all sides of an issue, on knowing that truth and honesty do not always coincide with social dicta, and who may even cherish a subterranean outlaw streak that, like being ready to violently defend one's family, reputation, and country, is by tradition male.

Men, being so much freer than women in society, used to feel
they had less of a stake in the maintenance of certain churchly
conventions and enjoyed speaking irreverently about various
social truisms, including even the principle that people ought to
die on schedule, not cutting in ahead on their assigned place in
line. Contemporary women, after their triumphant irreverence
during the 1960s and 1970s, cannot be generalized about so
easily, however. They turn as skeptical and saturnine as any
man. In fact, women attempt suicide more frequently, but favor
pills or other methods, whereas two-thirds of the men who kill
themselves have used a gun. In 1985, 85 percent of suicides by
means of firearms were done by men. An overdose of medica-
tion hasn't the same finality. It may be reversible if the person
is discovered quickly, or be subject to benign miscalculation to
start with. Even if it works, perhaps it can be fudged by a kindly
doctor in the record-keeping. Like an enigmatic drowning or a
single-car accident that baffles the suspicions of the insurance
company, a suicide by drugs can be a way to avoid making a
loud statement, and merely illustrate the final modesty of a
person who didn't wish to ask for too much of the world's attention.

Unconsummated attempts at suicide can strike the rest of us
as self-pitying and self-aggrandizing, or plaintive plea-bargain-
ing — "childish," we say, though actually the suicide of children
is ghastly beyond any stunt of self-mutilation an adult may in-
dulge in because of the helplessness that echoes through the act.
It would be hard to define chaos better than as a world where
children decide that they don't want to live.

Love is the solution to all dilemmas, we sometimes hear, and
in those moments when the spirit bathes itself in beneficence
and manages to transcend the static of personalities rubbing fur
off of each other, indeed it is. Without love nothing matters,
Paul told the Corinthians, a mystery which, if true, has no ready
Darwinian explanation. Love without a significant sexual com-
ponent and for people who are unrelated to us serves little
practical purpose. It doesn't help us feed our families, win
struggles, thrive and prosper. It distracts us from the ordinary
business of sizing people up and making a living, and is not
even conducive to intellectual observation, because instead of

seeing them, we see right through them to the bewildered child and dreaming adolescent who inhabited their bodies earlier, the now-tired idealist who fell in love and out of love, got hired and quit, hired and fired, bought cars and wore them out, liked black-eyed Susans, blueberry muffins, and roosters crowing — liked roosters crowing better than skyscrapers but now likes skyscrapers better than roosters crowing. As swift as thought, we select the details that we need to see in order to be able to love them.

Yet at other times we'll dispense with these same poignancies and choose only their grunginess to look at, their pinched mouths and shifty eyes, their thirst for gin at noon and indifference to their kids, their greed for the best tidbit on the buffet table and penchant for poking their penises up the excretory end of other human beings. I tend to gaze quite closely at the faces of priests I meet on the street to see if a lifetime of love has marked them noticeably. Real serenity or asceticism I no longer expect, and I take for granted the beefy calm that frequently goes with Catholic celibacy, but I am watching for the marks of love and often see mere resignation or tenacity.

Many men are romantics, likely to plunge, go for broke, take action in a spirit of exigency rather than waiting for the problem to resolve itself. Then, on the contrary, still as romantics, they may drift into despairing passivity, stare at the TV all day long, and binge with a bottle. Women too may turn frenetic for a while and then throw up their hands; but though they may not seem as grandiosely fanciful and romantic at the outset, they are more often believers — at least I think they tend to believe in God or in humanity, the future, and so on. We have above us the inviting eternity of "the heavens," if we choose to look at it, lying on our backs in the summer grass under starlight, some of which had left its source before mankind became man. But because we live in our heads more than in nature nowadays, even the summer sky is a mine field for people whose memories are mined. With the sky no longer humbling, the sunshine only a sort of convenience, and no godhead located anywhere outside our own heads, every problem may seem insolubly interlocked. When the telephone has become impossible to answer at home, sometimes it finally becomes impossible to stride down the gangplank of a cruise ship in Mombasa too, although no telephones will ring for you there.

But if escapist travel is ruled out in certain emergencies, surely you can *pray*? Pray, yes; but to whom? That requires a bit of preparation. Rarely do people obtain much relief from praying if they haven't stood in line awhile to get a visa. It's an appealing idea that you can just *go*, and in a previous era perhaps you could have, like on an old-fashioned shooting safari. But it's not so simple now. What do you believe in? Whom are you praying to? What are you praying for? There's no crèche on the courthouse lawn; you're not supposed to adhere exactly even to what your parents had believed. Like psychotherapy, praying takes time, even if you know which direction to face when you kneel.

Love is powerfully helpful when the roof falls in — loving other people with a high and hopeful heart and as a kind of prayer. Yet that feat too requires new and sudden insights or long practice. The beatitude of loving strangers as well as friends — loving them on sight with a leap of empathy and intuition — is a form of inspiration, edging, of course, in some cases toward madness, as other states of beatitude can do. But there's no question that a genuine love for the living will stymie suicidal depressions not chemical in origin. Love is an elixir, changing the life of the lover like no other. And many of us have experienced this — a temporary lightening of our leery, prickly disapproval of much of the rest of the world when at a wedding or a funeral of shared emotion, or when we have fallen in love.

Yet the zest for life of those unusual men and women who make a great zealous success of living is due more often in good part to the craftiness and pertinacity with which they manage to overlook the misery of others. You can watch them watch life beat the stuffing out of the faces of their friends and acquaintances, yet they themselves seem to outwit the dense delays of social custom, the tedious tick-tock of bureaucratic obfuscation, accepting loss and age and change and disappointment without suffering punctures in their stomach lining. Breathlessness or strange dull pains from their nether organs don't nonplus them.

They fret and doubt in moderation, and love a lobster roast, squeeze lemon juice on living clams on the half shell to prove that the clams are alive, laugh as robins tussle a worm out of the ground or a kitten flees a dog. Like the problem drinkers, pork eaters, and chain smokers who nevertheless finish out their allotted years, succumbing to a stroke at a nice round biblical age when the best vitamin-eating vegetarian has long since died, their faces become veritable walnuts of fine character, with the same smile lines as the rarer individual whose grin has been affectionate all of his life.

We spend our lives getting to know ourselves, yet wonders never cease. During my adolescent years my states of mind, though undulant, seemed seamless; even when I was unhappy no cracks or fissures made me wonder if I was a danger to myself. My confidence was such that I treaded the slippery lips of waterfalls, fought forest fires, drove ancient cars cross-country night and day, and scratched the necks of menagerie leopards in the course of various adventures which enhanced the joy of being alive. The chemistry of the mind, because unfathomable, is more frightening. In the city, I live on the waterfront and occasionally will notice an agitated-looking figure picking his way along the pilings and stringpieces of the timbered piers nearby, staring at the sliding whorls on the surface of the Hudson as if teetering over an abyss. Our building, across the street, seems imposing from the water and over the years has acted as a magnet for a number of suicides — people who have dreaded the clammy chill, the onerous smothering essential to their first plan. One woman climbed out after jumping in and took the elevator to the roof (my neighbors remember how wringing wet she was) and leapt off, banging window ledges on the way down, and hit with the whap of a sack of potatoes, as others have.

Yet what is more remarkable than that a tiny minority of souls reach a point where they entrust their bodies to the force of gravity is that so few of the rest of us splurge an hour of a summer day gazing at the trees and sky. How many summers do we *have*? One sees prosperous families in the city who keep plants in their apartment windows that have grown so high they block the sunlight and appear to be doing the living for the tenants who are bolted inside. But beauty is nobody's sure salvation: not the beauty of a swimming hole if you get a cramp, and not the beauty of a woman if she doesn't care for you. The swimming hole looks inviting under the blue sky, with its amber bottom, green sedges sticking up in the shallows, and curls of gentle current over a waterlogged basswood tree two feet beneath the surface near the brook that feeds it. Come back at dusk, however, and the pond turns black — as dark as death, or on the contrary, a restful dark, a dark to savor. Take it as you will.

People with sunny natures do seem to live longer than people who are nervous wrecks; yet mankind didn't evolve out of the animal kingdom by being unduly sunny-minded. Life was fearful and phantasmagoric, supernatural and preternatural, as well as encompassing the kind of clockwork regularity of our well-governed day. It had numerous superstitious (from the Latin, "standing over") elements, such as we are likely to catch a whiff of only when we're peering at a dead body. And it was not just our optimism but our pessimistic premonitions, our dark moments as a species, our irrational, frightful speculations, our strange mutations upon the simple theme of love, and our sleepless, obsessive inventiveness — our dread as well as our faith — that made us human beings. Staking one's life on the more general good came to include risking suicide also. Brilliant, fecund people sometimes kill themselves.

"Joy to the world . . . Let heaven and nature sing, and heaven and nature sing . . . Repeat the sounding joy . . ." The famous Christmas carol invokes not only glee but unity: heaven with nature, not always a Christian combination. It's a rapturous hymn, and no one should refuse to surrender to such a pitch of revelation when it comes. But the flip side of rapture can be a riptide of panic, of hysterical gloom. Our faces are not molded as if joy were a preponderant experience. (Nor is a caribou's or a thrush's.) Our faces in repose look stoic or battered, and people of the sunniest temperament sometimes die utterly unstrung, doubting everything they have ever believed in or have done.

Let heaven and nature sing! the hymn proclaims. But *is* there such harmony? Are God and Mother Nature really the same? Are they even compatible? And will we risk burning our wings if we mount high enough to try to see? I've noticed that woods

soil in Italy smells the same as woods soil in New England when
you pick up a handful of it and enjoy its aromas — but is God
there the same? It can be precarious to wonder. I don't rule out
suicide as being unthinkable for people who have tried to live
full lives, and don't regard it as negating the work and faith and
satisfaction and fun and even ecstasy they may have known
before. In killing himself a person acknowledges his failures
during a time span when perhaps heaven and earth had caught
him like a pair of scissors — but not his life span. Man is different from animals in that he speculates, a high-risk activity.

MARY HOOD

Why Stop?

FROM THE GETTYSBURG REVIEW

Si monumentum requiris, circumspice.
— Wren

THERE IS an essential human ichor of awe, an instinct for reverence, a gracious sap which rises in us seasonally and flowers into devotions and wreaths. "Than longen folk to goon on pilgrimages." Goon indeed. Every sap has its sucker. SEE THE CONTINENTAL DIVIDE IN ACTION, the billboard in the Rockies invites. The parking lot is not empty. (When one sparrow decides to bathe, they all splash in.) Yet whether we queue up at the thronged-in-August, hell-hot gates of Graceland, candle and rose in hand, "the blisful holy martir for to seke," or shiver alone on the wintry bleak summit of the Kill Devil Hills contemplating the Wright brothers, who may have climbed the dune as we did but found quite another way down, it is all one expression of that wayfaring urge, now sublime, now ridiculous, which must not be confused with religious piety — whose zeal seeks the soul's perpetuation in a timeless future; homage, on the other hand, cherishes endurance of mortal report — fame — and acknowledges the past's claims upon us. We raise memorials against oblivion, not death. Death is, to the makers of monuments and pilgrimages, but one more occasion.

Apparently, any occasion will do. Near Jamestown, North Dakota, broods the world's largest concrete buffalo (three stories). South Dakota, not to be outdone, has erected a forty-foot-tall fiberglass pheasant. Although these monuments of civic pride stand in somewhat out-of-the-way places, seekers find them, eager to feel themselves dwarfed in the sweep of those great manmade shadows. The mood is festive, more aw shucks than awe. Yet even when a monument may have originally honored some historic glory beyond its place and pile, it can ultimately win its own fame as a landmark which travelers seek, not for the spirit of its intention of any love of history, but for itself alone, *because it's there.* The brochures and one's neighbors and co-workers label this sort a "must see" for no other reason than that many have seen it. Such a pilgrimage risks devolving into merest tourism. Still, if touring — travel for curiosity and rec-reation — is reverence's lowest expression, at worst a Pavlovian response to report of marvel or infamy, at least it is motion, and at best it offers some poignancy, if not poetry, to be recollected in whatever tranquillity the post-vacation letdown affords. At times we are moved only to laughter on the scene, out of em-barrassment, perhaps, at our being there at all, yet who would willingly miss an Alabama meteorite as long as it first missed us? Is not the Cardiff giant — ten and a half feet of midwestern gypsum sleeping in a Cooperstown museum — more popular now in his exposure to ridicule than ever he was when first exposed to light?

"Was this here then?" asks a child at the top of the San Jacinto monument in Texas, staring down at the curried swale where Sam Houston, that tough old bird, caught his worm by rising early. Tourists are all children at history's knee, begging for some snatch of song or scrap of idea to play with. Though all the world's a stage, we prefer the sideshow. " 'I know not,' said Rasselas, 'what pleasure the sight of the catacombs can afford; but since nothing else is offered, I am resolved to view them, and shall place this with many other things which I have done because I would do something.' "

Even now, in Providence, lines are forming to view the root of the apple tree which consumed Roger Williams in his grave. They say it curved around his skull, grew straight down his spine, branched for arms and legs, and turned up at his feet. "I'll believe that when I see it," we scoff, already loading the camera and car, keen to meddle ourselves in legend; like so many Mandevilles and Marco Polos, we'll bring home proof in our trunk. In Kodachrome: WE WERE THERE.

"Fame is proof that people are gullible," Emerson warns all pilgrims. But what cynic could fail to share the curator's pride in the key exhibit of the Jimmie Rodgers Museum in Mississippi, The Singing Brakeman's simple iron bedstead: "Over a hundred years old so far at least." For the small toll of admission we may wander around for hours, studying the trainman's guitar, signal flags, oilcan, cap, his wife's red dress, and the ordinary postal scale with which he weighed his replies to fan mail. We walk out into the present tense as though waking from a tender dream. And though roadside museums can offer the traveler the greatest opportunity for disappointment or suffocation, there yet remain these surprises and satisfactions, reminders that the quotidian has its charms and adventures.

LOOK WHAT'S HIDING
IN YOUR CUPBOARD!

urges an enthusiast's placard in the rice museum in Crowley, Louisiana. At an Acadian shrine a candid *genius loci* has scrawled this *caveat:*

Yes we have
mosquitoes we
don't give re-
funds.

Sometimes the spirit of a place "gives out glory, sometimes its little light must be sought to be seen," Eudora Welty notes of her own sorties down byroads. And sometimes, "generations have trod, have trod, have trod," as at San Juan Capistrano, where the returning swallows gull the punctual busloads in, to squint through lenses at those twittering walls and then further stretch their credulity and legs in the SACRED GIFT SHOP, whose harried clerks are more expert at making change than small talk.

Disappointment, from time to time, plagues every pilgrim. The shrine may be closed for the afternoon, or the week, or the duration. Roads and rivers may have altered course and given the lie to the sincerest maps. Rustic parlors suffer urbane renewals and portraits enjoy retouchings with a glossy wink toward beauty rather than authenticity. Mice and moss invade and creep. The arbors sag. The cobbles sleep under layers of asphalt. The jambs and sills of a birthplace may glower too low to have ever framed our heroes. Legend lengthens stature until truth cannot keep up. Doubts creep in with the unforecast rains. The winds and attendants may be contrary. One's will, or train, or diligence may falter. In short, "I have not the memory of Chinon," as Henry James sighs on his little tour in France, "I have only the regret." The most eagerly anticipated romantic tumults can eventuate as mere drips; honeymooners have been stranded high and dry at Niagara when for reasons of civil engineering the falls are shut down as though a tap had been turned. Authorized biographies and lyrical guidebooks may prove fiction or trumpery, and the reality leaves us unabashed and cold. "If the house is small the tablet is very big," Henry James observes on that same tour, when viewing the birthplace of Lamartine. We may either give up the hunt or become stoics. "Do I fail to find in the place to which I go the things that were reported to me? . . . I do not regret my pains," shrugs Montaigne. "I have learned that what was told me was not there."

If you seek a monument, look around, Sir Christopher Wren advises us from his grave. Even the most cursory glance around harvests treasures of homage. We honor Liberty, Justice, and the Boll Weevil with shrines of perpetual glory. We similarly remind the world of the site of the birth of the first English child in America, and upon the National Honor Roll list the date of the first live birth in an airplane. Lest we forget, earmuffs were patented in 1877, and the ball-point pen is having its centenary. There is a museum for moonshiners in Georgia and one for sponge divers in Florida. Besides labor, we celebrate rest: the hammock in South Carolina, rock skipping in Michigan and California.

When it seems as though no one else will, we honor ourselves. There was a ton or so of granite ordered carved and shipped south, the story goes, by a homesick native son relocated in the Midwest. When the shoulder-high marker arrived by freight on the L&N rail, was no one left alive in his native place to know and honor the man's beau geste? Did his patriotic love go unclaimed? Or was it simply too daunting a task, too monumental a labor in horse-and-buggy days, easier to offload it and set it there rather than try to trundle it over land to its intended homesite? Gentle mystery surrounds it even today. It stands facing west behind the superannuated Holly Springs depot — trains don't stop there anymore, and the kudzu gropes yearly nearer — in Cherokee County, Georgia. Its journey over, it has for almost a century announced to the setting sun:

Birthplace of
Julian M. Hughes
Feby. 3. 1860.

HERE EARLY ONE MORN I WAS BORN.
AMONG THE HILLS AND MIDST THE
CHARMS OF LOVELY CHEROKEE
IN DEAR OLD GEORGIA SO SWEET TO ME.

Mr. Hughes is famous for his having been born, if not for his poem. But perhaps the most cherished and lively posterities are reserved to fortune's children who have surprised and surpassed local custom in martyrdom for love. Every hamlet has its lovers' leap, or lane, or oak; its Frankie and Johnnie; its Helen or Romeo; the Hatfields and McCoys even tried for a second Troy. When Longfellow invented Evangeline and Gabriel, he could not have imagined that Dolores Del Rio would pose for the statue, or that it would be erected facing Bayou Teche a few paces from where the actual Evangeline (Emmeline Labiche) lies buried in the churchyard. The real story is sadder than poetry. (Isn't that what lovers always learn?) And then there is that bull moose in New England who became enthralled with a dairy cow; in all weathers he guarded her — lovelorn, dignified, loyal — the very exemplar of Longfellow's "affection that hopes, and endures, and is patient"; and didn't the country lanes clog with the traffic of pilgrims who wanted to pay their respects to that enchanted fool?

That nine days' wonder brought out the best in us; we didn't seek to disillusion the moose, or ride by to jeer at his amazing valentine. We cheered. But if fame can elicit the finest of our instincts, it can also draw forth the worst. Milton calls the fever for fame the "last infirmity of noble mind." And it is true that a man who will not take the slightest steps to alter his pace of living to prevent illness will run long risks to assure remembrance; in fact, he may be stimulated by the notion of death, though not craving its early sting — "Fame is the spur" — to raise advertisements to it thereafter. Didn't Cheops close the temples and exhaust four hundred thousand Egyptians in his service annually for a decade, merely to construct the smooth approaches to his future tomb? The pyramid itself required twenty years more to build. Cheops must have been as shrewd as he was determined, to know to begin early and live long, to keep alert till that bed was made, when so many could have rested if he'd slept sooner.

According to Herodotus, one wall of the tomb bears a grudging inscription complaining how much garlic, onions, and radishes the slaves on that project consumed. Cheops's expenses, beyond greengroceries and even with forced labor, were so staggering that he ordered his daughter into a brothel to procure by her own industry "a certain sum — how much I cannot say, for I was not told" — the historian modestly confesses. By her monumental exertions the daughter — who had begun to lust for a pyramid of her own — exacted from each client not only her father's levied tribute but also the gift of a building stone for herself. Thus, one by one she laid the foundations, 150 feet along each side, of her own tomb. The work was completed in her lifetime, or as the perpetual-care salesmen call it nowadays, "pre-need." Is there something as interesting as radishes, onions, and garlic inscribed on her death chamber? Herodotus does not mention it.

Fashions in tombs and inscriptions — and in monuments and literature — have changed over time. Yet from the beginning, we can be sure, there were both events and ways to remember. "Before the music, there were drums," Eudora Welty reminds us, in "Some Notes on River Country." Before there were alphabets and tools to carve them, there were the mute stones, to be shouldered upright, single, slow-weathering, massive, or accreted, toss on toss, into sun-bleached cairns. The stones are all that last long, say the Cheyenne. "When people pass and remember, they bring stones," Paco explains in Harriet Doerr's novel, *Stones for Ibarra,* voicing the primitive principle of reverence and respect which allows the most awful historic catastrophe to be witnessed in human perspective and sympathy, and claimed on a personal level. It is no longer a vainglorious and Kilroy boast of "I was there." It becomes rather a humble gesture of inclusion, present tense, a comprehension and admission of decent and deep kinship. According to myth, Fame is the last child of Mother Earth, brought forth in anguish at the deaths of her sons. Whether we chase it in granite or sandstone or marble, fame is the quarry. *Quisque Ibarra lapidenda est,* we might say; every Ibarra must have its stones. Considered in this way, remembrance is an act of mercy, as is burying the dead.

Monumental fashions ever change, reflecting the tastes — now sober, now giddy — of the era. Sir Christopher Wren, rebuilding St. Paul's after the Great Fire, got the dead back on their feet, preferring his nobles upright rather than reclining upon stone biers, under their own effigies, guarded by fabulous beasts and antic angels. Vengeances and jests abound; in Paris, Napoleon's eternal couch is so framed that all who approach must bow. Emerson's marker is an elephantine and unpolished hunk of pinkish rock; Thoreau's, in the same Massachusetts cemetery, is a plain tablet, ankle-high, announcing simply HENRY. The Victorians had, perhaps, the most generally elaborate funerary furnishings since the Chinese emperors and the pharaohs. No expense nor word nor feeling was spared; if there lacked wit, in these public performances and reminders, there was not room for it. Handkerchiefs were larger then, also.

But even before Victoria's reign and storm of tears, perhaps since the beginning of messages on stone, a certain uncandor has canted the proceedings. *Cum grano salis* ought to be the motto of the churchyard pilgrim, and the statue gazer and battlefield stalker. "In lapidary inscriptions a man is not upon oath," Samuel Johnson cautions. All the sweet old protocols and decorums of hero-making and worship failed in the aftershock of World War I. Literature and the survivors have been dusting off the fallout ever since. While valor had its finest hour, glory had its worst. On Peace Day, 1919, Virginia Woolf wrote, "I can't help listening to speaking as though it were writing and thus the flowers, which [were] brandished now and again, look terribly artificial. . . . A melancholy thing to see the incurable soldiers lying in bed at the Star and Garter with their backs to us, smoking cigarettes and waiting for the noise to be over."

There have been wars since, never a day in this century when there was not armed conflict somewhere on earth, but in the English-speaking world, stone has latterly learned a new bluntness and integrity, as has literature, and — intermittently — politics. That frankness achieves as well as honors heroic moments, as though truth and emotion finally have found a lasting, living style. The minimalist tendency to offer the anguished facts and allow the seeker to supply the emotional caption has culminated in a stark and dark modern monument, the Vietnam Veterans Memorial, a black wall furnished with no rhetoric, simply the names and dates, row on row, achieving, below ground level, the monitory and pathetic impact of that archaic epitaph on a Greek clifftop: *When my ship sank, the others sailed on.*

Perhaps the pendulum is already swinging back, and our memorials, unsparing and spare, will once again costume themselves to honor the drama of history. If old ways may return, new ways might also be discovered to make some statement mocking transience. Already, for a price, one may have one's ashes rocketed into space, to be outward bound forever, or till the stars fail. That's about as far as any pilgrim can go: *Hic jacet* for speed readers; "urn buriall" at the velocity of light.

On earth, in pioneer days, it was unusual to have surveyors at one's beck and call; landowners did their best to locate and abide by the boundaries and landmarks mentioned in their grant deeds. To assure that the bounds, once agreed upon, wouldn't alter, the settler would take his sons — to whom the land would pass at his death — and stand them at the corners of the lots and sections, near some memorable natural marker, or if none existed, a stone hauled in on a leather sling behind an ox; the child was beaten and left there alone all day, to watch and absorb his surroundings. No water, no food. The ordeal was repeated, day by day, corner by corner. It was a common enough practice to have a name: "beating the bounds." That purpose was to engrave, by suffering and privation and the child's eager willingness to please his elders, the exact location of the corners and lines upon the youth's impressionable memory. He would indelibly have a mental map of what was his to claim. He would know his limits. He would be able to recognize, in all weathers and seasons — for after the boundaries were learned, they were patrolled from time to time, to check for incursion or erosion — what was rightfully his to cherish, and how precious it was, for it had been both earned, and learned, by blood.

Pilgrims make the same journeys and suffer similar ordeals, though the boundaries are less clear, and larger, and the patrols longer. We find out by patience and witness who we are, where we belong, how much we hold in common with the rest of humanity. Sometimes there is but a rubble; at other times incised and magnificent stones speak to us, invite us to stop and look around. Sometimes we must suffer to find it; at other times we lose our way, confuse one place for another, or miss our exit. We must try again. "Have I left anything behind me unseen? I go back to see it; it is always in my way," says Montaigne, who knew the joys of taken pains.

There is a directory published by Lone Star Legends — you may purchase it in the gift shop at the Alamo — which advertises that near Cotulla, Texas, twenty-five miles southeast of farm/market road 468 on private property — GATES LOCKED, we are warned — there is a historical marker celebrating the fact that "O. Henry came to Fort Ewell for his mail." Who would not detour many anxious miles over washboard or desolate roads to relish that or any such legend in cast bronze in its own natural context? However, the editors of the directory point out on the back cover, "This book is published so that you can read the inscriptions on 2,850 Texas roadside historical markers without having to stop. You will not only save time but also be rewarded with knowledge." The guidebook — a menu of morsels to whet any pilgrim's appetite — is poignantly titled *Why Stop?*

Why stop? As Satchmo answered, when asked to define jazz, if you've gotta ask, you're never gonna know.

WILLIAM KITTREDGE

Who Owns the West?

FROM HARPER'S MAGAZINE

AFTER A HALF MILE in soft rain on the slick hay-field stubble, I would crouch behind the levee and listen to the gentle clatter of the water birds, and surprise them into flight — maybe a half-dozen mallard hens and three green-headed drakes lifting in silhouetted loveliness against the November twilight, hanging only yards from the end of my shotgun. This was called jump shooting or meat hunting, and it almost always worked. But I wish someone had told me reasons you should not necessarily kill the birds every time. I wish I'd been told to kill ducks maybe only once or twice a winter, for a fine meal with children and friends, and that nine times out of ten I was going to be happier if I let the goddamned birds fly away.

In 1959, on the MC Ranch, in the high desert country of southeastern Oregon, an agricultural property my family owned, I was twenty-seven, prideful with a young man's ambition, and happy as such a creature can be, centered in the world of my upbringing, king of my mountain, and certain I was deep into the management of perfection. It was my responsibility to run a ranch-hand cookhouse and supervise the labors of from ten to twenty-five workingmen. Or, to put it most crudely, as was often done, "hire and fire and work the winos."

Think of it as a skill, learnable as any other. In any profession there are rules, the most basic being enlightened self-interest. Take care of your men and they will take care of you.

And understand their frailties, because you are the one responsible for taking care. Will they fall sick to death in the bunkhouse, and is there someone you can call to administer mercy if they do? What attention will you give them as they die?

Some thirty-six miles west of our valley, over the Warner Mountains in the small lumbering and ranching town of Lakeview, a workingman's hotel functions as a sort of hiring hall. There was a rule of thumb about the men you would find there. The best of them wore a good pair of boots laced up tight over wool socks; this meant they were looking for a laboring job. The most hapless would be wearing low-cut city shoes, no socks, no laces. They were looking for a place to hide, and never to be hired. It was a rule that worked.

On bright afternoons when many people were scrambling to survive in the Great Depression, my mother was young and fresh as she led me on walks along the crumbling small-town streets of Malin, Oregon, in the Klamath Basin just north of the California border. This was before we moved to the MC Ranch; I was three years old and understood the world as concentric circles of diminishing glory centered on the sun of her smile. Outside our tight circle was my father, an energetic stranger who came home at night and before he touched anything, even me or my mother, rolled up his sleeves over his white forearms and scrubbed his hands in the kitchen sink with coarse lava soap. Out beyond him were the turkey herders, and beyond them lay the vast agricultural world, on the fringes of the Tule Lake Reclamation District, where they worked.

What the herders did in the turkey business, as it was run by my father, was haul crates full of turkeys around on old flatbed trucks. When they got to the back side of some farm property where nobody was likely to notice, they parked and opened the doors on those crates and turned the turkeys out to roam and feed on grasshoppers. Sometimes they had permission, sometimes my father had paid a fee; and some of the time it was theft, grazing the turkeys for free. Sometimes they got caught, and my father paid the fee then. And once in a while they had to reload the turkeys into their crates and move on while some farmer watched with a shotgun.

The barnyard turkey, you have to understand, is a captive, bitter creature. (Some part of our alienation, when we are most

isolated, is ecological. We are lonely and long to share in what
we regard as the dignity of wild animals — this is the phantom
so many of us pursue as we hunt, complicating the actual killing
into a double-bind sort of triumph.) My upbringing taught me
to consider the domesticated turkey a rapacious creature, eyes
dull with the opaque gleam of pure selfishness, without soul. I
had never heard of a wild one. The most recent time I had
occasion to confront turkeys up close was in the fall of 1987,
driving red scoria roads in the North Dakota badlands. I came
across farmstead turkeys, and true or not, I took that as a sign
we were where agriculture meant subsistence. No doubt my
horror of turkeys had much to do with my fear of the men who
herded them.

From the windows of our single-bedroom apartment on the
second floor of the only brick building in Malin, where I slept
on a little bed in the living room, we could look south across the
rich, irrigated potato- and barley-raising country of the Tule
Lake basin and see to California and the lava-field badlands
where the Modoc Indians had hidden out from the U.S. Army
in the long-ago days of their rebellion. I wonder if my mother
told me stories of those natives in their caves, and doubt it, but
not because she didn't believe in the arts of make-believe. It's
just that my mother would have told me other stories. She grew
up loving opera. My grandfather, as I will always understand
him, even though we were not connected by blood, earned the
money for her music lessons as a blacksmith for the California/
Oregon Power Company in Klamath Falls — sharpening steel,
as he put it. So it is unlikely my mother was fond of stories about
desperate natives and hold-out killings and the eventual hanging of Captain Jack, the Modoc war chief, at Fort Klamath. That
was just the sort of nastiness she was interested in escaping; and
besides, we were holding to defensive actions of our own.

After all, my father was raising turkeys for a living in a most
haphazard fashion. So my mother told me stories about Christmas as perfection realized: candied apples glowing in the light
of an intricately decorated tree, and little toy railroads which
tooted and circled the room as if the room were the world.

But we live in a place more complex than paradise, some
would say richer, and I want to tell a story about my terror on

Christmas Eve, and the way we were happy anyhow. The trouble began on a sunny afternoon with a little snow on the ground, when my mother took me for my first barbershop haircut, a step into manhood as she defined it. I was enjoying the notion of such ceremony, and even the snipping of the barber's gentle shears as I sat elevated to manly height by the board across the arms of his chair — until Santa Claus came in, jerked off his cap and the fringe of snowy hair and his equally snowy beard, and stood revealed as an unshaven man in a Santa Claus suit who looked like he could stand a drink from the way his hands were shaking.

The man leered at my kindly barber and muttered something. I suppose he wanted to know how long he would have to wait for a shave. Maybe he had been waiting all day for a barbershop shave. A fine, brave, hung over sort of waiting, all the while entombed in that Santa Claus suit. I screamed. I like to think I was screaming against chaos, in defense of my mother and notions of a proper Christmas, and maybe because our Santa Claus who was not a Santa, with his corded, unshaven neck, even looked remotely like a turkey as this story turns edgy and nightmarish.

My father's turkeys had been slaughtered the week before Thanksgiving in a couple of boxcars pulled onto a siding in Tule Lake, and shipped to markets in the East. Everyone was at liberty and making ready to ride out winter on whatever he had managed to accumulate. So the party my parents threw on the night before Christmas had ancient ceremonial resonances. The harvest was done, the turkeys were slaughtered, and the dead season of cold winds was at hand. It was a time of release into meditation and winter, to await rebirth.

But it was not a children's party. It is difficult to imagine my father at a children's party. As I recall from this distance it was a party for the turkey herders, those men who had helped my father conspire his way through that humiliating summer with those terrible creatures. At least the faces I see in my dream of that yellow kitchen are the faces of those men. Never again, my mother said, and my father agreed; better times were coming and everybody got drunk.

I had been put down to sleep on the big bed in my parents'

bedroom, which was quite a privilege in itself, and it was only late in the night that I woke to a sense of something gone wrong. The sacred place where I lived with my mother had been invaded by loud laughter and hoedown harmonica music and people dancing and stomping. As I stood in the doorway looking into the kitchen in my pajamas, nobody saw me for a long moment — until I began my hysterical momma's-boy shrieking.

The harmonica playing stopped, and my mother looked shamefaced toward me from the middle of the room, where she had been dancing with my father while everyone watched. All those faces of people who are now mostly dead turned to me, and it was as if I had gotten up and come out of the bedroom into the actuality of a leering nightmare, vivid light and whiskey bottles on the table and those faces glazed with grotesque intentions.

Someone saved it, one of the men, maybe even my father, by picking me up and ignoring my wailing as the harmonica music started again, and then I was in my mother's arms as she danced, whirling around the kitchen table and the center of all attention in a world where everything was possible and good, while the turkey herders watched and smiled and thought their private thoughts, and it was Christmas at last in my mother's arms, as I have understood it ever since.

For years the faces of the turkey herders in their otherness, in that bright kitchen, were part of a dream I dreaded as I tried to go to sleep. In struggling against the otherness of the turkey herders I made a start toward indifference to the disenfranchised. I was learning to inhabit distance, from myself and people I should have cared for.

A couple of years later my family moved the hundred miles east to the MC Ranch. My grandfather got the place when he was sixty-two years old, pledging everything he had worked for all his life, unable to resist owning such a kingdom. The move represented an enormous change in our fortunes.

Warner Valley is that place which is sacred to me as the main staging ground for my imagination. I see it as an inhabited landscape where the names of people remind me of places, and the places remind me of what happened there — a thicket of stories to catch the mind if it might be falling.

It was during the Second World War that wildlife biologists from up at the college in Corvallis told my father the sandhill cranes migrating through Warner were rare and vanishing creatures, to be cherished with the same intensity as the ring-necked Manchurian pheasants, which had been imported from the hinterlands of China. The nests of sandhill cranes, with their large, off-white speckled eggs, were to be regarded as absolutely precious. "No matter what," I heard my father say, "you don't break those eggs."

My father was talking to a tall, gray-faced man named Clyde Bolton, who was stuck with a day of riding a drag made of heavy timbers across Thompson Field, breaking up cow shit in the early spring before the irrigating started, so the chips wouldn't plug up the John Deere mowing machines come summer and haying. Clyde was married to Ada Bolton, the indispensable woman who cooked and kept house for us, and he had a damaged heart which kept him from heavy work. He milked the three or four cows my father kept, and tended the chickens and the house garden, and took naps in the afternoon. He hadn't hired out for field work, and he was unhappy.

But help was scarce during those years when so many of the able-bodied were gone to the war, and there he was, take it or leave it. And anyway, riding that drag wouldn't hurt even a man with a damaged heart. Clyde was a little spoiled — that's what we used to say. Go easy on the hired help long enough, and they will sour on you. A man, we would say, needs to get out in the open air and sweat and blow off the stink.

This was a Saturday morning in April after the frost had gone out, and I was a boy learning the methodologies of field work. The cranes' nests my father was talking about were hidden down along unmowed margins — in the yellow remnants of knee-high meadow grass from the summer before, along the willow-lined sloughs through the home fields. "The ones the coons don't get," my father said.

I can see my father's gray-eyed good humor and his stockman's fedora pushed back on his head as he studied Clyde, and hear the ironic rasp in his voice. At that time my father was more than ten years younger than I am now, a man recently come to the center of his world. And I can see Clyde Bolton hitching his suspenders and snorting over the idea of keeping an eye out for the nest of some sandhill crane. I can see his disdain.

This going out with Clyde was as close to any formal initiation as I ever got on the ranch. There really wasn't much of anything for me to do, but it was important I get used to the idea of working on days when I was not in school. It wouldn't hurt a damned bit. A boy should learn to help out where he can, and I knew it, so I was struggling to harness the old team of matched bay geldings, Dick and Dan, and my father and Clyde were not offering to help because a boy would never make a man if you helped him all the time.

"You see what you think out there," my father said, and he spoke to Clyde seriously, man to man, ignoring me. They were deeply serious all at once and absorbed into what I understood as the secret lives of men. It was important to watch them for clues.

My father acted like he was just beginning to detail Clyde's real assignment. You might have thought we faced a mindless day spent riding that drag behind a farting old team. But no, it seemed Clyde's real mission involved a survey of conditions, and experienced judgment.

"Them swales been coming to swamp grass," my father said. "We been drowning them out." He went on to talk about the low manure dams which spread irrigation water across the swales. Clyde would have the day to study those damns, and figure where they should be relocated.

Once we believed work done well would see us through. But it was not true. Once it seemed the rewards of labor would be naturally rationed out with at least a rough kind of justice. But we were unlettered and uninstructed in the true nature of our ultimate values. Our deep willingness to trust in our native goodness was not enough.

But we tried. This is what I am writing of here, that trying and also about learning to practice hardening of the heart. Even back then I might have suspected my father wasn't much worried about swamp grass in the swales, and that Clyde Bolton knew he wasn't, and that it wasn't the point of their negotiations. My father was concerned about dignity, however fragile, as an ultimate value.

"Your father was the damnedest son of a bitch," one of the ranch hands once told me. "He'd get you started on one thing, and make you think you were doing another thing which was more important, and then he would go off and you wouldn't see him for days, and pretty soon it was like you were working on your own place."

It was not until I was a man in the job my father perfected that I learned the sandhill cranes were not endangered at all. It didn't matter. Those birds were exotic and lovely as they danced their mating dances in our meadows, each circling the other with gawky tall-bird elegance, balanced by their extended fluttering wings as they seized the impulse and looped across the meadows with their long necks extended to the sky and their beaks open to whatever ecstasy birds can know. I think my father was simply trying to teach me and everyone else on the property that certain vulnerabilities should be cherished and protected at whatever inconvenience.

I have to wish there had been more such instruction, and that it had been closer to explicit in a philosophical sense. Most of all I wish my father had passed along some detailed notion of how to be boss. It was a thing he seemed to do naturally. I wish he had made clear to me the dangers of posturing in front of people who are in some degree dependent on your whims, posturing until you have got yourself deep into the fraud of maintaining distance and mystery in place of authenticity.

A man once told me to smoke cigars. "They see you peel that cellophane," he said, "and they know you don't live like they do."

My father set up the Grain Camp on a sagebrush hill slope, beneath a natural spring on the west side of Warner Valley. And it was an encampment, short on every amenity except running water in the early days — a double row of one-room shacks, eight in all, trucked in from a nearby logging camp abandoned in the late 1930s. There were also two shacks tacked across one another in a T shape to make a cookhouse, one cabin for the cooking and another for the long table where everyone ate.

The men, who lived two to a cabin in the busy seasons, sweltering on that unshaded hill slope in the summers, and waking in the night to the stink of drying work clothes as they fed split wood to their little stoves in the winter, were a mix of transients and what we called homesteaders, men who stayed with us for more than an occasional season, often years in the same cabin, which became known as theirs. Those men have my heart as I write this, men who were my friends and my mentors, some of whom died at the Grain Camp and have been inconspicuously dead for many years. Louie Hanson, Vance Beebe, Jake O'Rourke, Lee Mallard, so many others. I would like the saying of their names to be an act of pure celebration.

When I came home from the air force in the fall of 1957, I was twenty-five years old and back to beginnings after most of eight years away, a woeful figure from American mythology, the boss's kid and heir to the property, soon to inherit, who didn't know anything. Then in the spring of 1958, the myth came directly home to roost. I found myself boss at the Grain Camp.

There was no choice but to plead ignorance and insinuate myself into the sympathies of the old hands. Ceremony demanded that I show up twice a day to sit at the head of the long table for meals, breakfast and noon, and in the course of those appearances negotiate my way through the intricacies of managing eight thousand acres of irrigated land. For a long time I was bluffing, playing a hand I didn't understand, risking disgrace and reaping it plenty enough. The man who saved my bacon mostly was an old alcoholic Swede in filthy coveralls named Louie Hanson, who sat at my right hand at the table.

About five-thirty on a routine morning, after a hot shower and instant coffee, I would drive the three or so miles from the house to the Grain Camp. The best cabin, walls filled with sawdust for insulation, belonged to Louie. He had worked for my father since our beginnings in Warner, hiring out in 1937 to build dikes with a secondhand Caterpillar RD-6, the first track layer my father bought, and made his way up to Cat mechanic, and into privileges, one of which was occasional drinking. Theoretically, we didn't allow any drinking. Period. Again, there were rules. You need to drink, go to town. Maybe your job will be waiting when you get back. Unless you were one of the old hands. Then your job was secure. But nobody was secure if he got to drinking on the job, or around camp.

Except for Louie. Every morning in winter he would go down to the Cat shop to build his fire before breakfast, and dig a couple of beers from one of the bolt-rack cubbyholes, pop the tops, and set the bottles on the stove to heat. When they were steaming he would take them off, drink the beer in a few long draughts, and be set to seize the day.

So it would not be an entirely sober man I greeted when I came early to get him for breakfast and knocked on the door to his cabin. Louie would be resting back on the greasy tarp that covered his bed, squinting through the smoke from another Camel, sipping coffee from a filthy cup and looking up to grin. "Hell, you own the place," he would say, "you're in."

Louie would blink his eyes. "Chee-rist. You got enough water in Dodson Lake?" He was talking about one of the huge grain fields we flooded every spring. And I wouldn't know. Did I have enough water in Dodson Lake? Louie would look at me directly. "Get a south wind and you are going to lose some dikes." I knew what that meant: eroded levee banks, washouts, catastrophe, 450 acres of flooded alfalfa.

Up at the breakfast table, while Louie reached for the pounded round steak, I would detail a couple of men to start drawing down the water in Dodson Lake, a process involving the opening of huge valves, pulling head-gate boards, running the eighteen-inch pump. All of which would have been unnecessary if I had known what I was doing in the first place. Which everybody knew and nobody mentioned. All in all a cheap mistake, easily covered — wages for the men and electricity to run the pump, wasted time and a little money, maybe a couple hundred bucks. Without Louie's intercession, maybe twenty thousand.

The deeply fearful are driven to righteousness, as we know, and they are the most fearsome fools we have. This is a story I have told as a tavern-table anecdote, in which I call our man the Murderer, since I have no memory of his real name. Call the story "The Day I Fired the Murderer." It is designed, as told in taverns, to make me appear winsome and ironic, liberated, guilty no more. Which of course implies there was guilt. And there was, in a way that cornered me into thinking it was anger that drove me, and that my anger was mostly justifiable.

I had been boss at the Grain Camp for four or five years, and I had come to understand myself as a young man doing good work, employing the otherwise unemployable (which was kind of true), and also as someone whose efforts were continually confounded by the incompetence of the men who worked for me. We were farming twenty-four hours a day through early May while the Canada honkers hatched their downy young and the tulips pushed up through the crusted flower beds and the Lombardy poplar broke their buds and the forsythia bloomed lurid yellow against the cookhouse wall. But I don't think of such glories when I remember those spring mornings. I remember the odor of dank peat turning up behind those disc Cats as we went on farming twenty-four hours a day, and how much I loved breaking ground.

Before sunrise on those mornings I would come awake and go piss, then stand in my undershorts on the screened-in veranda attached to the house where I lived with my wife and young children. I would shiver with chill and happiness as I smelled the world coming awake. Far out across our valley the lights on our D-7 disc Cats would flicker as lights do when seen through a screen, moving almost imperceptibly. I would take my binoculars and open the screen door and gaze out to those lights as if I might catch one of my night-shift Catskinners at some dog-fuckery, but really all I wanted to see was the machinery moving. Those Cats would clank along at two or three miles an hour all through the hours of darkness, turning a thirty-six-foot swatch — a hundred acres every night and another hundred acres on the day shift. The upturned soil would mellow in the air for a day, and then we would harrow it and seal it with dust and drill it to barley. In ten days or so the seedlings would break earth, and those orderly drill-rows undulating over the tilled ground toward the sundown light were softly yellow-green and something alive I had seen to completion.

It came to a couple hundred acres of barley every day for fifteen days, three-thousand-some-odd acres in all. By the end of harvest in late September, at roughly a ton per acre, that came to 3,000 tons of barley at $50 a ton, or $150,000, real money in the early 1960s in our end of the world.

We drained the wetlands and thought that made them ours. We believed the world was made to be useful; we ditched and named the intersections of our ditches: Four Corners, Big Pump, Center Bridge, Beatty Bridge. We thought such naming made the valley ours.

And we thought the people were ours.

The man I call the Murderer was one of those men who rode the disc Cats, circling toward the sunrise. My involvement with him that spring had started the previous fall, when someone from the Oregon Board of Parole called and asked if we would participate in what they called their Custody Release Program. They would send us a parolee if we would guarantee a job; in return we got an employee who was forbidden to drink or quit, on penalty of being sent back to prison. If there was "anything," we could call and the State Police would come take him away. It seemed like a correct idea; it had been twenty-some years since the Murderer killed his wife in an act of drunken bewilderment he couldn't recall.

Frail and dark-eyed in a stiff new evergreen-colored workshirt, with the sleeves rolled to expose thin white arms, pensive and bruised and looking incapable of much beyond remorse, the Murderer spent the winter feeding bales to the drag at our feed mill, a cold, filthy job, and as monotonous an enterprise as it is possible to imagine this side of automation. So when it came time to go farming in the spring, I sat him up at the controls of a D-7, taught him to pull frictions and grease the rollers and called him a Catskinner, which is to say, gave him some power. The Murderer responded by starting to talk. Bright, misinformed chatter at the breakfast table.

All I remember is annoyance. Then it rained, and we couldn't work. My crew went off to town for a couple of days with my blessing, and the Murderer went with them. That was against our rules, his and mine. And he came back drunk, and I fired him on the spot. He came up to breakfast drunk, terribly frightened and unable to be sober, lowering himself into my mercies, which did not exist.

Only in the imagination can we share another person's specific experiences. I was the ice queen, which means no stories,
please, there is no forgiveness for you and never will be, just
roll your goddamned bed and be gone. If I fired him, he would
go back to prison. I knew that. I am sure I imagined some
version of his future — isolation again in the wrecked recognition that in this life he was not to be forgiven.

Stories bind us by reminding us that our lives all participate
in the same fragilities, and this should soften us so that we stay
humane. But I didn't want to be humane; I wanted to be correct. If I had not ignored his devastation as I no doubt saw it,
imagined it, I might have found a way to honor common sense
and taken him riding around with me that day as he sobered
up, and listened to his inane chatter. But I sent him down the
road, and thought I was doing the right thing. There were rules.
As I tell the story I mean to say, See, I am not like that anymore.
See. But we know this is only another strategy.

I fired a lot of men, and Louie Hanson more than once, after
on-the-job binges. But Louie wouldn't go away; he understood
the true nature of our contract. I needed his assurances exactly
as he needed his life at the Grain Camp. After a few days Louie
would sober up, and one morning he would be at the breakfast
table like nothing had happened. In fact, he was fired the day
he died.

He was too drunk to make sense by three in the afternoon,
feeding shots of whiskey to the chore man, which meant I had
to take some action. So I told him to clear out. What he did was
go off to visit an old woman he had known years before in a
small town just down into California.

"A fancy woman," Louie said after drawing himself up to fine
old-man lewdness. "Screw you, I am going to see a woman I
should have been seeing." He was seventy-seven years old and
unkillable so far as I knew as he drove away in his old Plymouth,
squinting through his cracked eyeglasses.

A stranger in a pickup truck hauled him home late in the
night, and Louie, having wrecked the Plymouth, was ruined, a
cut over one eye, hallucinating as he lay curled into himself like
an old knot, reeking with vomit, sick on the floor, unwilling even

to open his eyes, complaining that his eyeglasses were lost. This descent into nowhere had happened before. Let him lie. And he did, facing the wall for three days.

By then it was clear something extraordinary and terrible was afoot, but Louie refused to hear of the hospital in Lakeview. They'll kill you, he said. Around the time of World War I, in the Imperial Valley of Califorñia near Calexico, his back had been broken when a bridge caved in under the weight of a steel-wheeled steam tractor. The doctors got him on morphine for the pain, and then fed him alcohol to get him off morphine, and that was it for the rest of his life, he said. Booze.

They just left me there, he would say, half drunk and grinning like it was a fine joke. Maybe he felt the doctors had already killed him. I called his son in Napa, California, who came overnight in an old car and talked Louie onto his feet, as I should have done, and into a trip over the Warner Mountains to the hospital.

All that should have been my responsibility. Days before, I should have ignored his wounded objections. The doctors wouldn't kill him, and I knew it. He would have lived some more, not for long maybe, but some more. But such obligations were a bit beyond my job description, and I fell back on excuses.

Louie Hanson died in the automobile, slumped sideways against his son — dead with a broken rib through one lung, which would have been fixable a day or so earlier. I went to the funeral but wouldn't look in the coffin. There was nothing I wanted to know about the look of things in coffins.

There had been an afternoon when I stood on a ditch bank with a dented bucket of carrot slices marinated in strychnine, poisoning badgers and dreading every moment I could foresee, all things equally unreal, my hand in the rubber glove, holding the slice of carrot which was almost luminous, clouds over Bidwell Mountain, the sound of my breathing. I would have to move soon if I was ever going to get home. I was numb with dread and sorrowed for myself because I felt nothing but terror, and I had to know this was craziness. There is no metaphor for that condition; it is precisely like nothing.

By craziness I mean nearly catatonic fearfulness generated by the conviction that nothing you do connects to any other particular thing inside your daily life. Mine was never real craziness, although some fracturing of ice seemed to lie just around the corner of each moment. It was easy to imagine vanishing into complete disorientation. My trouble could be called "paralyzed before existential realities," a condition I could name, having read Camus like any boy of my time. But such insight was useless. Nothing was valuable unless it helped toward keeping the lid on my own dis-ease.

The Fee Point reaches into the old tule beds on the east side of Warner. A homesteader shack out there was my father's first Grain Camp cookhouse, in 1938. I see my mother at the Fee in a soft summery wind, a yellow cotton dress, a young woman on a summer day, gazing out to plow-ground fields being cut from the swamps.

Close to thirty years later my Catskinners crushed that shack into a pile of weathered gray junk lumber, dumped on the diesel, and burned it. It was January and we all warmed our hands on the flames, then drank steaming coffee and ate cold roast beef sandwiches sent out from another cookhouse.

In Latin *"familia"* means residence and family, which I take to mean community, an interconnection of stories. As I lie down to sleep I can stand out at Fee Point and see my mother and those Catskinners and the old shack burning, although I have not lived on the ranch in Warner Valley for twenty years. It's a fact of no more than sentimental interest except as an example of the ways we are inhabited by stories, and the ways they connect.

Water birds were a metaphor for abundance beyond measure in my childhood. A story about water birds: On a dour November afternoon, my father sat on a wooden case of shotgun shells in the deep tules by Pelican Lake like a crown prince of shotgunning, and dropped 123 ducks for an Elks Club feed. The birds were coming north to water from the grain fields and fighting a stiff head wind. They flared and started to settle, just over him, and they would not stop coming into the long red flame from his shotgun as darkness came down from the east. The dead birds fell collapsed to the water and washed back to shore in the wind. Eventually it was too dark to shoot, and the dead birds were heaped in the back of his pickup and he hauled them to town; he dumped them off to the woman he had hired to do the picking and went on to a good clear-hearted night at the poker table, having discharged a civic duty.

When someone had killed too many birds, their necks would be strung together with baling twine, and they would be hung from spikes in an old crab-apple tree back of our house, to freeze and be given away to anyone who might come visiting. When time came to leave, we would throw in three or four Canada honkers as a leave-taking gift, frozen and stiff as cordwood, and give you the name of the lady in town who did the picking.

What is the crime here?

It is not my father's. In later years men came to me and told me he was the finest man they ever worked for, and I envy that fineness, by which, I think, they meant fair and convivial — and just, in terms of an implied contract. From an old hand who had worked for room and board and no wages through the Great Depression, that was a kind of ultimate praise. They knew he hadn't broken any promises, and he had sense enough to know that finally you can't really help anybody die, no matter how much you owe them.

But there was an obvious string of crimes. Maybe we should have known the world wasn't made for our purposes, to be remodeled into our idea of an agricultural paradise, and that Warner Valley wasn't there to have us come along and drain the swamps, and level the peat ground into alfalfa land. No doubt we should have known the water birds would quit coming. But we had been given to understand that places we owned were to be used as we saw fit. The birds were part of all that.

What went wrong? Rules of commerce or cowardice or what? Bad thinking? Failure to identify what was sacred? All of the above? Did such failures lead me to treat men as if they were tools, to be used?

Probably. But that is no excuse for participating in the kind of cold-heartedness we see everywhere, the crime we commit while we all claim innocence.

One night in Lakeview I was dancing with a woman we all knew as the Crop Duster's Wife. She came to the taverns every night, and she was beautiful in an overbruised sort of way, but she wouldn't go find a bed with any of us. She was, she claimed, married forever to a man who was off in Arkansas dusting cotton from an old Steerman biplane. She said she just hoped he didn't wreck that Steerman into some Arkansas church. We sat at the bar and I was drunk and started telling her about Louie Hanson and how he died, eager to confess my craziness. Maybe I thought a woman who waited for a man who flew crop-dusting aircraft would understand. Maybe I thought she would fall for a crazy man.

"There is nothing to dislike but the meanness," she said, picking at her words. "You ought to be glad you ever knew those old farts."

Failures of the sympathy, she was saying, if I read her right, originate in failures of the imagination, which is a betrayal of self. Like so many young men, I could only see myself in the mirror of a woman. Offering the utility of that reflection, and solace, was understood to be the work of women, their old job, inhabit the house and forgive, at least until they got tired of it.

In those days a woman who wanted to be done with such duties might do something like buy herself a wedding ring, and make up a story about a faraway romantic husband who flew his Steerman every morning to support her. This woman might say people like me were no cure for her loneliness. But she might excuse my self-centered sorrowing. She might say we don't have any choice, it's the creature we are. Or she might tell me to wise up and understand that sympathy can be useful only if it moves us to quit the coldness of the heart.

It is possible to imagine a story in which the Murderer does not return to prison, but lives on at the Grain Camp for years and years, until he has forgiven himself and is healed — a humorous old man you could turn to for sensible advice. In the end all of us would be able to forgive and care for ourselves. We would have learned to mostly let the birds fly away, because it is not necessarily meat we are hunting.

LEONARD KRIEGEL

Falling into Life

FROM THE AMERICAN SCHOLAR

IT IS NOT the actual death a man is doomed to die but the deaths
his imagination anticipates that claim attention as one grows
older. We are constantly being reminded that the prospect of
death forcefully concentrates the mind. While that may be so, it
is not a prospect that does very much else for the imagination
— other than to make one aware of its limitations and imbal-
ances.

Over the past five years, as I have moved into the solidity of
middle age, my own most formidable imaginative limitation has
turned out to be a surprising need for symmetry. I am possessed
by a peculiar passion: I want to believe that my life has been
balanced out. And because I once had to learn to fall in order
to keep that life mine, I now seem to have convinced myself that
I must also learn to fall into death.

Falling into life wasn't easy, and I suspect that is why I hunger
for such awkward symmetry today. Having lost the use of my
legs during the polio epidemic that swept across the eastern
United States during the summer of 1944, I was soon immersed
in a process of rehabilitation that was, at least when looked at in
retrospect, as much spiritual as physical.

That was a full decade before the discovery of the Salk vaccine
ended polio's reign as the disease most dreaded by America's
parents and their children. Treatment of the disease had been
standardized by 1944: following the initial onslaught of the
virus, patients were kept in isolation for a period of ten days to
two weeks. Following that, orthodox medical opinion was con-

tent to subject patients to as much heat as they could stand. Stiff paralyzed limbs were swathed in heated, coarse woolen towels known as "hot packs." (The towels were that same greenish brown as blankets issued to American GIs, and they reinforced a boy's sense of being at war.) As soon as the hot packs had baked enough pain and stiffness out of a patient's body so that he could be moved on and off a stretcher, the treatment was ended, and the patient faced a series of daily immersions in a heated pool.

I would ultimately spend two full years at the appropriately named New York State Reconstruction Home in West Haverstraw. But what I remember most vividly about the first three months of my stay there was being submerged in a hot pool six times a day, for periods of between fifteen and twenty minutes. I would lie on a stainless steel slab, my face alone out of water, while the wet heat rolled against my dead legs and the physical therapist was at my side working at a series of manipulations intended to bring my useless muscles back to health.

Each immersion was a baptism by fire in the water. While my mind pitched and reeled with memories of the "normal" boy I had been a few weeks earlier, I would close my eyes and focus not, as my therapist urged, on bringing dead legs back to life but on my strange fall from the childhood grace of the physical. Like all eleven-year-old boys, I had spent a good deal of time thinking about my body. Before the attack of the virus, however, I thought about it only in connection with my own lunge toward adolescence. Never before had my body seemed an object in itself. Now it was. And like the twenty-one other boys in the ward — all of us between the ages of nine and twelve — I sensed I would never move beyond the fall from grace, even as I played with memories of the way I once had been.

Each time I was removed from the hot water and placed on a stretcher by the side of the pool, there to await the next immersion, I was fed salt tablets. These were simply intended to make up for the sweat we lost, but salt tablets seemed to me the cruelest confirmation of my new status as spiritual debtor. Even today, more than four decades later, I still shiver at the mere thought of those salt tablets. Sometimes the hospital orderly would literally have to pry my mouth open to force me to swallow them. I dreaded the nausea the taste of salt inspired in me. Each time I was resubmerged in the hot pool, I would grit my teeth — not from the flush of heat sweeping over my body but from the thought of what I would have to face when I would again be taken out of the water. To be an eater of salt was far more humiliating than to endure pain. Nor was I alone in feeling this way. After lights-out had quieted the ward, we boys would furtively whisper from cubicle to cubicle of how we dreaded being forced to swallow salt tablets. It was that, rather than the pain we endured, that anchored our sense of loss and dread.

Any recovery of muscle use in a polio patient usually took place within three months of the disease's onset. We all knew that. But as time passed, every boy in the ward learned to recite stories of those who, like Lazarus, had witnessed their own bodily resurrection. Having fallen from physical grace, we also chose to fall away from the reality in front of us. Our therapists were skilled and dedicated, but they weren't wonder-working saints. Paralyzed legs and arms rarely responded to their manipulations. We could not admit to ourselves, or to them, that we were permanently crippled. But each of us knew without knowing that his future was tied to the body that floated on the stainless steel slab.

We sweated out the hot pool and we choked on the salt tablets, and through it all we looked forward to the promise of rehabilitation. For, once the stiffness and pain had been baked and boiled out of us, we would no longer be eaters of salt. We would not be what we once had been, but at least we would be candidates for re-entry into the world, admittedly made over to face its demands encased in leather and steel.

I suppose we might have been told that our fall from grace was permanent. But I am still grateful that no one — neither doctors nor nurses nor therapists, not even that sadistic orderly, himself a former polio patient, who limped through our lives and through our pain like some vengeful presence — told me that my chances of regaining the use of my legs were nonexistent. Like every other boy in the ward, I organized my needs around whatever illusions were available. And the illusion I needed above any other was that one morning I would simply wake up and rediscover the "normal" boy of memory, once again playing baseball in French Charley's Field in Bronx Park rather than roaming the fields of his own imagination. At the age of eleven, I needed to weather reality, not face it. And to this very day, I silently thank those who were concerned enough about me, or indifferent enough to my fate, not to tell me what they knew.

Like most boys, sick or well, I was an adaptable creature — and rehabilitation demanded adaptability. The fall from bodily grace transformed each of us into acolytes of the possible, pragmatic Americans for whom survival was method and strategy. We would learn, during our days in the New York State Reconstruction Home, to confront the world that was. We would learn to survive the way we were, with whatever the virus had left intact.

I had fallen away from the body's prowess, but I was being led toward a life measured by different standards. Even as I fantasized about the past, it disappeared. Rehabilitation, I was to learn, was ahistorical, a future devoid of any significant claim on the past. Rehabilitation was a thief's primer of compensation and deception: its purpose was to teach one how to steal a touch of the normal from an existence that would be striking in its abnormality.

When I think back to those two years in the ward, the boy who made his rehabilitation most memorable was Joey Tomashevski. Joey was the son of an upstate dairy farmer, a Polish immigrant who had come to America before the Depression and whose English was even poorer than the English of my own shtetl-bred father. The virus had left both of Joey's arms so lifeless and atrophied that I could circle where his bicep should have been with pinky and thumb and still stick the forefinger of my own hand through. And yet, Joey assumed that he would make do with whatever had been left him. He accepted without question the task of making his toes and feet over into fingers and hands. With lifeless arms encased in a canvas sling that looked like the breadbasket a European peasant might carry to market, Joey would sit up in bed and demonstrate how he could maneuver fork and spoon with his toes.

I would never have dreamed of placing such confidence in

my fingers, let alone my toes. I found, as most of the other boys in the ward did, Joey's unabashed pride in the flexibility and control with which he could maneuver a forkful of mashed potatoes into his mouth a continuous indictment of my sense of the world's natural order. We boys with dead legs would gather round his bed in our wheelchairs and silently watch Joey display his dexterity with a vanity so open and naked that it seemed an invitation to being struck down yet again. But Joey's was a vanity already tested by experience. For he was more than willing to accept whatever challenges the virus threw his way. For the sake of demonstrating his skill to us, he kicked a basketball from the auditorium stage through the hoop attached to a balcony some fifty feet away. When one of our number derisively called him lucky, he proceeded to kick five of seven more balls through that same hoop.

I suspect that Joey's pride in his ability to compensate for what had been taken away from him irritated me, because I knew that, before I could pursue my own rehabilitation with such singular passion, I had to surrender myself to what was being demanded of me. And that meant I had to learn to fall. It meant that I had to learn, as Joey Tomashevski had already learned, how to transform absence into opportunity. Even though I still lacked Joey's instinctive willingness to live with the legacy of the virus, I found myself being overhauled, re-created in much the same way as a car engine is rebuilt. Nine months after I arrived in the ward, a few weeks before my twelfth birthday, I was fitted for double long-legged braces bound together by a steel pelvic band circling my waist. Lifeless or not, my legs were precisely measured, the steel carefully molded to form, screws and locks and leather joined to one another for my customized benefit alone. It was technology that would hold me up — another offering on the altar of compensation. "You get what you give," said Jackie Lyons, my closest friend in the ward. For he, too, was now a novitiate of the possible. He, too, now had to learn how to choose the road back.

Falling into life was not a metaphor; it was real, a process learned only through doing, the way a baby learns to crawl, to stand, and then to walk. After the steel bands around calves and thighs and pelvis had been covered over by the rich-smelling leather, after the braces had been precisely fitted to allow my fear-ridden imagination the surety of their holding presence, I was pulled to my feet. For the first time in ten months, I stood. Two middle-aged craftsmen, the hospital bracemakers who worked in a machine shop deep in the basement, held me in place as my therapist wedged two wooden crutches beneath my shoulders.

They stepped back, first making certain that my grip on the crutches was firm. Filled with pride in their technological prowess, the three of them stood in front of me, admiring their skill. Had I been created in the laboratory of Mary Shelley's Dr. Frankenstein, I could not have felt myself any more the creature of scientific pride. I stood on the braces, crutches beneath my shoulders slanting outward like twin towers of Pisa. I flushed, swallowed hard, struggled to keep from crying, struggled not to be overwhelmed by my fear of falling.

My future had arrived. The leather had been fitted, the screws had been turned to the precise millimeter, the locks at the knees and the bushings at the ankles had been properly tested and retested. That very afternoon I was taken for the first time to a cavernous room filled with barbells and Indian clubs and crutches and walkers. I would spend an hour each day there for the next six months. In the rehab room, I would learn how to mount two large wooden steps made to the exact measure of a New York City bus's. I would swing on parallel bars from one side to the other, my arms learning how they would have to hurl me through the world. I balanced Indian clubs like a circus juggler because my therapist insisted it would help my coordination. And I was expected to learn to fall.

I was a dutiful patient. I did as I was told because I could see no advantage to doing anything else. I hungered for the approval of those in authority — doctors, nurses, therapists, the two bracemakers. Again and again, my therapist demonstrated how I was to throw my legs from the hip. Again and again, I did as I was told. Grabbing the banister with my left hand, I threw my leg from the hip while pushing off my right crutch. Like some baby elephant (despite the sweat lost in the heated pool, the months of inactivity in bed had fattened me up considerably), I dangled from side to side on the parallel bars. Grunting with effort, I did everything demanded of me. I did it with an unabashed eagerness to please those who had power over my life. I wanted to put myself at risk. I wanted to do whatever was supposed to be "good" for me. I believed as absolutely as I have ever believed in anything that rehabilitation would finally placate the hunger of the virus.

But when my therapist commanded me to fall, I cringed. For the prospect of falling terrified me. Every afternoon, as I worked through my prescribed activities, I prayed that I would be able to fall when the session ended. Falling was the most essential "good" of all the "goods" held out for my consideration by my therapist. I believed that. I believed it so intensely that the belief itself was painful. Everything else asked of me was given — and given gladly. I mounted the bus stairs, pushed across the parallel bars until my arms ached with the effort, allowed the medicine ball to pummel me, flailed away at the empty air with my fists because my therapist wanted me to rid myself of the tension within. The slightest sign of approval from those in authority was enough to make me puff with pleasure. Other boys in the ward might not have taken rehabilitation seriously, but I was an eager servant cringing before the promise of approval.

Only I couldn't fall. As each session ended, I would be led to the mats that took up a full third of the huge room. "It's time," the therapist would say. Dutifully, I would follow her, step after step. Just as dutifully, I would stand on the edge of those two-inch-thick mats, staring down at them until I could feel my body quiver. "All you have to do is let go," my therapist assured me. "The other boys do it. Just let go and fall."

But the prospect of letting go was precisely what terrified me. That the other boys in the ward had no trouble in falling added to my shame and terror. I didn't need my therapist to tell me the two-inch-thick mats would keep me from hurting myself. I knew there was virtually no chance of injury when I fell, but that knowledge simply made me more ashamed of a cowardice that was as monumental as it was unexplainable. Had it been able to rid me of my sense of my own cowardice, I would happily have settled for bodily harm. But I was being asked to surrender myself to the emptiness of space, to let go and crash down to the mats below, to feel myself suspended in air when nothing stood between me and the vacuum of the world. *That* was the prospect that overwhelmed me. *That* was what left me sweating with rage and humiliation. The contempt I felt was for my own weakness.

I tried to justify what I sensed could never be justified. Why should I be expected to throw myself into emptiness? Was this sullen terror the price of compensation, the badge of normality? Maybe my refusal to fall embodied some deeper thrust than I could then understand. Maybe I had unconsciously seized upon some fundamental resistance to the forces that threatened to overwhelm me. What did matter that the ground was covered by the thick mats? The tremors I feared were in my heart and soul.

Shame plagued me — and shame is the older brother to disease. Flushing with shame, I would stare down at the mats. I could feel myself wanting to cry out. But I shriveled at the thought of calling more attention to my cowardice. I would finally hear myself whimper, "I'm sorry. But I can't. I can't let go."

Formless emptiness. A rush of air through which I would plummet toward obliteration. As my "normal" past grew more and more distant, I reached for it more and more desperately, recalling it like some movie whose plot has long since been forgotten but whose scenes continue to comfort through images disconnected from anything but themselves. I remembered that there had been a time when the prospect of falling evoked not terror but joy: football games on the rain-softened autumn turf of Mosholu Parkway, belly-flopping on an American Flyer down its snow-covered slopes in winter, rolling with a pack of friends down one of the steep hills in Bronx Park. Free falls from the past, testifying not to a loss of the self but to an absence of barriers.

My therapist pleaded, ridiculed, cajoled, threatened, bullied. I was sighed over and railed at. But I couldn't let go and fall. I couldn't sell my terror off so cheaply. Ashamed as I was, I wouldn't allow myself to be bullied out of terror.

A month passed — a month of struggle between me and my therapist. Daily excursions to the rehab room, daily practice runs through the future that was awaiting me. The daily humiliation of discovering that one's own fear had been transformed into a public issue, a subject of discussion among the other boys in the ward, seemed unending.

And then, terror simply evaporated. It was as if I had served enough time in that prison. I was ready to move on. One Tuesday afternoon, as my session ended, the therapist walked resignedly alongside me toward the mats. "All right, Leonard. It's time again. All you have to do is let go and fall." Again, I stood above the mats. Only this time, it was as if something beyond my control or understanding had decided to let my body's fall from grace take me down for good. I was not seized by the usual paroxysm of fear. I didn't feel myself break out in a terrified sweat. It was over.

I don't mean that I suddenly felt myself spring into courage. That wasn't what happened at all. The truth was I had simply been worn down into letting go, like a boxer in whose eyes one recognizes not the flicker of defeat — that issue never having been in doubt — but the acceptance of defeat. Letting go no longer held my imagination captive. I found myself quite suddenly faced with a necessary fall — a fall into life.

So it was that I stood above the mat and heard myself sigh and then felt myself let go, dropping through the quiet air, crutches slipping off to the sides. What I didn't feel this time was the threat of my body slipping into emptiness, so mummified by the terror before it that the touch of air pre-empted even death. I dropped. I did not crash. I dropped. I did not collapse. I dropped. I did not plummet. I felt myself enveloped by a curiously gentle moment in my life. In that sliver of time before I hit the mat, I was kissed by space.

My body absorbed the slight shock and I rolled onto my back, braced legs swinging like unguided missiles into the free air, crutches dropping away to the sides. Even as I fell through the air, I could sense the shame and fear drain from my soul, and I knew that my sense of my own cowardice would soon follow. In falling, I had given myself a new start, a new life.

"That's it!" my therapist triumphantly shouted. "You let go! And there it is!"

You let go! And there it is! Yes, and you discover not terror but the only self you are going to be allowed to claim anyhow. You fall free, and then you learn that those padded mats hold not courage but the unclaimed self. And if it turned out to be not the most difficult of tasks, did that make my sense of jubilation any less?

From that moment, I gloried in my ability to fall. Falling became an end in itself. I lost sight of what my therapist had desperately been trying to demonstrate for me — that there was a purpose in learning how to fall. For she wanted to teach me through the fall what I would have to face in the future. She wanted to give me a wholeness I could not give myself. For she knew that mine would be a future so different from what confronts the "normal" that I had to learn to fall into life in order not to be overwhelmed.

From that day, she urged me to practice falling as if I were a religious disciple being urged by a master to practice spiritual discipline. Letting go meant allowing my body to float into space, to turn at the direction of the fall and follow the urgings of emptiness. For her, learning to fall was learning the most essential of American lessons: how to turn incapacity into capacity.

"You were afraid of hurting yourself," she explained to me. "But that's the beauty of it. When you let go, you can't hurt yourself."

An echo of the streets and playgrounds I called home until I met the virus. American slogans: go with the flow, roll with the punch, slide with the threat until it is no longer a threat. They were simply slogans, and they were all intended to create strength from weakness, a veritable world's fair of compensation.

I returned to the city a year later. By that time, I was a willing convert, one who now secretly enjoyed demonstrating his ability to fall. I enjoyed the surprise that would greet me as I got to my feet, unscathed and undamaged. However perverse it may seem, I felt a certain pleasure when, as I walked with a friend, I felt a crutch slip out of my grasp. Watching the thrust of concern darken his features, I felt myself in control of my own capacity. For falling had become the way my body sought out its proper home. It was an earthbound body, and mine would be an earthbound life. My quest would be for the solid ground beneath me. Falling with confidence, I fell away from terror and fear.

Of course, some falls took me unawares, and I found myself letting go too late or too early. Bruised in ego and sometimes in body, I would pull myself to my feet to consider what had gone wrong. Yet I was essentially untroubled. Such defeats were part of the game, even when they confined me to bed for a day or two afterward. I was an accountant of pain, and sometimes heavier payment was demanded. In my mid-thirties, I walked my two-year-old son's babysitter home, tripped on the curbstone, and broke my wrist. At forty-eight, an awkward fall triggered by a carelessly unlocked brace sent me smashing against the bathtub and into surgery for a broken femur. It took four months for me to learn to walk on the crutches all over again. But I learned. I already knew how to fall.

I knew such accidents could be handled. After all, pain was not synonymous with mortality. In fact, pain was insurance against an excessive consciousness of mortality. Pain might validate the specific moment in time, but it didn't have very much to do with the future. I did not yet believe that falling into life had anything to do with falling into death. It was simply a way for me to exercise control over my own existence.

It seems to me today that, when I first let my body fall to those mats, I was somehow giving myself the endurance I would need to survive in this world. In a curious way, falling became a way of celebrating what I had lost. My legs were lifeless, useless, but their loss had created a dancing image in whose shadowy gyrations I recognized a strange but potentially interesting new self. I would survive. I knew that now. I could let go, I could fall, and, best of all, I could get up.

To create an independent self, a man had to rid himself of both the myths that nurtured him and the myths that held him back. Learning to fall had been the first lesson in how I yet might live successfully as a cripple. Even disease had its inviolate principles. I understood that the most dangerous threat to the sense of self I needed was an inflated belief in my own capacity. Falling rid a man of excess baggage; it taught him how each of us is dependent on balance.

But what really gave falling legitimacy was the knowledge that I could get to my feet again. That was what taught me the rules of survival. As long as I could pick myself up and stand on my own two feet, brace-bound and crutch-propped as I was, the fall testified to my ability to live in the here and now, to stake my claim as an American who had turned incapacity into capacity. For such a man, falling might well be considered the language of everyday achievement.

But the day came, as I knew it must come, when I could no longer pick myself up. It was then that my passion for symmetry in endings began. On that day, spurred on by another fall, I found myself spinning into the inevitable future.

The day was actually a rainy night in November of 1983. I had just finished teaching at the City College Center for Worker Education, an off-campus degree program for working adults, and had joined some friends for dinner. All of us, I remember, were in a jovial, celebratory mood, although I no longer remember what it was we were celebrating. Perhaps it was simply the satisfaction of being good friends and colleagues at dinner together.

We ate in a Spanish restaurant on Fourteenth Street in Manhattan. It was a dinner that took on, for me at least, the intensity of a time that would assume greater and greater significance as I grew older, one of those watershed moments writers are so fond of. In the dark, rain-swept New York night, change and possibility seemed to drift like a thick fog all around us.

Our mood was still convivial when we left the restaurant around eleven. The rain had slackened off to a soft drizzle and the street glistened beneath the play of light on the wet black creosote. At night, rain in the city has a way of transforming proportion into optimism. The five of us stood around on the slicked-down sidewalk, none of us willing to be the first to break the richness of the mood by leaving.

Suddenly, the crutch in my left hand began to slip out from under me, slowly, almost deliberately, as if the crutch had a mind of its own and had not yet made the commitment that would send me down. Apparently, I had hit a slick patch of city sidewalk, some nub of concrete worn smooth as medieval stone by thousands of shoppers and panhandlers and tourists and students who daily pounded the bargain hustlings of Fourteenth Street.

Instinctively, I at first tried to fight the fall, to seek for balance by pushing off from the crutch in my right hand. But as I recognized that the fall was inevitable, I simply went slack — and for the thousandth time my body sought vindication in its ability to let go and drop. These good friends had seen me fall before. They knew my childish vanities, understood that I still thought of falling as a way to demonstrate my control of the traps and uncertainties that lay in wait for us all.

Thirty-eight years earlier, I had discovered that I could fall into life simply by letting go. Now I made a different discovery — that I could no longer get to my feet by myself. I hit the wet ground and quickly turned over and pushed up, trying to use one of the crutches as a prop to boost myself to my feet, as I had been taught to do as a boy of twelve.

But try as hard as I could, I couldn't get to my feet. It wasn't that I lacked physical strength. I knew that my arms were as powerful as ever as I pushed down on the wet concrete. It had nothing to do with the fact that the street was wet, as my friends insisted later. No, it had to do with a subtle, if mysterious, change in my own sense of rhythm and balance. My body had decided — *and decided on its own, autonomously* — that the moment had come for me to face the question of endings. It was the body that chose its time of recognition.

It was, it seems to me now, a distinctively American moment. It left me pondering limitations and endings and summations. It left me with the curiously buoyant sense that mortality had quite suddenly made itself a felt presence rather than the rhetorical strategy used by the poets and novelists I taught to my students. This was what writers had in mind when they spoke of the truly common fate, this sense of ending coming to one unbidden. This had brought with it my impassioned quest for symmetry. As I lay on the wet ground — no more than a minute or two — all I could think of was how much I wanted my life to balance out. It was as if I were staring into a future in which time itself had evaporated.

Here was a clear, simple perception, and there was nothing

mystical about it. There are limitations we recognize and those that recognize us. My friends, who had nervously been standing around while I tried to get to my feet, finally asked if they could help me up. "You'll have to," I said. "I can't get up any other way."

Two of them pulled me to my feet while another jammed the crutches beneath my arms, as the therapist and the two brace-makers had done almost four decades earlier. When I was standing, they proceeded to joke about my sudden incapacity in that age-old way men of all ages have, as if words might codify loss and change and time's betrayal. I joined in the joking. But what I really wanted was to go home and contemplate this latest fall in the privacy of my apartment. The implications were clear: I would never again be an eater of salt, I would also never again get to my feet on my own. A part of my life had ended. But that didn't depress me. In fact, I felt almost as exhilarated as I had thirty-eight years earlier, when my body surrendered to the need to let go and I fell into life.

Almost four years have passed since I fell on the wet sidewalk of Fourteenth Street. I suppose it wasn't a particularly memorable fall. It wasn't even particularly significant to anyone who had not once fallen into life. But it was inevitable, the first time I had let go into a time when it would no longer even be necessary to let go.

It was a fall that left me with the knowledge that I could no longer pick myself up. That meant I now needed the help of others as I had not needed their help before. It was a fall that left me burning with this strange passion for symmetry, this desire to balance my existence out. When the day comes, I want to be able to fall into my death as nakedly as I once had to fall into my life.

Do not misunderstand me. I am not seeking a way out of mortality, for I believe in nothing more strongly than I believe in the permanency of endings. I am not looking for a way out of this life, a life I continue to find immensely enjoyable — even if I can no longer pull myself to my own two feet. Of course, a good deal in my life has changed. For one thing, I am increasingly impatient with those who claim to have no use for endings of any sort. I am also increasingly embarrassed by the thought of the harshly critical adolescent I was, self-righteously convinced that the only way for a man to go to his end was by kicking and screaming.

But these are, I suppose, the kinds of changes any man or woman of forty or fifty would feel. Middle-aged skepticism is as natural as adolescent acne. In my clearer, less passionate moments, I can even laugh at my need for symmetry in beginnings and endings as well as my desire to see my own eventual death as a line running parallel to my life. Even in mathematics, let alone life, symmetry is sometimes too neat, too closed off from the way things actually work. After all, it took me a full month before I could bring myself to let go and fall into life.

I no longer talk about how one can seize a doctrine of compensation from disease. I don't talk about it, but it still haunts me. In my heart, I believe it offers a man the only philosophy by which he can actually live. It is the only philosophy that strips away both spiritual mumbo jumbo and the procrustean weight of existential anxiety. In the final analysis, a man really is what a man does.

Believing as I do, I wonder why I so often find myself trying to frame a perspective that will prove adequate to a proper sense of ending. Perhaps that is why I find myself sitting in a bar with a friend, trying to explain to him all that I have learned from falling. "There must be a time," I hear myself tell him, "when a man has the right to stop thinking about falling."

"Sure," my friend laughs. "Four seconds before he dies."

DAVID QUAMMEN

Strawberries Under Ice

FROM OUTSIDE MAGAZINE

1. The Gradient of Net Mass Balance

ANTARCTICA is a gently domed continent squashed flat, like a dent in the roof of a Chevy, by the weight of its ice. That burden of ice amounts to seven million cubic miles. Melt it away and the Antarctic interior would bounce upward; Earth itself would change shape. This grand cold fact has, to me, on the tiny and personal scale, a warm appeal. Take away ice and the topography of my own life changes drastically too.

Ice is lighter than water but still heavy. The stuff answers gravity. Ice is a solid but not an absolute solid. The stuff flows. Slowly but inexorably it runs downhill. We think of iciness as a synonym for cold, but cold is relative and ice happens to function well as insulation against heat loss: low thermal conductivity. Also it *releases* heat to immediate surroundings in the final stage of becoming frozen itself. Ice warms. On a certain night, roughly thirteen years ago, it warmed me.

When a tongue of ice flows down a mountain valley, we call it a glacier. When it flows out in all directions from a source point at high elevation, like pancake batter poured on a griddle, we call it a sheet. Out at the Antarctic circumference are glaciers and seaborne shelves, from which icebergs calve off under their own weight. Both sheets and glaciers are supplied with their substance, their impetus, their ice, by snow and other forms of precipitation back uphill at the source. While old ice is continually lost by calving and melting in the lowlands, new ice is deposited in the highlands, and any glacier or sheet receiving more new ice than it loses old, through the course of a year, is a glacier or sheet that is growing. The scientists would say that its net mass balance is positive.

The Antarctic sheet, for instance, has a positive balance. But this is not an essay about Antarctica.

Each point on a great ice body has its own numerical value for mass balance. Is the ice right here thicker or thinner than last year? Is the glacier, at this spot, thriving or dying? The collective profile of all those individual soundings — more ice or less? thriving or dying? — is called the gradient of net mass balance. This gradient tells, in broad perspective, what has been lost and what has been gained. On that certain night, thirteen years ago, I happened to be asking myself exactly the same question: *What's been lost and what, if anything, gained?* Because snow gathers most heavily in frigid sky-scraping highlands, the gradient of net mass balance correlates steeply with altitude. Robust glaciers come snaking down out of the Alaskan mountains. Also because snow gathers most heavily in frigid sky-scraping highlands, I had taken myself on that day to a drifted-over pass in the Bitterroot Mountains, all hell-and-gone up on the state border just west of the town of Tarkio, Montana, and started skiing up from there.

I needed as much snow as possible. I carried food and a goose-down bag and a small shovel. It was December 31, 1975.

I hadn't come to measure depths or calculate gradients. I had come to insert myself into a cold white hole. First, of course, I had to dig it. This elaborately uncomfortable enterprise seems to have been part of a long foggy process of escape and purgation, much of which you can be spared. Suffice that my snow cave, to be dug on New Year's Eve into a ten-foot-high cornice on the leeward side of the highest ridge I could ski to, and barely large enough for one person, would be at the aphelion of that long foggy process. At the perihelion was Oxford University.

At Oxford University during one week in late springtime there is a festival of crew races on the river, girls in long dresses, boys in straw hats, champagne and strawberries. This event is called Eights Week, for the fact of eight men to a crew. It is

innocent. More precisely: it is no more obnoxious, no more
steeped in snobbery and dandified xenophobia and intellectual
and social complacence, thaṅ any other aspect of Oxford University. The strawberries are served under heavy cream. Sybar-
itism is mandatory. For these and other reasons, partly personal, partly political, I had fled the place screaming during
Eights Week of 1972, almost precisely coincident (by no coincidence) with Richard Nixon's announcement of the blockade of
Haiphong Harbor. Nixon's blockade and Oxford's strawberries
had nothing logically in common, but they converged to produce in me a drastic reaction to what until then had been just a
festering distemper.

It took me another year to arrive in Montana. I had never
before set foot in the state. I knew no one there. But I had
heard that it was a place where, in the early weeks of September,
a person could look up to a looming horizon and see fresh snow.
I had noted certain blue lines on a highway map, knew the lines
to be rivers, and imagined those rivers to be dark mountain
streams flashing with trout. I arrived during the early weeks of
September, and lo, it was all true.

I took a room in an old-fashioned boardinghouse. I looked
for a job. I started work on a recklessly ambitious and doomed
novel. I sensed rather soon that I hadn't come to this place
temporarily. I began reading the writers — Herodotus, Euri-
pides, Coleridge, Descartes, Rousseau, Thoreau, Raymond
Chandler — for whom a conscientious and narrow academic
career had left no time. I spent my nest egg and then sold my
Volkswagen bus for another. I learned the clownish mortifica-
tion of addressing strangers with: "Hi, my name is Invisible and
I'll be your waiter tonight." I was twenty-six, just old enough to
realize that this period was not some sort of prelude to my life
but the thing itself. I knew I was spending real currency, hard
and finite, on a speculative venture at an unknowable rate of
return: the currency of time, energy, stamina. Two more years
passed before I arrived, sweaty and chilled, at that high cold
cornice in the Bitterroots.

By then I had made a small handful of precious friends in
this new place, and a menagerie of acquaintances, and I had
learned also to say: "You want that on the rocks or up?" Time

was still plentiful but stamina was low. Around Christmas that year, two of the precious friends announced a New Year's Eve party. Tempting, yet it seemed somehow a better idea to spend the occasion alone in a snow cave.

So here I was. There had been no trail up the face of the ridge, and lifting my skis through the heavy snow had drenched and exhausted me. My thighs felt as though the Chicago police had worked on them with truncheons. I dug my hole. That done, I changed out of the soaked, freezing clothes. I boiled and ate some noodles, drank some cocoa; if I was smart enough to have encumbered my pack with a bottle of wine, I don't remember it. When dark came, I felt the nervous exhilaration of utter solitude and, behind that like a metallic aftertaste, loneliness. I gnawed on my thoughts for an hour or two, then retired. The night turned into a clear one, and when I crawled out of the cave at 3 A.M. of the new year to empty my bladder, I found the sky rolled out in a stunning pageant of scope and dispassion and cold grace.

It was too good to waste. I went back into the cave for my glasses.

The temperature by now had gone into the teens below zero. I stood there beside the cornice in cotton sweatpants, gaping up. "We never know what we have lost, or what we have found," says America's wisest poet, Robert Penn Warren, in the context of a meditation about John James Audubon and the transforming power of landscape. We never know what we have lost, or what we have found. All I did know was that the highway maps called it Montana, and that I was here, and that in the course of a life a person could travel widely but could truly open his veins and his soul to just a limited number of places.

After half an hour I crawled back into the cave, where ten feet of snow and a rime of ice would keep me warm.

2. *Ablation*

Trace any glacier or ice sheet downhill from its source and eventually you will come to a boundary where the mass balance of ice is zero. Here, nothing is lost, over the course of time, and nothing is gained. This boundary is called the equilibrium line. Above the equilibrium line is the zone of accumulation. Below is the zone of ablation. Ablation is the scientists' fancy word for loss.

Down here, in the zone of ablation, the mass balance is negative. At this end the glacier is shrinking. The continual loss of ice results from several different processes: wind erosion, surface melting, evaporation (ice does evaporate), underside melting of an ice shelf where it rests on the warmer seawater. Calving off of icebergs. Calving is the scientists' quaint word for that event when a great hunk of ice — as big as a house or, in some cases, as big as a county — tears away from the leading edge of the sheet or the glacier and falls thunderously into the sea. Wind erosion and evaporation and most of those other ablative processes work on the ice slowly, incrementally. Calving, on the other hand, is abrupt.

The occurrence of a calving event depends on a number of physical factors, one of which is the strength of the ice itself. That factor, strength, is hard to measure. Certain experiments done on strength-testing machines have yielded certain arcane numbers. But those numbers offer no absolute guide to the performance of different types of ice under different conditions. They only suggest in a relative way that, although ice may flow majestically under its own weight, although it may stretch like caramel, although it may bend like lead, it gives back rock-like resistance to a force coming down on it suddenly. None of this cold information was available to me on the day now in mind, and if it had been I wouldn't have wanted it.

On the day now in mind I had been off skiing, again, with no thought for the physical properties of ice, other than maybe some vague awareness of the knee strain involved in carving a turn across boilerplate. I came home to find a note in my door.

The note said that a young woman I knew, the great love of a friend of mine, was dead. The note didn't say what had happened. I should call a number in Helena for details. It was not only shocking but ominous. Because I knew that the young woman had lately been working through some uneasy and confusing times, I thought of all the various grim possibilities involving despair. Then I called Helena, where a houseful of friends were gathered for communal grieving and food and loud music. I learned that the young woman had died from a fall. A freak accident. In the coldest sense of cold consolation, there was in this information some relief.

She had slipped on a patch of sidewalk ice the night before and hit her head. A nasty blow, a moment or two of unconsciousness, but she had apparently been all right. She went home alone and was not all right and died before morning. I suppose she was about twenty-seven. This is exactly why head trauma cases are normally put under close overnight observation, but I wasn't aware of that at the time, and neither, evidently, were the folks who had helped her up off that icy sidewalk. She had seemed dazed but healthy. Even after the fall, her death was preventable. Of course most of us will die preventable deaths; hers was only more vividly so, and earlier.

I had known her, not well, through her sweetheart and the network of friends now assembled in that house in Helena. These friends of hers and mine were mostly a group of ecologists who had worked together, during graduate school, as waiters and bartenders and cooks; I met them in that context and they had nurtured my sanity to no small degree when that context began straining it. They read books, they talked about ideas, they knew a spruce from a hemlock, they slept in snow caves: a balm of good company to me. They made the state of Montana into a place that was not only cold, true, hard, and beautiful, but damn near humanly habitable. The young woman, now dead, was not herself a scientist, but she was one of them in all other senses. She came from a town up on the High Line.

I had worked with her too, and seen her enliven long afternoons that could otherwise be just a tedious and not very lucrative form of self-demeanment. She was one of those rowdy, robust people — robust in good times, just as robust when she was angry or miserable — who are especially hard to imagine dead. She was a rascal of wit. She could be hilariously crude. We all knew her by her last name, because her first seemed too ladylike and demure. After the phone call to Helena, it took me a long time to make the mental adjustment of tenses: She *had been* a rascal of wit.

The memorial service was scheduled for such-and-such day in that town up on the High Line. We drove up together on winter roads, myself and two of the Helena friends, a husband-and-wife pair of plant ecologists. Places available for sleeping, spare rooms and floors; make contact by phone; meet at the church. We met at the church and sat lumpish while a local pastor discoursed with transcendent irrelevance about what we could hardly recognize as her life and death. It wasn't his fault; he didn't know her. There was a reception with the family, followed by a post-wake on our own at a local bar, a fervent gathering of young survivors determined not only to cling to her memory but to cling to one another more appreciatively now that such a persuasive warning knell of mortality had been rung. Then, sometime after dark, while the wind came up and the temperature dropped away as though nothing was under it and a new storm raked in across those wheatlands, the three of us started driving back south. It had been my first trip to the High Line.

Aside from the note in the door, this is the part I remember most clearly. The car's defroster wasn't working. I had about four inches of open windshield. It was a little Honda that responded to wind like a shuttlecock, and on slick pavement the rear end flapped like the tail of a trout. We seemed to be rolling down a long dark tube coated inside with ice, jarred back and forth by the crosswinds, nothing else visible except the short tongue of road ahead and the streaming snow and the trucks blasting by too close in the other lane. How ironic, I thought, if we die on the highway while returning from a funeral. I hunched over the wheel, squinting out through that gap of windshield, until certain muscles in my right shoulder and neck shortened themselves into a knot. The two plant ecologists kept me awake with talk. One of them, from the back seat, worked at the knot in my neck. We talked about friendship and the message of death as we all three felt we had heard it, which was to cherish the living while you have them. Seize, hold, appreciate. Pure friendship, uncomplicated by romance or blood, is one of the most nurturing human relationships and one of the most easily taken for granted. This was our consensus, spoken and unspoken.

These two plant ecologists had been my dear friends for a few years, but we were never closer than during that drive. Well after midnight, we reached their house in Helena. I slept on sofa cushions. In the morning they got me to a doctor for the paralytic clench in my neck. That was almost ten years ago and I've hardly seen them since.

The fault is mine, or the fault is nobody's. We got older and busier and trails diverged. They began raising children. I traveled to Helena less and less. Mortgages, serious jobs, deadlines; and the age of sleeping on sofa cushions seemed to have passed. I moved, they moved, opening more geographical distance. Montana is a big place and the roads are often bad. These facts offered in explanation sound even to me like excuses. The ashes of the young woman who slipped on the ice have long since been sprinkled onto a mountaintop or into a river, I'm not sure which. Nothing to be done now either for her or about her. The two plant ecologists I still cherish, in intention anyway, at a regrettable distance, as I do a small handful of other precious friends, who seem to have disappeared from my life by wind erosion or melting.

3. Leontiev's Axiom

The ice mass of a mountain glacier flows down its valley in much the same complicated pattern as a river flowing in its bed. Obviously the glacier is much slower. Like the water of a river, though, the ice of a glacier does not all flow at the same rate. There are eddies and tongues and slack zones, currents and swells, differential vectors of mix and surge. Any such swirl of independently mobile molecules is known to the scientists as turbulent flow. Turbulent flow is what makes a glacier unfathomable.

Turbulent flow is also what distinguishes a river from, say, a lake. When a river itself freezes, the complexities of turbulent flow interact with the peculiar physics of ice formation to produce a whole rat's nest of intriguing and sometimes inconvenient surprises. Because of turbulence, the water of a river cools down toward the freezing point uniformly, not in stratified lay-

ers as in a lake. Eventually the entire mass of flowing water
drops below 32 degrees Fahrenheit and small disks of frazil ice
appear. Again because of turbulence, this frazil ice doesn't all
float on the surface (despite being lighter than water) but mixes
throughout the river's depth. Frazil ice has a tendency to adhe-
sion, so some of it sticks to riverbed rocks. Some of it gloms on
to bridge pilings and culverts, growing thick as a soft cold fur.
Some of it aggregates with other frazil ice, forming large dollops
of drifting slush. Meanwhile huge slabs of harder sheet ice,
formed along the banks and broken free as the river changes
level, may also be floating downstream. The slabs of sheet ice
and the dollops of frazil ice go together like bricks and mortar.
Stacking up at a channel constriction, they can lock themselves
into an ice bridge. Generally, when such an ice bridge forms,
the river will have room to flow underneath. If the river is very
shallow and the slabs of sheet ice are large, possibly not. A
clogging phenomenon can occur.

And the Madison River, where it runs north through Montana, happens to be very shallow.

Upstream from the lake that sits five miles north of Ennis, the
Madison River is a magnificent stretch of habitat for stoneflies
and caddisflies and trout and blue herons and fox and eagles
and, half the year anyway, fishermen. The water is warmed at
its geothermal source in Yellowstone Park, cooled again by its
Montana tributaries, rich in nutrients and oxygen, clear, lam-
bent, unspoiled. Thanks to these graces, it is probably much too
renowned for its own good. Upstream from the highway bridge
at Ennis, it gets an untoward amount of attention. This is where
the famous salmonfly hatch happens: boat traffic like the Hen-
ley Regatta during that dizzy two weeks of June while the insects
swarm and the fish gluttonize. This is the stretch of the Madison
for fishermen who crave trophies but not solitude. Downstream
from the Ennis bridge it becomes a different sort of river. It
becomes a different sort of place.

Downstream from the Ennis bridge, for that five-mile stretch
to the lake, the Madison is a broken-up travesty of a river that
offers mediocre fishing and clumsy floating and no trophy trout
and not many salmonflies and I promise you fervently you
wouldn't like it. This stretch is called the channels. The river

braids out into a maze of elbows and sloughs and streams separated by hundreds of small and large islands, some covered only
with grass and willow, some shaded with buckling old-growth
cottonwoods, some holding thickets of water birch and woods
rose and raspberry scarcely tramped through by a single fisherman in the course of a summer. The deer love these islands
and, in May, so do the nesting geese. Mosquitoes are bad here.
The walking is difficult and there are bleached cottonwood
deadfalls waiting to tear your waders. I adore that five miles of
river more than any piece of landscape in the world.

Surrounding the braidwork of channels is a zone of bottomland roughly two miles wide, a great flat swath of subirrigated
meadow only barely above the river's springtime high-water
level. This low meadow area is an unusual sort of no man's land
that performs a miraculous service: protecting the immediately
riparian vicinity of the channels from the otherwise inevitable
arrival of ranch houses, summer homes, resort lodges, motels,
all-weather roads, development, spoliation, and every other sort
of venal doom. Tantalizing and vulnerable as it may appear on
a July afternoon, the channels meadowland is an ideal place to
raise bluegrass and Herefords and sandhill cranes but, for reasons we'll come to, is not really good for much else.

By late December the out-of-state fishermen are long gone,
the duck hunters more recently, and during a good serious
stretch of weather the dark river begins to flow gray and woolly
with frazil ice. If the big slabs of sheet ice are moving too, a
person can stand on the Ennis highway bridge and hear the two
kinds of ice rubbing, hissing, whispering to each other as though
in conspiracy toward mischief, or maybe revenge. (Through the
three winters I lived in Ennis myself, I stood on that bridge
often, gawking and listening. There aren't too many other
forms of legal amusement in a Montana town of a thousand
souls during the short days and long weeks of midwinter.) By
this time the lake, five miles downstream, will have already frozen over. Then the river water cools still further, the frazil thick-
ens, the slabs bump and tumble into those narrow channels until
somewhere, at a point of constriction down near the lake, mortar meets brick. And the clogging phenomenon begins.

Soon the river is choked with its own ice. All the channels are nearly or totally blocked. But water is still arriving from up-stream, and that water has to go somewhere. So it flows out across the bottomland. It pours out over its banks and, moving quickly, faster than a man can walk, it covers a large part of that meadow area with water. Almost as quickly, the standing flood-water becomes ice.

If you have been stubborn or foolish enough to build your house out on that flat, on a pretty spot at the edge of the river, you now have three feet of well-deserved ice in your living room. "Get back away from me" is what the river has told you. "Show some goddamn respect." There are memories of this sort of ice-against-man encounter. It hasn't happened often, that a person should come along so mule-minded as to insist on flout-ing the reality of the ice, but often enough for a few vivid ex-empla. Back in 1863, for instance, a settler named Andrew Odell, who had built his cabin out on the channel meadows, woke up one night in December to find river water already lapping onto his bed. He grabbed his blanket and fled, knee deep, toward higher ground on the far side of a spring creek that runs parallel to the channels a half mile east. That spring creek is now called Odell Creek, and it marks a rough eastern boundary of the zone that gets buried in ice. Nowadays you don't see any cabins or barns in the flat between Odell Creek and the river.

Folks in Ennis call this salubrious event the Gorge. The Gorge doesn't occur every year, and it isn't uniform or predictable when it does. Two or three winters may go by without serious weather, without a Gorge, without that frozen flood laid down upon thousands of acres, and then there will come a record year. A rancher named Ralph Paugh remembers one particular Gorge, because it back-flooded all the way up across Odell to fill his barn with a two-foot depth of ice. This was on Christmas Day, 1983. "It come about four o'clock," he recalls. "Never had got to the barn before." His barn has sat on that rise since 1905. He has some snapshots from the 1983 episode, showing vistas and mounds of whiteness. "That pile there, see, we piled that up with the dozer when we cleaned it out." Ralph also remem-bers talk about the Gorge in 1907, the year he was born; that one took out the old highway bridge, so for the rest of the winter

schoolchildren and mailmen and whoever else had urgent reason for crossing the river did so on a trail of planks laid across
ice. The present bridge is a new one, but the Gorge of the
Madison channels is immemorial.

I used to lace up my Sorels and walk on it. Cold sunny afternoons of January or February, bare willows, bare cottonwoods,
exquisite solitude, fox tracks in an inch of fresh snow, and down
through three feet of ice below my steps and the fox tracks were
spectacular bits of Montana that other folk, outlanders, coveted
only in summer.

Mostly I wandered these places alone. Then one year a certain biologist of my recent acquaintance came down for a visit
in Ennis. I think this was in late April. I know that the river had
gorged that year and that the ice was now melting away from
the bottomland, leaving behind its moraine of fertile silt. The
channels themselves, by now, were open and running clear. The
first geese had arrived. This biologist and I spent that day in the
water, walking downriver through the channels. We didn't fish.
We didn't collect aquatic insects or study the nesting of *Branta
canadensis*. The trees hadn't yet come into leaf and it was no day
for a picnic. We just walked in the water, stumbling over boul-
ders, bruising our feet, getting wet over the tops of our waders.
We saw the Madison channels, fresh from cold storage, before
anyone else that year. We covered only about three river miles
in the course of the afternoon, but that was enough to exhaust
us, and then we stumbled out across the muddy fields and
walked home on the road. How extraordinary, I thought, to
come across a biologist who would share my own demented
appreciation for such an arduous, stupid, soggy trek. So I married her.

The channels of the Madison River are a synecdoche. They
are the part that resonates so as to express the significance of
that whole. To understand how I mean that, it might help to
know Leontiev's Axiom. Konstantin Leontiev was a cranky Russian thinker from the last century. He trained as a physician,
worked as a diplomat in the Balkans, wrote novels and essays
that aren't read much today, and at the end of his life flirted
with becoming a monk. By most of the standards you and I
likely share, he was an unsavory character. But even a distem-

pered and retrograde czarist of monastic leanings is right about
something once in a while.

Leontiev wrote: "To stop Russia from rotting, one would have
to put it under ice."

In my mind, in my dreams, that great flat sheet of Madison
River whiteness spreads out upon the whole state of Montana. I
believe, with Leontiev, in salvation by ice.

4. Sources

The biologist whose husband I am sometimes says to me: "All
right, so where do we go when Montana's been ruined? Alaska?
Norway? Where?" This is a dark joke between us. She grew up
in Montana, loves the place the way some women might love an
incorrigibly self-destructive man, with pain and fear and pity,
and she has no desire to go anywhere else. I grew up in Ohio,
discovered home in Montana only fifteen years ago, and I feel
the same. But still we play at the dark joke. "Not Norway," I say,
"and you know why." We're each half Norwegian and we've
actually eaten lutefisk. "How about Antarctica," I say. "Antarctica should be O.K. for a while yet."

On the desk before me now is a pair of books about Antarctica. Also here is a book on the Arctic, another book titled *The
World of Ice,* a book of excerpts from Leontiev, a master's thesis
on the subject of goose reproduction and water levels in the
Madison channels, an excerpt from an unpublished fifty-year-
old manuscript on the history of Ennis, Montana, a cassette tape
of a conversation with Ralph Paugh, and a fistful of photocopies
of technical and not-so-technical articles. One of the less technical articles is titled "Ice on the World," from a recent issue of
National Geographic. In this article is a full-page photograph of
strawberry plants covered with a thick layer of ice.

These strawberry plants grew in central Florida. They were
sprayed with water, says the caption, because subfreezing tem-
peratures had been forecast. The growers knew that a layer of
ice, giving insulation, even giving up some heat as the water
froze, would save them.

In the foreground is one large strawberry. The photocopy
shows it dark gray, but in my memory it's a death-defying red.

JUDY RUIZ

Oranges and Sweet Sister Boy

FROM IOWA WOMAN

I AM SLEEPING, hard, when the telephone rings. It's my brother,
and he's calling to say that he is now my sister. I feel something
fry a little, deep behind my eyes. Knowing how sometimes
dreams get mixed up with not-dreams, I decide to do a reality
test at once. "Let me get a cigarette," I say, knowing that if I
reach for a Marlboro and it turns into a trombone or a snake or
anything else on the way to my lips that I'm still out in the large
world of dreams.

The cigarette stays a cigarette. I light it. I ask my brother to
run that stuff by me again.

It is the Texas Zephyr at midnight — the woman in a white suit, the
man in a blue uniform; she carries flowers — I know they are flowers.
The petals spill and spill into the aisle, and a child goes past this
couple who have just come from their own wedding — goes past
them and past them, going always to the toilet but really just going
past them; and the child could be a horse or she could be the police
and they'd not notice her any more than they do, which is not at all
— the man's hands high up on the woman's legs, her skirt up,
her stockings and garters, the petals and finally all the flowers
spilling out into the aisle and his mouth open on her. My mother.
My father. I am conceived near Dallas in the dark while a child
passes, a young girl who knows and doesn't know, who witnesses,
in glimpses, the creation of the universe, who feels an odd hurt as
her own mother, fat and empty, snores with her mouth open, her
false teeth slipping down, snores and snores just two seats behind
the Creators.

News can make a person stupid. It can make you think you can do something. So I ask The Blade question, thinking that if he hasn't had the operation yet that I can fly to him, rent a cabin out on Puget Sound. That we can talk. That I can get him to touch base with reality.

"Begin with an orange," I would tell him. "Because oranges are mildly intrusive by nature, put the orange somewhere so that it will not bother you — in the cupboard, in a drawer, even a pocket or a handbag will do. The orange, being a patient fruit, will wait for you much longer than say a banana or a peach."

I would hold an orange out to him. I would say, "This is the one that will save your life." And I would tell him about the woman I saw in a bus station who bit right into her orange like it was an apple. She was wild looking, as if she'd been outside for too long in a wind that blew the same way all the time. One of the dregs of humanity, our mother would have called her, the same mother who never brought fruit into the house except in cans. My children used to ask me to "start" their oranges for them. That meant to make a hole in the orange so they could peel the rind away, and their small hands weren't equipped with fingernails that were long enough or strong enough to do the job. Sometimes they would suck the juice out of the hole my thumbnail had made, leaving the orange flat and sad.

The earrings are as big as dessert plates, filigree gold-plated with thin dangles hanging down that touch her bare shoulders. She stands in front of the Alamo while a bald man takes her picture. The sun is absorbed by the earrings so quickly that by the time she feels the heat, it is too late. The hanging dangles make small blisters on her shoulders, as if a centipede had traveled there. She takes the famous river walk in spiked heels, rides in a boat, eats some Italian noodles, returns to the motel room, soaks her feet, and applies small band-aids to her toes. She is briefly concerned about the gun on the nightstand. The toilet flushes. She pretends to be sleeping. The gun is just large and heavy. A .45? A .357 magnum? She's never been good with names. She hopes he doesn't try to. Or that if he does, that it's not loaded. But he'll say it's loaded just for fun. Or he'll pull the trigger and the bullet will lodge in her medulla oblongata, ripping through her womb first, taking everything else vital on the way.

In the magazine articles, you don't see this: "Well, yes. The
testicles have to come out. And yes. The penis is cut off." What
you get is tonsils. So-and-so has had a "sex change" operation.
A sex change operation. How precious. How benign. Doctor,
just what do you people do with those penises?

News can make a person a little crazy also. News like, "We
regret to inform you that you have failed your sanity hearing."

The bracelet on my wrist bears the necessary information about
me, but there is one small error. The receptionist typing the
information asked me my religious preference. I said, "None."
She typed, "Neon."

Pearl doesn't have any teeth and her tongue looks weird. She says,
"Pumpkin pie." That's all she says. Sometimes she runs her hands
over my bed sheets and says pumpkin pie. Sometimes I am under
the sheets. Marsha got stabbed in the chest, but she tells everyone
she fell on a knife. Elizabeth — she's the one who thinks her shoe is
a baby — hit me in the back with a tray right after one of the cooks
gave me extra toast. There's a note on the bulletin board about a
class for the nurses: "How Putting A Towel On Sometime's Face
Makes Them Stop Banging Their Spoon/OR Reduction of Disrup-
tive Mealtime Behavior By Facial Screening — 7 P.M. — Conference
Room." Another note announces the topic for remotivation class:
"COWS." All the paranoid schizophrenics will be there.

Here, in the place for the permanently bewildered, I fit right in.
Not because I stood at the window that first night and listened to the
trains. Not because I imagined those trains were bracelets, the jew-
elry of earth. Not even because I imagined that one of those bracelets
was on my own arm and was the Texas Zephyr where a young couple
made love and conceived me. I am eighteen and beautiful and committed to the state hospital by a district court judge for a period of
one day to life. Because I am a paranoid schizophrenic.

I will learn about cows.

So I'm being very quiet in the back of the classroom, and I'm
peeling an orange. It's the smell that makes the others begin to
turn around, that mildly intrusive nature. The course is called
"Women and Modern Literature," and the diaries of Virginia
Woolf are up for discussion except nobody has anything to say.

I, of course, am making a mess with the orange; and I'm wanting to say that my brother is now my sister.

Later, with my hands still orangey, I wander in to leave something on a desk in a professor's office, and he's reading so I'm
being very quiet, and then he says, sort of out of nowhere,
"Emily Dickinson up there in her room making poems while her
brother was making love to her best friend right downstairs on
the dining room table. A regular thing. Think of it. And Walt
Whitman out sniffing around the boys. Our two great American
poets." And I want to grab this professor's arm and say, "Listen.
My brother called me and now he's my sister, and I'm having
trouble making sense out of my life right now, so would you
mind not telling me any more stuff about sex." And I want my
knuckles to turn white while the pressure of my fingers leaves
imprints right through his jacket, little indentations he can in-
terpret as urgent. But I don't say anything. And I don't grab his
arm. I go read a magazine. I find this:

> "I've never found an explanation for why the human race has so
> many languages. When the brain became a language brain, it ob-
> viously needed to develop an intense degree of plasticity. Such plas-
> ticity allows languages to be logical, coherent systems and yet be
> extremely variable. The same brain that thinks in words and symbols
> is also a brain that has to be freed up with regard to sexual turn-on
> and partnering. God knows why sex attitudes have been subject to
> the corresponding degrees of modification and variety as language.
> I suspect there's a close parallel between the two. The brain doesn't
> seem incredibly efficient with regard to sex."

John Money said that. The same John Money who, with surgeon
Howard W. Jones, performed the first sex change operation in
the United States in 1965 at Johns Hopkins University and Hospital in Baltimore.

Money also tells about the *hijra* of India who disgrace their
families because they are too effeminate: "The ultimate stage of
the *hijra* is to get up the courage to go through the amputation
of penis and testicles. They had no anesthetic." Money also answers anyone who might think that "heartless members of the
medical profession are forcing these poor darlings to go and get
themselves cut up and mutilated," or who think the medical

profession should leave them alone. "You'd have lots of patients willing to get a gun and blow off their own genitals if you don't do it. I've had several who got knives and cut themselves trying to get rid of their sex organs. That's their obsession!"

Perhaps better than all else, I understand obsession. It is of the mind. And it is language-bound. Sex is of the body. It has no words. I am stunned to learn that someone with an obsession of the mind can have parts of the body surgically removed. This is my brother I speak of. This is not some lunatic named Carl who becomes Carlene. This is my brother.

So while we're out in that cabin on Puget Sound, I'll tell him about LuAnn. She is the sort of woman who orders the in-season fruit and a little cottage cheese. I am the sort of woman who orders a double cheeseburger and fries. LuAnn and I are sitting in her car. She has a huge orange, and she peels it so the peel falls off in one neat strip. I have a sack of oranges, the small ones. The peel of my orange comes off in hunks about the size of a baby's nail. "Oh, you bought the *juice* oranges," LuAnn says to me. Her emphasis on the word "juice" makes me want to die or something. I lack the courage to admit my ignorance, so I smile and breathe "yes," as if I know some secret, when I'm wanting to scream at her about how my mother didn't teach me about fruit and my own blood pounds in my head wanting out, out.

> There is a pattern to this thought as there is a pattern for a jump-suit. Sew the sleeve to the leg, sew the leg to the collar. Put the garment on. Sew the mouth shut. This is how I tell about being quiet because I am bad, and because I cannot stand it when he beats me or my brother.

"The first time I got caught in your clothes was when I was four years old and you were over at Sarah what's-her-name's babysitting. Dad beat me so hard I thought I was going to die. I really thought I was going to die. That was the day I made up my mind I would *never* get caught again. And I never got caught again." My brother goes on to say he continued to go through my things until I was hospitalized. A mystery is solved.

He wore my clothes. He played in my makeup. I kept saying,

back then, that someone was going through my stuff. I kept
saying it and saying it. I told the counselor at school. "Someone
goes in my room when I'm not there, and I *know* it — goes in
there and wears my clothes and goes through my stuff." I was
assured by the counselor that this was not so. I was assured by
my mother that this was not so. I thought my mother was doing
it, snooping around for clues like mothers do. It made me a
little crazy, so I started deliberately leaving things in a certain
order so that I would be able to prove to myself that someone,
indeed, was going through my belongings. No one, not one
person, ever believed that my room was being ransacked; I was
accused of just making it up. A paranoid fixation.

And all the time it was old Goldilocks.

So I tell my brother to promise me he'll see someone who coun-
sels adult children from dysfunctional families. I tell him he
needs to deal with the fact that he was physically abused on a
daily basis. He tells me he doesn't remember being beaten except on three occasions. He wants me to get into a support
group for families of people who are having a sex change. Support groups are people who are in the same boat. Except no one
has any oars in the water.

I tell him I know how it feels to think you are in the wrong
body. I tell him how I wanted my boyfriend to put a gun up
inside me and blow the woman out, how I thought wearing
spiked heels and low-cut dresses would somehow help my crisis,
that putting on an ultrafeminine outside would mask the male-
ness I felt needed hiding. I tell him it's the rule, rather than the
exception, that people from families like ours have very spooky
sexual identity problems. He tells me that his sexuality is a birth
defect. I recognize the lingo. It's support-group-for-transsex-
uals lingo. He tells me he sits down to pee. He told his therapist
that he used to wet all over the floor. His therapist said, "You
can't aim the bullets if you don't touch the gun." Lingo. My
brother is hell-bent for castration, the castration that started
before he had language: the castration of abuse. He will simply
finish what was set in motion long ago.

I will tell my brother about the time I took ten sacks of oranges
into a school so that I could teach metaphor. The school was for

special students — those who were socially or intellectually impaired. I had planned to have them peel the oranges as I spoke about how much the world is like the orange. I handed out the oranges. The students refused to peel them, not because they wanted to make life difficult for me — they were enchanted with the gift. One child asked if he could have an orange to take home to his little brother. Another said he would bring me ten dollars the next day if I would give him a sack of oranges. And I knew I was at home, that these children and I shared something that *makes* the leap of mind the metaphor attempts. And something in me healed.

A neighbor of mine takes pantyhose and cuts them up and sews them up after stuffing them. Then she puts these things into Mason jars and sells them, you know, to put out on the mantel for conversation. They are little penises and little scrotums, complete with hair. She calls them "Pickled Peters."

A friend of mine had a sister who had a sex change operation. This young woman had her breasts removed and ran around the house with no shirt on before the stitches were taken out. She answered the door one evening. A young man had come to call on my friend. The sex-changed sister invited him in and offered him some black bean soup as if she were perfectly normal with her red surgical wounds and her black stitches. The young man left and never went back. A couple years later, my friend's sister/brother died when s/he ran a car into a concrete bridge railing. I hope for a happier ending. For my brother, for myself, for all of us.

My brother calls. He's done his toenails: Shimmering Cinnamon. And he's left his wife and children and purchased some nightgowns at a yard sale. His hair is getting longer. He wears a special bra. Most of the people he works with know about the changes in his life. His voice is not the same voice I've heard for years; he sounds happy.

My brother calls. He's always envied me, my woman's body. The same body I live in and have cursed for its softness. He asks me how I feel about myself. He says, "You know, you are really our father's first-born son." He tells me he used to want to be me because I was the only person our father almost loved.

The drama of life. After I saw that woman in the bus station eat an orange as if it were an apple, I went out into the street and smoked a joint with some guy I'd met on the bus. Then I hailed a cab and went to a tattoo parlor. The tattoo artist tried to talk me into getting a nice bird or butterfly design; I had chosen a design on his wall that appealed to me — a symbol I didn't know the meaning of. It is the Yin-Yang, and it's tattooed above my right ankle bone. I suppose my drugged, crazed consciousness knew more than I knew: that yin combines with yang to produce all that comes to be. I am drawn to androgyny.

Of course there is the nagging possibility that my brother's dilemma is genetic. Our father used to dress in drag on Halloween, and he made a beautiful woman. One year, the year my mother cut my brother's blond curls off, my father taped those curls to his own head and tied a silk scarf over the tape. Even his close friends didn't know it was him. And my youngest daughter was a body builder for a while, her lean body as muscular as a man's. And my sons are beautiful, not handsome: they look androgynous.

Then there's my grandson. I saw him when he was less than an hour old. He was naked and had hiccups. I watched as he had his first bath, and I heard him cry. He had not been named yet, but his little crib had a blue card affixed to it with tape. And on the card were the words "Baby Boy." There was no doubt in me that the words were true.

When my brother was born, my father was off flying jets in Korea. I went to the hospital with my grandfather to get my mother and this new brother. I remember how I wanted a sister, and I remember looking at him as my mother held him in the front seat of the car. I was certain he was a sister, certain that my mother was joking. She removed his diaper to show me that he was a boy. I still didn't believe her. Considering what has happened lately, I wonder if my child-skewed consciousness knew more than the anatomical proof suggested.

I try to make peace with myself. I try to understand his decision to alter himself. I try to think of him as her. I write his woman name, and I feel like I'm betraying myself. I try to be open-minded, but something in me shuts down. I think we humans are in big trouble, that many of us don't really have a clue as to what acceptable human behavior is. Something in me says no to all this, that this surgery business is the ultimate betrayal of the self. And yet, I want my brother to be happy.

It was in the city of San Antonio that my father had his surgery. I rode the bus from Kansas to Texas, and arrived at the hospital two days after the operation to find my father sitting in the solarium playing solitaire. He had a type of cancer that particularly thrived on testosterone. And so he was castrated in order to ease his pain and to stop the growth of tumors. He died six months later.

Back in the sleep of the large world of dreams, I have done surgeries under water in which I float my father's testicles back into him, and he — the brutal man he was — emerges from the pool a tan and smiling man, parting the surface of the water with his perfect head. He loves all the grief away.

I will tell my brother all I know of oranges, that if you squeeze the orange peel into a flame, small fires happen because of the volatile oil in the peel. Also, if you squeeze the peel and it gets into your cat's eyes, the cat will blink and blink. I will tell him there is no perfect rhyme for the word "orange," and that if we can just make up a good word we can be immortal. We will become obsessed with finding the right word, and I will be joyous at our legitimate pursuit.

I have purchased a black camisole with lace to send to my new sister. And a card. On the outside of the card there's a drawing of a woman sitting by a pond and a zebra is off to the left. Inside are these words: "The past is ended. Be happy." And I have asked my companions to hold me and I have cried. My self is wet and small. But it is not dark. Sometimes, if no one touches me, I will die.

Sister, you are the best craziness of the family. Brother, love what you love.

SHELBY STEELE

On Being Black and Middle Class

FROM COMMENTARY

NOT LONG AGO a friend of mine, black like myself, said to me
that the term "black middle class" was actually a contradiction
in terms. Race, he insisted, blurred class distinctions among
blacks. If you were black, you were just black and that was that.
When I argued, he let his eyes roll at my naiveté. Then he went
on. For us, as black professionals, it was an exercise in self-
flattery, a pathetic pretension, to give meaning to such a distinction. Worse, the very idea of class threatened the unity that was
vital to the black community as a whole. After all, since when
had white America taken note of anything but color when it
came to blacks? He then reminded me of an old Malcolm X line
that had been popular in the sixties. Question: What is a black
man with a Ph.D.? Answer: A nigger.

For many years I had been on my friend's side of this argument. Much of my conscious thinking on the old conundrum of
race and class was shaped during my high school and college
years in the race-charged sixties, when the fact of my race took
on an almost religious significance. Progressively, from the mid-
sixties on, more and more aspects of my life found their explanation, their justification, and their motivation in race. My
youthful concerns about career, romance, money, values, and
even styles of dress became a subject to consultation with various
oracular sources of racial wisdom. And these ranged from a
figure as ennobling as Martin Luther King, Jr., to the under-

SHELBY STEELE   235

world elegance of dress I found in jazz clubs on the South Side
of Chicago. Everywhere there were signals, and in those days I
considered myself so blessed with clarity and direction that I
pitied my white classmates who found more embarrassment
than guidance in the fact of *their* race. In 1968, inflated by my
new power, I took a mischievous delight in calling them cultur-
ally disadvantaged.

But now, hearing my friend's comment was like hearing a
priest from a church I'd grown disenchanted with. I understood
him, but my faith was weak. What had sustained me in the
sixties sounded monotonous and off the mark in the eighties.
For me, race had lost much of its juju, its singular capacity to
conjure meaning. And today, when I honestly look at my life
and the lives of many other middle-class blacks I know, I can
see that race never fully explained our situation in American
society. Black though I may be, it is impossible for me to sit in
my single-family house with two cars in the driveway and a
swing set in the back yard and *not* see the role class has played
in my life. And how can my friend, similarly raised and similarly
situated, not see it?

Yet despite my certainty I felt a sharp tug of guilt as I tried to
explain myself over my friend's skepticism. He is a man of many
comedic facial expressions and, as I spoke, his brow lifted in
extreme moral alarm as if I were uttering the unspeakable. His
clear implication was that I was being elitist and possibly (dare
he suggest?) anti-black — crimes for which there might well be
no redemption. He pretended to fear for me. I chuckled along
with him, but inwardly I did wonder at myself. Though I never
doubted the validity of what I was saying, I felt guilty saying it.
Why?

After he left (to retrieve his daughter from a dance lesson) I
realized that the trap I felt myself in had a tiresome familiarity
and, in a sort of slow-motion epiphany, I began to see its outline.
It was like the suddenly sharp vision one has at the end of a
burdensome marriage when all the long-repressed incompati-
bilities come undeniably to light.

What became clear to me is that people like myself, my friend,
and middle-class blacks generally are caught in a very specific
double bind that keeps two equally powerful elements of our

identity at odds with each other. The middle-class values by which we were raised — the work ethic, the importance of education, the value of property ownership, of respectability, of "getting ahead," of stable family life, of initiative, of self-reliance, etc. — are, in themselves, raceless and even assimilationist. They urge us toward participation in the American mainstream, toward integration, toward a strong identification with the society — and toward the entire constellation of qualities that are implied in the word "individualism." These values are almost rules for how to prosper in a democratic, free-enterprise society that admires and rewards individual effort. They tell us to work hard for ourselves and our families and to seek our opportunities whenever they appear, inside or outside the confines of whatever ethnic group we may belong to.

But the particular pattern of racial identification that emerged in the sixties and that still prevails today urges middle-class blacks (and all blacks) in the opposite direction. This pattern asks us to see ourselves as an embattled minority, and it urges an adversarial stance toward the mainstream, an emphasis on ethnic consciousness over individualism. It is organized around an implied separatism.

The opposing thrust of these two parts of our identity results in the double bind of middle-class blacks. There is no forward movement on either plane that does not constitute backward movement on the other. This was the familiar trap I felt myself in while talking with my friend. As I spoke about class, his eyes reminded me that I was betraying race. Clearly, the two indispensable parts of my identity were a threat to each other.

Of course when you think about it, class and race are both similar in some ways and also naturally opposed. They are two forms of collective identity with boundaries that intersect. But whether they clash or peacefully coexist has much to do with how they are defined. Being both black and middle class becomes a double bind when class and race are defined in sharply antagonistic terms, so that one must be repressed to appease the other.

But what is the "substance" of these two identities, and how does each establish itself in an individual's overall identity? It seems to me that when we identify with any collective we are basically identifying with images that tell us what it means to be a member of that collective. Identity is not the same thing as the fact of membership in a collective; it is, rather, a form of self-definition, facilitated by images of what we wish our membership in the collective to mean. In this sense, the images we identify with may reflect the aspirations of the collective more than they reflect reality, and their content can vary with shifts in those aspirations.

But the process of identification is usually dialectical. It is just as necessary to say what we are *not* as it is to say what we are — so that finally identification comes about by embracing a polarity of positive and negative images. To identify as middle class, for example, I must have both positive and negative images of what being middle class entails; then I will know what I should and should not be doing in order to be middle class. The same goes for racial identity.

In the racially turbulent sixties the polarity of images that came to define racial identification was very antagonistic to the polarity that defined middle-class identification. One might say that the positive images of one lined up with the negative images of the other, so that to identify with both required either a contortionist's flexibility or a dangerous splitting of the self. The double bind of the black middle class was in place.

The black middle class has always defined its class identity by means of positive images gleaned from middle- and upper-class white society, and by means of negative images of lower-class blacks. This habit goes back to the institution of slavery itself, when "house" slaves both mimicked the whites they served and held themselves above the "field" slaves. But in the sixties the old bourgeois impulse to dissociate from the lower classes (the "we-they" distinction) backfired when racial identity suddenly called for the celebration of this same black lower class. One of the qualities of a double bind is that one feels it more than sees it, and I distinctly remember the tension and strange sense of dishonesty I felt in those days as I moved back and forth like a bigamist between the demands of class and race.

Though my father was born poor, he achieved middle-class standing through much hard work and sacrifice (one of his favorite words) and by identifying fully with solid middle-class values — mainly hard work, family life, property ownership, and education for his children (all four of whom have advanced degrees). In his mind these were not so much values as laws of nature. People who embodied them made up the positive images in his class polarity. The negative images came largely from the blacks he had left behind because they were "going nowhere."

No one in my family remembers how it happened, but as time went on, the negative images congealed into an imaginary character named Sam, who, from the extensive service we put him to, quickly grew to mythic proportions. In our family lore he was sometimes a trickster, sometimes a boob, but always possessed of a catalogue of sly faults that gave up graphic images of everything we should not be. On sacrifice: "Sam never thinks about tomorrow. He wants it now or he doesn't care about it." On work: "Sam doesn't favor it too much." On children: "Sam likes to have them but not to raise them." On money: "Sam drinks it up and pisses it out." On fidelity: "Sam has to have two or three women." On clothes: "Sam features loud clothes. He likes to see and be seen." And so on. Sam's persona amounted to a negative instruction manual in class identity.

I don't think that any of us believed Sam's faults were accurate representations of lower-class black life. He was an instrument of self-definition, not of sociological accuracy. It never occurred to us that he looked very much like the white racist stereotype of blacks, or that he might have been a manifestation of our own racial self-hatred. He simply gave us a counterpoint against which to express our aspirations. If self-hatred was a factor, it was not, for us, a matter of hating lower-class blacks but of hating what we did not want to be.

Still, hate or love aside, it is fundamentally true that my middle-class identity involved a dissociation from images of lower-class black life and a corresponding identification with values and patterns of responsibility that are common to the middle class everywhere. These values sent me a clear message: be both an individual and a responsible citizen; understand that the quality of your life will approximately reflect the quality of effort you put into it; know that individual responsibility is the basis of freedom and that the limitations imposed by fate (whether fair or unfair) are no excuse for passivity.

Whether I live up to these values or not, I know that my acceptance of them is the result of lifelong conditioning. I know also that I share this conditioning with middle-class people of all races and that I can no more easily be free of it than I can be free of my race. Whether all this got started because the black middle class modeled itself on the white middle class is no longer relevant. For the middle-class black, conditioned by these values from birth, the sense of meaning they provide is as immutable as the color of his skin.

I started the sixties in high school feeling that my class-conditioning was the surest way to overcome racial barriers. My racial identity was pretty much taken for granted. After all, it was obvious to the world that I was black. Yet I ended the sixties in graduate school a little embarrassed by my class background and with an almost desperate need to be "black." The tables had turned. I knew very clearly (though I struggled to repress it) that my aspirations and my sense of how to operate in the world came from my class background, yet "being black" required certain attitudes and stances that made me feel secretly a little duplicitous. The inner compatibility of class and race I had known in 1960 was gone.

For blacks, the decade between 1960 and 1969 saw racial identification undergo the same sort of transformation that national identity undergoes in times of war. It became more self-conscious, more narrowly focused, more prescribed, less tolerant of opposition. It spawned an implicit party line, which tended to disallow competing forms of identity. Race-as-identity was lifted from the relative slumber it knew in the fifties and pressed into service in a social and political war against oppression. It was redefined along sharp adversarial lines and directed toward the goal of mobilizing the great mass of black Americans in this warlike effort. It was imbued with a strong moral authority, useful for denouncing those who opposed it and for celebrating those who honored it as a positive achievement rather than as a mere birthright.

The form of racial identification that quickly evolved to meet this challenge presented blacks as a racial monolith, a singular people with a common experience of oppression. Differences within the race, no matter how ineradicable, had to be minimized. Class distinctions were one of the first such differences to be sacrificed, since they not only threatened racial unity but also seemed to stand in contradiction to the principle of equality which was the announced goal of the movement for racial progress. The discomfort I felt in 1969, the vague but relentless sense of duplicity, was the result of a historical necessity that put my race and class at odds, that was asking me to cast aside the distinction of my class and identify with a monolithic view of my race.

If the form of this racial identity was the monolith, its substance was victimization. The civil rights movement and the more radical splinter groups of the late sixties were all dedicated to ending racial victimization, and the form of black identity that emerged to facilitate this goal made blackness and victimization virtually synonymous. Since it was our victimization more than any other variable that identified and unified us, moreover, it followed logically that the purest black was the poor black. It was images of him that clustered around the positive pole of the race polarity; all other blacks were, in effect, required to identify with him in order to confirm their own blackness.

Certainly there were more dimensions to the black experience than victimization, but no other had the same capacity to fire the indignation needed for war. So, again out of historical necessity, victimization became the overriding focus of racial identity. But this only deepened the double bind for middle-class blacks like me. When it came to class we were accustomed to defining ourselves against lower-class blacks and identifying with at least the values of middle-class whites; when it came to race we were now being asked to identify with images of lower-class blacks and to see whites, middle class or otherwise, as victimizers. Negative lining up with positive, we were called upon to reject what we had previously embraced and to embrace what we had previously rejected. To put it still more personally, the Sam figure I had been raised to define myself against had now become the "real" black I was expected to identify with.

The fact that the poor black's new status was only passively earned by the condition of his victimization, not by assertive, positive action, made little difference. Status was status apart from the means by which it was achieved, and along with it came a certain power — the power to define the terms of access to that status, to say who was black and who was not. If a lower-class black said you were not really "black" — a sellout, an Uncle Tom — the judgment was all the more devastating because it carried the authority of his status. And this judgment soon enough came to be accepted by many whites as well.

In graduate school I was once told by a white professor, "Well, but . . . you're not really black. I mean, you're not disadvantaged." In his mind my lack of victim status disqualified me from the race itself. More recently I was complimented by a black student for speaking reasonably correct English, "proper" English as he put it. "But I don't know if I really want to talk like that," he went on. "Why not?" I asked. "Because then I wouldn't be black no more," he replied without a pause.

To overcome his marginal status, the middle-class black had to identify with a degree of victimization that was beyond his actual experience. In college (and well beyond) we used to play a game called "nap matching." It was a game of one-upmanship, in which we sat around outdoing each other with stories of racial victimization, symbolically measured by the naps of our hair. Most of us were middle class and so had few personal stories to relate, but if we could not match naps with our own biographies, we would move on to those legendary tales of victimization that came to us from the public domain.

The single story that sat atop the pinnacle of racial victimization for us was that of Emmett Till, the Northern black teenager who, on a visit to the South in 1955, was killed and grotesquely mutilated for supposedly looking at or whistling at (we were never sure which, though we argued the point endlessly) a white woman. Oh, how we probed his story, finding in his youth and Northern upbringing the quintessential embodiment of black innocence, brought down by a white evil so portentous and apocalyptic, so gnarled and hideous, that it left us with a feeling not far from awe. By telling his story and others like it, we came to *feel* the immutability of our victimization, its utter indigenousness, as a thing on this earth like dirt or sand or water.

Of course, these sessions were a ritual of group identification, a means by which we, as middle-class blacks, could be at one with our race. But why were we, who had only a moderate experience of victimization (and that offset by opportunities our parents never had), so intent on assimilating or appropriating an identity that in so many ways contradicted our own? Because, I think, the sense of innocence that is always entailed in feeling victimized filled us with a corresponding feeling of entitlement, or even license, that helped us endure our vulnerability on a largely white college campus.

In my junior year in college I rode to a debate tournament with three white students and our faculty coach, an elderly English professor. The experience of being the lone black in a group of whites was so familiar to me that I thought nothing of it as our trip began. But then halfway through the trip the professor casually turned to me and, in an isn't-the-world-funny sort of tone, said that he had just refused to rent an apartment in a house he owned to a "very nice" black couple because their color would "offend" the white couple who lived downstairs. His eyebrows lifted helplessly over his hawkish nose, suggesting that he too, like me, was a victim of America's racial farce. His look assumed a kind of comradeship: he and I were above this grimy business of race, though for expediency we had occasionally to concede the world its madness.

My vulnerability in this situation came not so much from the professor's blindness to his own racism as from his assumption that I would participate in it, that I would conspire with him against my own race so that he might remain comfortably blind. Why did he think I would be amenable to this? I can only guess that he assumed my middle-class identity was so complete and all-encompassing that I would see his action as nothing more than a trifling concession to the folkways of our land, that I would in fact applaud his decision not to disturb propriety. Blind to both his own racism and to me — one blindness serving the other — he could not recognize that he was asking me to betray my race in the name of my class.

His blindness made me feel vulnerable because it threatened to expose my own repressed ambivalence. His comment pressured me to choose between my class identification, which had contributed to my being a college student and a member of the debating team, and my desperate desire to be "black." I could have one but not both; I was double-bound.

Because double binds are repressed there is always an element of terror in them: the terror of bringing to the conscious mind the buried duplicity, self-deception, and pretense involved in serving two masters. This terror is the stuff of vulnerability, and since vulnerability is one of the least tolerable of all human feelings, we usually transform it into an emotion that seems to restore the control of which it has robbed us; most often, that emotion is anger. And so, before the professor had even finished his little story, I had become a furnace of rage. The year was 1967, and I had been primed by endless hours of nap-matching to feel, at least consciously, completely at one with the victim-focused black identity. This identity gave me the license, and the impunity, to unleash upon this professor one of those volcanic eruptions of racial indignation familiar to us from the novels of Richard Wright. Like Cross Damon in *Outsider,* who kills in perfectly righteous anger, I tried to annihilate the man. I punished him not according to the measure of his crime but according to the measure of my vulnerability, a measure set by the cumulative tension of years of repressed terror. Soon I saw that terror in *his* face, as he stared hollow-eyed at the road ahead. My white friends in the back seat, knowing no conflict between their own class and race, were astonished that someone they had taken to be so much like themselves could harbor a rage that for all the world looked murderous.

Though my rage was triggered by the professor's comment, it was deepened and sustained by a complex of need, conflict, and repression in myself of which I had been wholly unaware. Out of my racial vulnerability I had developed the strong need of an identity with which to defend myself. The only such identity available was that of me as victim, him as victimizer. Once in the grip of this paradigm, I began to do far more damage to myself than he had done.

Seeing myself as a victim meant that I clung all the harder to my racial identity, which, in turn, meant that I suppressed my class identity. This cut me off from all the resources my class values might have offered me. In those values, for instance, I might have found the means to a more dispassionate response, the response less of a victim attacked by a victimizer than of an individual offended by a foolish old man. As an individual I might have reported this professor to the college dean. Or I might have calmly tried to reveal his blindness to him, and possibly won a convert. (The flagrancy of his remark suggested a hidden guilt and even self-recognition on which I might have capitalized. Doesn't confession usually signal a willingness to face oneself?) Or I might have simply chuckled and then let my silence serve as an answer to his provocation. Would not my composure, in any form it might take, deflect into his own heart the arrow he'd shot at me?

Instead, my anger, itself the hair-trigger expression of a long-repressed double bind, not only cut me off from the best of my own resources, it also distorted the nature of my true racial problem. The righteousness of this anger and the easy catharsis it brought buoyed the delusion of my victimization and left me as blind as the professor himself.

As a middle-class black I have often felt myself *contriving* to be "black." And I have noticed this same contrivance in others — a certain stretching away from the natural flow of one's life to align oneself with a victim-focused black identity. Our particular needs are out of sync with the form of identity available to meet those needs. Middle-class blacks need to identify racially; it is better to think of ourselves as black and victimized than not black at all; so we contrive (more unconsciously than consciously) to fit ourselves into an identity that denies our class and fails to address the true source of our vulnerability.

For me this once meant spending inordinate amounts of time at black faculty meetings, though these meetings had little to do with my real racial anxieties or my professional life. I was new to the university, one of two blacks in an English department of over seventy, and I felt a little isolated and vulnerable, though I did not admit it to myself. But at these meetings we discussed the problems of black faculty and students within a framework of victimization. The real vulnerability we felt was covered over by all the adversarial drama the victim/victimized polarity inspired, and hence went unseen and unassuaged. And this, I think, explains our rather chronic ineffectiveness as a group. Since victimization was not our primary problem — the university had long ago opened its doors to us — we had to contrive to make it so, and there is not much energy in contrivance. What I got at these meetings was ultimately an object lesson in how fruitless struggle can be when it is not grounded in actual need.

At our black faculty meetings, the old equation of blackness with victimization was ever present — to be black was to be a victim; therefore, not to be a victim was not to be black. As we contrived to meet the terms of this formula there was an inevitable distortion of both ourselves and the larger university. Through the prism of victimization the university seemed more impenetrable than it actually was, and we more limited in our powers. We fell prey to the victim's myopia, making the university an institution from which we could seek redress but which we could never fully join. And this mind-set often led us to look more for compensations for our supposed victimization than for opportunities we could pursue as individuals.

The discomfort and vulnerability felt by middle-class blacks in the sixties, it could be argued, was a worthwhile price to pay considering the progress achieved during that time of racial confrontation. But what may have been tolerable then is intolerable now. Though changes in American society have made it an anachronism, the monolithic form of racial identification that came out of the sixties is still very much with us. It may be more loosely held, and its power to punish heretics has probably diminished, but it continues to catch middle-class blacks in a double bind, thus impeding not only their own advancement but even, I would contend, that of blacks as a group.

The victim-focused black identity encourages the individual to feel that his advancement depends almost entirely on that of the group. Thus he loses sight not only of his own possibilities but of the inextricable connection between individual effort and individual advancement. This is a profound encumbrance today, when there is more opportunity for blacks than ever before, for it reimposes limitations that can have the same oppressive effect as those the society has only recently begun to remove.

It was the emphasis on mass action in the sixties that made the victim-focused black identity a necessity. But in the eighties and beyond, when racial advancement will come only through a multitude of individual advancements, this form of identity inadvertently adds itself to the forces that hold us back. Hard work, education, individual initiative, stable family life, property ownership — these have always been the means by which ethnic groups have moved ahead in America. Regardless of past or present victimization, these "laws" of advancement apply absolutely to black Americans also. There is no getting around this. What we need is a form of racial identity that energizes the individual by putting him in touch with both his possibilities and his responsibilities.

It has always annoyed me to hear from the mouths of certain arbiters of blackness that middle-class blacks should "reach back" and pull up those blacks less fortunate than they — as though middle-class status were an unearned and essentially passive condition in which one needed a large measure of noblesse oblige to occupy one's time. My own image is of reaching back from a moving train to lift on board those who have no tickets. A noble enough sentiment — but might it not be wiser to show them the entire structure of principles, effort, and sacrifice that puts one in a position to buy a ticket any time one likes? This, I think, is something members of the black middle class can realistically offer to other blacks. Their example is not only a testament to possibility but also a lesson in method. But they cannot lead by example until they are released from a black identity that regards that example as suspect, that sees them as "marginally" black, indeed that holds *them* back by catching them in a double bind.

To move beyond the victim-focused black identity we must learn to make a difficult but crucial distinction: between actual victimization, which we must resist with every resource, and identification with the victim's status. Until we do this we will continue to wrestle more with ourselves than with the new opportunities which so many paid so dearly to win.

ROBERT STONE

Keeping the Future at Bay

FROM HARPER'S MAGAZINE

THE LATE GREAT journalist A. J. Liebling, who imagined the city of New Orleans with the intensity of a true lover, once described it as a combination of Paterson, New Jersey, and Port-au-Prince. Liebling was conjuring up the city before 1960, in most of which Stanley Kowalski would still have been comfortable without a shirt. The high life and the low life were curiously turned and very restricted. It was a poor, peculiar, happy place, where the fateful gaiety of carnival really did last all year long — an antic spirit that savored very much of mortality and the imperfectness of things. Only local black people and a handful of hipsters knew to call it the Big Easy.

With the oil boom, New Orleans acquired a belt of Chiclet suburbs where alligators fled the new white middle class that fled the inner city, divided, ironically, by integration. Million-dollar condominiums were nailed together everywhere in the Vieux Carré. Until 1960 a French Quarter address still carried with it more than a suggestion of bohemian impropriety, and the Monteleone was the only big hotel actually in the Quarter. A few years later there were half a dozen, all of them oozing old-timeyness and simulated essence of magnolia, with menu prose that implied they had been standing at least since Kate Chopin's day. One of them, the Bourbon Orleans, occupied the shell of the convent of the Sisters of the Holy Family. The Sisters were small brown Creole ladies of an ineffable delicacy, and I have often wondered whither they were removed. The convent, as I remember, had fewer stories than the hotel has, although the hotel is no higher. Above Canal Street, the city acquired several brutal square skyscrapers of the sort that seem to require a rooftop sign reading BULLSHIT WALKS — they manage to be tall and squat at the same time.

The New Orleans of my recollection ascended no higher than the white cupola atop the Hibernia Bank Building. I seem to remember chimes that sounded "Abide with Me" over the rattle of the St. Charles streetcar and the newsie's cry and the police whistles. I'll never be sure how much of what I remember is imagined, so readily does this city lend itself to dreams. Memory is subverted, tainted by fantasies that thrive in the languid shadows. People who grew up here tell me it is the same for them, that the way in which they recall lining up for frozen Sno Balls or going to parochial school takes on a certain spin.

At the same time, reality has always been relentless in New Orleans. My daughter was born in Huey Long's Charity Hospital under legal segregation, which meant that everything was done twice, separately, often cheerfully and in theoretical equality but under circumstances that are horrible to contemplate today. There was nothing insubstantial about the poverty, violence, and general squalor that poor people, white or black, endured in the land of dreams. Yet in the worst of times an absurd magic might intrude itself. In the waiting room outside the maternity ward, I fell into conversation with a Cajun farmer who assured me that St. Joseph took special care of first-born children. It was good to hear a friendly word in that hard-boiled but unsanitary place.

Politics had a way of coming to you in Louisiana, circa 1960, even of coming at you, no matter how you tried to hide. For one thing, the desegregation battles were being fought in the streets and in the small towns of the Deep South. About the time I showed up, other young people from the North were appearing all over the South to help in the struggle for black civil rights. I was not among them; instead I was ingloriously supporting my new career as a beatnik, selling encyclopedias door to door in towns such as Bogalusa and Picayune. By some perverse synchronicity I always seemed to appear with my cheap suit and dissembling sales pitch at the very moment when the townsfolk had sworn unspeakable violence against the next

fast-talking scut of a Yankee agitator with the nerve to show his
nose. Northern accents were instantly detected and explana-
tions urgently required. In several places I was rescued by the
police; in others, I was not. I got to see the inside of a couple of
Mississippi and northeast Louisiana jails. To this day, when people from the movement tell war stories and talk Southern pris-
ons, I'm tempted to casually put in my observations on the St.
Tammany Parish lockup compared with the jail in Pearl River
County. But at the time I was a subscriber to art for art's sake,
wanting to be left alone.

The last thing Louisiana needed in 1960 was a few more
beatniks, but there we were. It was existential. We got by with
odd jobs and passing the goblet after poetry readings. There
was a bar on Burgundy Street that featured bunches of bananas
as part of its decor; on evenings when the paying customers
found our performance insufficiently stirring, they would toss
bananas at us to indicate their displeasure. A poet I know
would take the bananas home and eat them with rice and Wor-
cestershire sauce. In those days, the *vie de bohème* was undertaken without state assistance. The only thing forthcoming
from the municipal welfare authorities, should we have been rash
enough to approach them in our penury, would have been a
couple of expletives and the advice to get out of town. We went
from day to day, eating when we worked, fasting otherwise. Our
poverty was not a game; there were no rich relatives back home
to bail us out. On the other hand we always felt just on the edge
of vision, an available cop-out, shameful but perhaps eventually
necessary. One could always go home, get a steady job, maybe
save enough to go to college. Our style, if not our lack of means,
was voluntary.

But around us in those years another kind of poverty ruled,
one that afforded its subjects no redeeming posture. The timeless poverty of the Deep South had not been relieved at that
time, if indeed it has since. For all that things had improved
since the Depression of the thirties, poverty lay like a dark en-
chantment over that part of the country, laving the edges of the
city and flourishing well inside it. Its victims were more often
black than white (although plenty were white). This poverty was
deathly mean and formidable; it embittered people and made

them dangerous; it stunted hope and destroyed even the imagination. Because I was young and male, the aspect of the poor South that most arrested my attention then was its anger and violence. I was looking for experience, wanting to learn. I got it and I learned. Eventually, I saw that poverty and the culture it promotes have a political dimension. Politics, it turned out, was not something I could ignore.

Of course it would have been hard to ignore politics in New Orleans in any case, if in a definition of politics one chooses to include the caperings and adventures of Louisiana politicians. When I first came to the city, Huey Long's younger brother Earl was at the end of his long career, and his eccentricities were prized and recounted angrily or affectionately all over town. When I came to write my first novel, which like all first novelists I made the receptacle of every single thing I knew, I found Louisiana and its politics inevitable. I thought *A Hall of Mirrors* was quite fair to America in important ways, although probably unfair to New Orleans in unimportant ones. I tried never to let on how in love I was with the big soupy city, but it came through anyway. The idea of the Republicans convening in the Superdome aroused in my breast a fierce possessiveness to which I was not in the least entitled.

The town the Republicans came to was a poor place again. Ten years ago, when I had last passed through, New Orleans was on a roll. The squat skyscrapers were shinier and the Quarter was extremely spiffy; some residents worried that progress might sweep the old city beyond recall. Preservation has always been a little difficult in New Orleans, where politicians have traditionally been available for a good time. The old breed of shady white politician had been replaced by a new breed of shady black politician, but money was still green. Subsequently, however, oil took its downturn and the city went back to living off the out-of-towners while waiting for the wheel to come around. In the Vieux Carré, the old walls looked patched and peeled now, and balconies were sagging. The *Times-Picayune* ran a story on the "demolition by neglect" of some of the older buildings. The owners of these buildings, the story said, "either didn't want to spend the money or hoped to let an old building decay so badly that the city would finally allow the owner to tear it down and put the property to more profitable use, such as turning it into a hotel or a parking lot."

My personal standard of measure is the building my wife and I lived in on St. Philip; ten years ago it had been newly renovated, but this August it looked worse than it did when we moved in. Some New Orleans residents I talked to say that the hard times have at least served to maintain the Quarter's character — which depends somewhat on its characters, many of whom may be priced out when the boom comes back. But in the quiet streets away from the hustle and din of Bourbon, the steamy air hung timeless and fragrant and it might have been long ago. You could hear children playing on some of the patios, and caged canaries sang in the balcony windows. All over town the ironwork was dressed in patriotic bunting as the city got itself up for the convention, the old soul sister never more herself than when getting ready for a party. Even good-time girls have their authenticity.

The Louisiana Superdome, the actual site of the four-day convention, is a wonder of the modern age. If the purpose of the vaulted Gothic cathedrals was to remind humanity that God was above, the Superdome serves to remind us that what yawns eternally overhead today is space. Together with the Hyatt Regency and an adjoining shopping mall, to which it is attached by a concrete caul, the Superdome forms an air conditioned island of spic-and-span order right in the middle of funk's own hometown. Within this bastion you can watch the NFL Saints, go to bed, or sip an apéritif at a sidewalk café the temperature of a meat locker. During the convention, the entire complex was as busy as a hive, with delegates, guests, and journalists lining up for food and drink. In the shopping mall, the outer reaches of the Hyatt, and all around the Superdome itself, hucksters were selling Ollie North videotapes, Ronald Reagan masks, political chachkas of every kind. It would not be too much to say that a carnival atmosphere prevailed. Strolling this enormous carnival, I saw ghosts. I took the 1960 census here.

Yes, right here, house to house in the summer heat, I carried my census book, knocking on doors when there were doors to knock on, yoo-hooing into shanties, poking my nose into people's kitchens. The people endured my questions: Place of birth? Estimated yearly income? Mother's full name? Father's? Condition of residence? We didn't ask that one; the answer was always "dilapidated," and we checked the appropriate square.

Where the counter dispensing Libertarian Republican literature stood was once a row of shacks before which half-naked children played among rusting automobile skeletons. On the site of the campaign-button boutique was a storefront church, the Sanctified Temple of the Lord God, in whose window was the painted text: "Sufficient unto the day is the evil thereof." (When I first saw that text in the church window I didn't understand what it meant, though I've since learned.) Under the dome itself, where the band played "Happy Days Are Here Again," was a kind of hotel, unlike the Hyatt Regency, in which solitary people lived in rooms divided at the top by chicken wire, and with candles for light. Where the podium was erected — of course I exaggerate here, but not by much, a block or two — was the house in which I apprehended one of the very few political truths I know. Let me describe the scene.

It is July 1960 and I am alone, deep in the heart of the black slum where many years later the Superdome will rise. I am not, as I certainly would be today, afraid. Not at all, in fact. I've been coming back here for weeks and everybody knows my white face by now. Some people are rather short with me, but many others sit me down with a cool drink and tell me the story of their lives. Never have I known heat like this. Never have I seen such poverty.

I am Tail-end Charlie for the census, I get the hard cases — the brothels, skid row, the B-girl dorms, the transvestites who scared the last census taker away. It's an aspiring young novelist's dream. I'm also assigned to the poorest black areas back-of-town to get people the regulars missed. The fact is, I'm having rather a good time of it. I have taken to the South in a big way. I feel very romantically about it. I've also fallen hard for blackness, in the mindless old-time hipper-than-thou beatnik way. In the weeks I've been in this back-of-town, I've been listening to black speech and watching black moves, and I dig it. It's ringing my young literary bells. It's got something, all right; the rhythms and the raps are sounding in my dreams; I think I'm ready to signify.

Late one afternoon, up against the Illinois Central yards, I check out a ramshackle wooden house suspected of being a household. No one, over the summer, has responded to the bureau's attempts at communication. So I knock . . . and this time there's an answer, a female voice asks me in. Inside, half a dozen people are gathered around a bed. Beside it, a single candle burns at the feet of a plaster Virgin. Cloth blinds have been drawn over the windows to keep back the killing sun, and the candle provides the only light in the room. I advance on the bed. The people in the room have turned to watch me. Looking over their shoulders, I see that lying there, with clean white sheets drawn almost up to her chin, is a very old woman. Her skin is a café-au-lait color and engraved with fine wrinkles. Her toothless face is like an old turtle's. She breathes slowly and with difficulty. She's clearly dying.

I am delighted to learn that the folks in the room are attendant relatives from two different households, an overwhelming tactical coup, census-wise. In my brisk impatience to record the statistical details of everyone's life, it takes me a moment to register the fact that these people are strangely unforthcoming. Looking up from my forms, I confront their eyes. Their eyes are calmly questioning, almost humorous. I stand and stare and return to my jottings, and then suddenly it hits me: someone is dying here. These people have come to attend a death. Perhaps this is not the best of times for census taking? After this death-defying leap of understanding, the rest follows unbidden.

That had this been a white middle-class household I would never have been allowed past the door.

That had this been a white middle-class household I would never have dreamed of entering a sickroom, approaching a deathbed, asking cold irrelevant questions of people who had come to mourn and pray.

That what has happened here is entirely determined by the politics of race and class — how blinding it can be, how dehumanizing, how denying of basic human dignity.

So I left, and walking along Dryades Street in the paralyzing glare, the rest of the wave hit me. The question of why I, a white person from out of town, should have been taking the census here. That there were no black census takers.

So the voice of God was in that wave. A poor thing, a less than

dazzling exercise of the social sensibilities, but mine nevertheless. In the many years since then, I have tried to keep that frail
candle of insight flickering. Through the absurdity and bloody-
mindedness of Race Relations in America, a subject so double-
dipped in hype, phoniness, hustling, hypocrisy, lies, stupidity,
malice, blind ambition, ignorance, groveling, sniveling, and
foolishness that it defies coherence, I've tried to keep it burning.
Life doesn't often pause to allow us a moment of common sense.
Watching the Republicans convene among the ghosts, I tried to
hold it to my heart.

The hotel in which I stayed was beside a freeway and of a
singular crumminess. Unluckily for the management, the New
York delegation was housed there, and in no time at all, a media
blitz of ridicule descended on the unfortunate place. A block
the other side of Canal stood the Iberville Housing Project,
another place I remembered from long ago. In my memory, the
Iberville project had both black and white tenants, the officially
segregated housing blocks alternating racially, so that passersby
could see poor Southern kids, black and white, playing together.
Now the project was officially integrated — and all black. Unemployment in the project ran up to 70 percent. Late one night,
in a welter of blue lights visible from the hotel bar, the police
picked up the body of an unidentified black male in his twenties.
He had been shot through the head, apparently another victim
of the crack wars. It occurred to me that I might have counted
him back in 1960; he might have been one of the babies. There
were so many.
    At the Calliope Street houses, a project that stands in what's
left of the slum the Superdome replaced, residents had their
usual route to Canal Street blocked by chain-link fences installed around the Dome for security purposes. Forced to walk
the long way round, they were able to see the limousines scoot-
ing past, creating a significant juxtaposition no self-respecting
reporter could resist. To Calliope Street went the working press,
eliciting forlorn quotes. These are from the *Times-Picayune:*

> "Ask the politicians if they can cut out the shooting out here," said
> Mayola Brumfield, 40, cradling her granddaughter on a porch step.
>   "Tell them I need a job — bad," said Brenda Sumling, 26.

To all of which the unwritten coda was: Good luck.

A few hundred yards and a world away from Calliope Street, the President was now speaking. I missed a bit of his speech; I had decided to walk from the hotel to the Superdome and cover some of the old ground. This foolish exercise in nostalgia soon found me wandering through Fritz Lang's worst movie, a godforsaken wilderness of cement over which whirled a vortex of ascending and descending freeway ramps. Ghostly figures darted on the edge of the open spaces. I hurried, sweating mightily in the heat, feeling whiter than Moby-Dick and equally pursued. Imagine my relief, then, when I gained admission to the great stadium and heard the dear, familiar voice.

It is not entirely facetious to speak of the President's voice as dear and familiar. Ronald Reagan is one of the most interesting phenomena this country affords, and no examination of contemporary American reality should be undertaken without reference to him. In the Superdome on August 15, he was giving the assembled delegates and their guests enormous pleasure, making them laugh, bringing them to their feet with fierce patriotic cries, and occasionally reducing them to tears.

"Twilight? Not in America. Here it's a sunrise every day. Fresh new opportunities. Dreams to build."

One had the feeling he might have gone on and on and on. What could be dearer or more familiar, a happy mating of *Ursprache* and Muzak, the refined essence of every sunlit daydream crooned in a reassuring, cheery baritone.

Where have we heard it before?

But where have we not heard it?

It's the primal voice of the electronic age, the medium *and* the message, the voice that never sleeps, that cajoles, inspires, and commands wherever cathodes glow. We can no more resist it than oncoming night. For just about as long as Ronald Reagan has been alive, this voice has whispered in our dreams, a manifestation of American reality. Flick a switch and there it is, unresponding but constant, everywhere, every hour. It seems to emanate from some invisible consensus, the voice we have all agreed to hear. It is not the voice of a man; its name is legion. It is inside us. Our consciousness ebbs and flows to its undulation, obedient as tides to the moon. Hearing it, we mistake it for our own.

Dutch Reagan, the man on the radio, is speaking in the voice of American popular culture. No one does it better. One of American popular culture's principal artifacts is a sentimentalized view of America, touched by the dreams of the immigrants, rubes, and carnies who created it. Its media are semaphores, not much good for conveying subtleties. In the language of American popular culture, words cast no shadows. The land to which it speaks is a land without irony, a land without contradictions, a land, in fact, that doesn't exist and never did. All the same, it's the real thing, the McCoy. That's a paradox, the only paradox you have to know in Ronald Reagan's business.

He was a poor kid, his old man drank. God knows what he's really like. But now he's American popular culture's greatest creation since the Wizard of Oz, another glib Midwesterner. Only Reagan's charm is authentic. Otherwise, as a voice or an image on a screen, he's always been the agent of someone else's agenda. Part of America's willingness to forgive him for the disasters of his administration may relate to the sense he gives of having been dragged in arsy-varsy, a secondary figure in his own career, along for the ride. His most effective public gesture is that humorous shrug of incomprehension, a mannerism that appears strangely genuine. To see him do it is to laugh with him, to share his amused befuddlement at the mess the world's in. It's also reassuring. If things are this bad and he's not worried, why should we be?

Inside the Superdome on that Monday night, he was breaking their hearts for a while. And why not? He had perfected his routine before a lot of them were born. Then a balloon popped. For a fraction of a second his rhythm broke, he seemed to lose forward motion. He misspoke a word or two. People looked from the monitors to the podium, but the man himself was too far away, a tiny figure.

It's difficult not to speculate on his inner life. Everybody has one. What resides at the core? What does he mean, "It's morning again in America"? Why should it be morning?

Suddenly, he regains his timing and I have the answer to that. I have only to look at him on the monitor and I know. It's because morning is time for brunch. Brunch is what he's making me think of. Maybe everyone in the audience all across America is listening and thinking of something equally scrumptious. I see it shining plain: it's 11 A.M. and we're in Pacific Palisades and the sun is sparkling on Santa Monica Bay. There will be croissants and honeydew. It's brunch, the California Eucharist, the sustaining reality at the President's core. It makes me feel like cheering, but when the monitors fade, he's gone.

Off the convention floor there were a few swell parties. One was thrown at the Fairmont Hotel by the National Rifle Association, a luncheon with free booze. From the very beginning of the convention, a certain coldness had been in evidence between the working press and the convening Republicans. At the NRA party, this mutual lack of appreciation occasionally threatened to bear fruit. The electronic media had stashed their equipment in the center of the hired ballroom, and the resultant mountain of hardware served as a rallying point for the reporters. From within the laager, a newsman might proceed in reasonable safety to the bar and then, fortified, venture forth in search of a survivalist troglodyte who might be baited into grunting threats and imprecations against decent folk.

In fact there were no camouflage suits to be seen at the NRA's party, the celebrants being, on the whole, better dressed than the press. But though the scene was mainly good-natured, there were volcanic domes of anger over which the crust sat lightly. Among the angriest were the several divines the NRA seemed to have assembled. There was a priest of the old school with a face that would have looked a lot more appetizing on a plate with parsley and horseradish than it did on the front of his head. There was an intense young man in a yarmulke who seemed ready to cast the first stone. I asked the priest if he was a member of the association, a question that reduced him to inchoate rage. He eyed my press pass as if it were a turd or a squirting boutonniere. He was not a member. Before long he was at the podium telling jokes, and I got the feeling that he and I went back a long way together and it was time to go.

The religious dimension was not overlooked in New Orleans. On Tuesday morning, Jerry Falwell spoke to a student symposium on the Tulane campus on the subject of the Moral Majority. Falwell was dapper, brisk, and genial. He allowed that the folly of the Bakkers and Jimmy Swaggart had "hurt the cause of Christ." He said he found the fall of the Bakkers unremarkable; he had been detecting a materialist element in their theology for a long time. In response to a question, he hinted, as he has several times lately, that he was about to undertake a program of civil disobedience. He compared *Roe* v. *Wade* with the Dred Scott decision. He sounded less like the leader of any "majority" than like the organizer of a major pressure group setting out to make trouble for the misguided.

Generally the convention was short on conflict. One of its minor dramas was the public fall of Falwell's fellow preacher, Pat Robertson. Robertson's camp had harbored the only organized disgruntlement left alive by convention time. Over the course of the year his delegates in states such as Michigan and Georgia managed to threaten the seamless fabric of Republican good fellowship. But in the end, Robertson simply failed to gather the money or the votes to back up his candidacy. The opening of the convention found him in the position of a man who had thrown a roundhouse right at the bouncer and connected with the incorporeal air. A muted anti-clericalism prevailed among the party pros. On Tuesday night, Robertson took his wages in the form of an opportunity to address the convention. He was less than electrifying. As his speech progressed, it was possible to stand at the exits and watch the crowds streaming out into the night, bound for Antoine's and Mahogany Hall. His press conference the next morning at the Intercontinental Hotel had a somber, penitential tone.

Barely a dozen reporters were present. These were equally divided between the Old Sweats, who had followed Robertson through the primaries, and the Marginals, who included this writer and an amiably nerdish young man in a baseball hat inscribed with the words ATHEIST AND PROUD. The young man described himself as "Chicago bureau chief" for the American Atheist Press. A beefy front-page type from *USA Today* asked him if there are also Rome and Jerusalem bureau chiefs. While waiting for Pat, several journalists interviewed the bureau chief, who recounted for them the variety of insults, threats, and putdowns visited upon him over the previous two days by godly Republicans. Presently Robertson arrived, smiling his smile and looking philosophical. He and the atheist were old pals; indeed, Robertson looked grateful for the company. Most of the reporters wanted to know about Robertson's plans for the future; they were assured that he would carry on. It was hard to believe, though. As Robertson left the room, the Chicago bureau chief of the American Atheist Press was pursuing his press secretary, Barbara Gattullo.

"Barbara, can Pat be on my radio show?"

Iowa was long gone. It was deepest Palookaville.

On the very same morning that Pat Robertson was facing the music, a state judge on the other side of the Mississippi was writing a footnote to another American religious career. Debra Arleen Murphree, the temptress before whose allure the redoubtable Jimmy Swaggart's Christian resolve did a fast fade, was dispatched to the Jefferson Parish Jail for six months, having copped a misdemeanor for prostitution. This timely retribution at the height of the convention may have preserved the career of some anonymous Republican state committeeman, who, atremble with self-destructive lust, might have flung himself on her scented settee down there on the Airline Highway.

As the convention opened, the Republicans had little to offer sensation seekers except a degree of suspense over George Bush's choice of a running mate. Bush himself had said that he would not announce a choice until Thursday, whereupon, it was thought, the selection might be dramatized at the anointing ceremony that evening. But as early as Sunday, rumors began to fly, and their flap and flutter was distracting. It was also believed that the notables on Bush's shortlist were not happy about having to spend the week standing around in their bathing suits. Robert Dole, who seemed to move through the convention in a storm of smiling, saturnine rage, made his displeasure public. Finally the rumors began to hint that Bush had not made up his own mind, a notion which invited mental images of the Vice President in one of his screwball-comedy states, dithering fatuously and plucking daisy petals. So on Tuesday, when the mighty paddle wheeler *Natchez* brought Bush down from Belle Chasse Naval Station to Spanish Plaza, Bush introduced Dan Quayle to the welcoming crowd and the word spread around town. Not all delegates, to say the least, were pleased with Bush's decision. Some of Jack Kemp's supporters, who were young, energetic, and numerous, cried real tears.

But the blow fell hardest on the remnants of what used to be called the Eastern Republican Establishment, now reduced to a grim band of *conversos* practicing their ancient faith in secret. For at least the last four years, they had been sporting kelly green slacks and white loafers, trying to pass as right-to-lifing Holy Rollers, while stealthily sipping scotch and dreaming that Nelson Rockefeller is alive in the heart of a mountain somewhere. Throughout the convention they had been buttonholing media acquaintances with assurances about George Bush's personal excellence. At any moment, they held, Bush would come into his own and reveal himself as the sensible and sophisticated Yalie he truly is. What they got was Quayle.

On Wednesday, while Pat Robertson was sparring with the Chicago bureau chief of the American Atheist Press, the conventional press was slapping Quayle around the grand ballroom of the Marriott. He was then hustled over to the Sheraton for a friendly session with the California Republican Caucus. Outside, party flacks were pointing out Quayle's valor in choosing to help defend Indianapolis from the San Francisco Mime Troupe. Inside all was groovy. Jack Kemp, a native Californian, signed on enthusiastically, prompting a few more tears from the young surfers. Senator Pete Wilson spoke. Quayle declared his ferocious impatience to campaign against Dukakis and Bentsen.

The press joke about the selection of Quayle was that "George Bush wanted a George Bush," but that wasn't it. Quayle had none of Bush's Washington experience. According to Germond and Witcover's piece in the *National Journal's Convention Daily,* Quayle's name did not appear on a shortlist of pickable senators compiled by Senator Mitch McConnell of Kentucky. Many people at the convention attributed the choice of Quayle to Roger Ailes, George Bush's media consultant, who happens also to be a consultant for Quayle. A dream deal in the Hollywood mode, a media fix so pure it could almost be called nonpolitical.

The following day, Thursday, the Republican Mainstream Committee met at the Howard Johnson Downtown. The Mainstream Republicans were many, but the room in which they met was very small indeed. The chairman of the meeting was Congressman Jim Leach from the First District of Iowa. The press attendance was meager, featuring those birds of ill omen, *Harper's Magazine* and the American Atheist Press. Many present at the Mainstream meeting were young, and they seemed idealistic in an old-fashioned, innocent way. Discussion tended to be rather abstract; there was talk of a struggle for the soul of the party, and of the necessity for a Republican party with some social responsibility. There were general expressions of support for the ticket and attempts to find common Republican ground. The only tangible expression of common ground expressed was an opposition to taxes. The Libertarian tendency seemed to predominate.

One of the Republicans at the meeting was Harriet Stinson of the California Republicans for Choice. The CRC had prepared a flyer it intended to distribute arguing a pro-choice position on the abortion issue. The flyers bore a few signatures that had once meant something in the Republican party — Barry Goldwater, Charles H. Percy, S. I. Hayakawa, and Rebecca Q. Morgan of the California State Senate. Harriet Stinson had Federal Expressed her flyers to a convention hotel, where the entire consignment disappeared. Asked if she believed that the consignment had been hijacked by an anti-abortionist faction, she replied that, indeed, she suspected that was the case.

Celeste King of the California Black Republican Council pointed out that when Vice President Bush landed at Spanish Plaza the only black on the platform was a high school kid playing the trumpet. King called the situation unacceptable.

So the Mainstream Republicans got nothing from George Bush's post-Reaganite Republican party. Black Republicans got practically nothing but the brief presence of Coretta Scott King in Bush's gallery, where she and the candidate acknowledged the applause of the convention. The Wall Street *conversos* got to hear the languid upscale tones of Governor Tom Kean's keynote address. Regarding the platform and the vice presidency, the right had everything its own way, and with the candidate's enthusiastic blessing. The moderates could lump it.

"The damn thing is," remarked one Mainstreamer, an alternate at the convention, "those people never could stand George

Bush." She meant the religious right and ultraconservatives. "He was always our man." By "our" she meant what the Robertson people liked to call the country-club set. She was watching "her man" being borne forward on the shields of the barbarians. Later in the week, Mainstreamers were speculating that everything might be different when Bush won election.

The delegates, alternates, and guests present in the Superdome performed a function somewhere between that of a studio audience and a laugh track. The audience could hardly behold the physical presence of its heroes; as mentioned, each speaker was a tiny figure unrecognizable across the Superdome's great spaces. Huge Orwellian monitors displayed talking heads at various points around the arena so that, in the stands and on the floor, people faced in different directions, watching different screens. As a result, there was little sense of unity, no true crowd to become a single animal with a single voice in the grand old style. There were milling, isolated groups. The sound system that carried the speeches was particularly poor. In some parts of the Dome the speaker's remarks were absolutely inaudible. For this reason, the prepared tapes that introduced the President on Monday night and George Bush on Thursday provoked a more emotional reaction than their remarks. Television speaks to isolation, and the 1988 Republican National Convention was television and little else. Being in the Superdome was a little like being on a movie set or behind the scenes at a television studio.

Late one night, CNN showed some footage of the 1952 Republican convention, at which General Douglas MacArthur was the keynote speaker. Plummy and orotund, the general's style was not well suited to a "cool medium." The cameras saved him from absurdity only by keeping their distance. The world that this footage evoked seemed hard to imagine. It appeared to be a grayer, riskier, and somehow more serious place, more than a little frightening. The Republicans in New Orleans thirty-six years later were trying hard not to affright a soul. As noted earlier, it was morning — all week, around the clock. The background colors on the monitors could adjust themselves as if by magic to tones complementary to the flesh and apparel of the speaker. The effect sought was similar to that of a beer commercial.

Amid this kind of flummery, it can be extremely difficult to maintain consistent standards. How to tell the wax from the Shinola? How to react, when references to love of country, honor, courage, and fidelity are shoveled into the hopper and ground into televised gruel to the throbbing of strings? Nihilism gapes beneath the pilgrim. The mind becomes taxed with the necessity of correctly perceiving the apparently obvious. Is American politics all a deception, designed to clothe a system of patronage? If it is, is that all right? And if American politics is all a deception, does not modern history show other systems to be equally so? Are we not apes with flags and speeches? Surely it will be necessary to go away somewhere and think about all this. Seen from within the core of its creation, such a media event reduces everything to the significance of Michelob Light.

No nation whose people are unable to recognize their own social superiors can be said to have lost its innocence. So the convention, like the country, continued to puzzle over George Bush's attempts to be a regular guy. Most of the week, the press eye-balled him like so many shrinks at a lunacy hearing, watching for popped synapses, spasms, and false moves. It must have taken considerable nerve to endure. There was a lot of slightly hysterical finger-pointing when he referred to his grandchildren as "the little brown ones"; fortunately, it soon stopped. Eventually, to the relief and disappointment of many, he more or less made it through. By the time he stepped away from the podium on Thursday night he appeared to have weathered the passage from goofy diffidence to button-eyed vulgarity.

The speech he made was of the sort generally described as "effective." Bush delivered it convincingly and it was extremely optimistic, from a certain point of view. It described America as a rising nation and predicted a second American Century. That is certainly a sort of patriotism, although not necessarily the sort we require at this period in our history. At one point, in summing up our country's achievements, he said we had "lit the world with our culture." I thought "lit" sounded a trifle electric. Later in his text, the Vice President was made to describe himself as a "quiet man," and this seemed an inspired phrase. "Quiet" is not entirely the word for the way George Bush appears, but it is an extremely sympathetic way of describing it.

"You are history," said George Bush to "the drug dealers," those swart banditos of American political song and legend. "Read my lips," he declared to any who might doubt his resolve to hold the line on taxes. This colorful lingo was a property of the new Bush, the one with the common touch, capable of exchanging the idiom of the country day school for that of the regional junior high.

So who is this George Bush? You have to believe he's a man who does good by stealth. No one in American public life is surrounded by so many favorable rumors and benign innuendos. Almost everyone who knows him personally says he's wonderful. Yet publicly he appears . . . "quiet."

The real point is that in order to become the Republican candidate for the presidency the Vice President has embraced some very intolerant and retrograde elements with whom he has not heretofore been associated. Perhaps, as he says of his stand on abortion, he has "changed his mind" on various issues.

Bush may well ride his successful convention appearances all the way to the White House. Then, perhaps, the inner excellence he's said to have will emerge in the fullness of time, expressed in policy. Perhaps not. And if George Bush doesn't care what he's really like, why should anyone else?

In August of 1988, Bush took charge of a Reagan-enchanted party, rigid with complacency. Against the backdrop of contemporary New Orleans, the party's convention looked even more unreal than its media specialists sought to make it. There are many other American landscapes upon which it would have appeared ephemeral and fantastic, not because of the lights and the music but because of what Bush might be induced to call "the vision thing." Again and again at this convention, speaker after Republican speaker affirmed that his party would carry this country into the future, as though it was a trick only they could manage. In fact they were promising to keep the future at bay. The future does not require the Republicans; it will come.

As the convention drew to a close, Bush left the podium and they released the balloons. It was a moment we'd all been waiting for, and it was quite amusing to watch the balloons and confetti drift down past the cold ironical smiles of the foreign press corps. Not all of them looked ready for another American Century. Guests, the press, the delegates, and alternates began filing toward the exits. Outside, the air was heavy with impending rain, smelling of history. People went in groups, searching for the buses or peering anxiously up Loyola Avenue for a taxi. The future we'd heard so much about was gathering in the darkness. The evening was ending as so many contemporary evenings do, in the search for a safe way home.

GAY TALESE

The Brave Tailors of Maida

FROM ESQUIRE

THERE IS A certain type of mild mental disorder that is endemic in the tailoring trade, and it began to weave its way into my father's psyche during his apprentice days in Italy, when he worked in the shop of a volatile craftsman named Francesco Cristiani, whose male forebears had been tailors for four successive generations and had, without exception, exhibited symptoms of this occupational malady.

Although it has never attracted scientific curiosity and therefore cannot be classified by an official name, my father once described the disorder as a form of prolonged melancholia that occasionally erupts into cantankerous fits — the result, my father suggested, of excessive hours of slow, exacting, microscopic work that proceeds stitch by stitch, inch by inch, mesmerizing the tailor in the reflected light of a needle flickering in and out of the fabric.

A tailor's eye must follow a seam precisely, but his pattern of thought is free to veer off in different directions, to delve into his life, to ponder his past, to lament lost opportunities, create dramas, imagine slights, brood, exaggerate — in simple terms, the man, when sewing, has too much time to think.

My father, who served as an apprentice each day before and after school, was aware that certain tailors could sit quietly at the workbench for hours, cradling a garment between their bowed heads and crossed knees, and sew without exercise or much physical movement, without any surge of fresh oxygen to clear their brains. Then, with inexplicable suddenness, my fa-

ther would see one of these men jump to his feet and take wild
umbrage at a casual comment of a co-worker, a trivial exchange
that was not intended to provoke. And my father would often
cower in a corner as spools and steel thimbles flew around the
room — and, if goaded by insensitive colleagues, the aroused
tailor might reach for the workroom's favorite instrument of
terror, the sword-length scissors.

There were also confrontations in the front of the store in
which my father worked, disputes between the customers and
the proprietor — the diminutive and vainglorious Francesco
Cristiani, who took enormous pride in his occupation and believed that he, and the tailors under his supervision, were incapable of making a serious mistake; if they were, he was not likely
to acknowledge it.

Once when a customer came in to try on a new suit but was
unable to slip into the jacket because the sleeves were too narrow, Francesco Cristiani not only failed to apologize to the
client; he behaved as if insulted by the client's ignorance of the
Cristiani shop's unique style in men's fashion. "You are not
supposed to put your arms *through* the sleeves of this jacket!"
Cristiani informed his client, in a superior tone. "This jacket is
only designed to be worn *over the shoulders!*"

On another occasion, when Cristiani paused in the Maida
square after lunch to listen to the band during its midday concert, he noticed that the new uniform that had been delivered
the day before to the third trumpeter showed a bulge behind
the collar whenever the musician lifted the instrument to his
lips.

Concerned that someone might notice it and cast aspersions
on his status as a tailor, Cristiani dispatched my father, then a
skinny boy of eight, to sneak up behind the bunting of the
bandstand and, with furtive finesse, pull down on the end of
the trumpeter's jacket whenever the bulge appeared. When the
concert was over, Cristiani contrived a subtle means by which
he was able to reacquire and repair the jacket.

Around this time, in the spring of 1911, there occurred a
catastrophe in the shop for which there seemed to be no possible
solution. The problem was so serious, in fact, that Cristiani's
first reaction was to leave town for a while rather than remain

in Maida to face the consequences. The incident that provoked such panic had taken place in Cristiani's workroom on the Saturday before Easter, and it centered on the damage done by an apprentice, accidentally but irreparably, to a new suit that had been made for one of Cristiani's most demanding customers — a man who was among the region's renowned *uomini rispettati*, men of respect, popularly known as the Mafia.

Before Cristiani became aware of the accident, he had enjoyed a prosperous morning in his shop collecting payment from several satisfied customers who had come in for the final try-on of their attire, which they would wear on the following day at the Easter *passeggiata*, the most exhibitionistic event of the year for the men of southern Italy. While the modest women of the village — except for the bolder wives of American immigrants — would spend the day after Mass discreetly perched on their balconies, the men would stroll in the square, chatting with each other as they walked arm in arm, smoking and shiftily examining the fit of each other's new suits. For despite the poverty in southern Italy, or perhaps because of it, there was excessive emphasis on appearances — it was part of the region's *fare bella figura* syndrome; and most of the men who assembled in the piazza of Maida, and in dozens of similar squares throughout the South, were uncommonly knowledgeable about the art of fine tailoring.

They could assess in a few seconds the craft of another man's suit, could appraise each dexterous stitch, could appreciate the mastery of a tailor's most challenging task, the shoulder, from which more than twenty individualized parts of the jacket must hang in harmony and allow for fluidity. Almost every prideful male, when entering a shop to select fabric for a new suit, knew by heart the twelve principal measurements of his tailored body, starting with the distance between the neckline and the waist of the jacket, and ending with the exact width of the cuffs above the shoes. Among such men were many customers who had been dealing with the Cristiani family firm all of their lives, as had their fathers and grandfathers before them. Indeed, the Cristianis had been making men's clothes in southern Italy since 1806, when the region was controlled by Napoleon Bonaparte; and when Napoleon's brother-in-law, Joachim Murat, who had been installed on the Naples throne in 1808, was assassinated in

1815 by a Spanish Bourbon firing squad in the village of Pizzo, a few miles south of Maida, the wardrobe that Murat left behind included a suit made by Francesco Cristiani's grandfather.

But now on this Holy Saturday in 1911, Francesco Cristiani confronted a situation that could not benefit from his family's long tradition in the trade. In his hands he held a new pair of trousers that had an inch-long cut across the left knee, a cut that had been made by an apprentice who had been idling with a pair of scissors atop the table on which the trousers had been laid out for Cristiani's inspection.

Although apprentices were repeatedly reminded that they were not to handle the heavy scissors — their main task was to sew on buttons and baste seams — some young men unwittingly violated the rule in their eagerness to gain tailoring experience. But what magnified the youth's delinquency in this situation was that the damaged trousers had been made for the *mafioso*, whose name was Vincenzo Castiglia.

A first-time customer from nearby Cosenza, Vincenzo Castiglia was so blatant about his criminal profession that, while being measured for the suit one month before, he had asked Cristiani to allow ample room inside the jacket for the holstered pistol. On that same occasion, however, Mr. Castiglia had made several other requests that elevated him in the eyes of his tailor as a man who had a sense of style and knew what might flatter his rather corpulent figure. For example, Mr. Castiglia had requested that the suit's shoulders be cut extra wide to give his hips a narrower appearance; and he sought to distract attention from his protruding belly by ordering a pleated waistcoat with wide pointed lapels and also a hole in the center of the waistcoat through which a gold chain could be looped and linked to his diamond pocket watch.

In addition, Mr. Castiglia specified that the hems of his trousers be turned up, in accord with the latest continental fashion; and, as he peered into Cristiani's workroom, he expressed satisfaction on observing that the tailors were all sewing by hand and not using the popularized sewing machine, which, despite its speed, lacked the capacity for the special molding of a fabric's seams and angles that was only possible in the hands of a talented tailor.

Bowing with appreciation, the tailor Cristiani assured Mr.

Castiglia that his shop would never succumb to the graceless mechanized invention, even though sewing machines were now widely used in Europe and also in America. With the mention of America, Mr. Castiglia smiled and said that he had once visited the New Land, and added that he had several relatives who had settled there. (Among them was a young cousin, Francesco Castiglia, who in future years, beginning in the era of Prohibition, would achieve great notoriety and wealth under the name Frank Costello.)

In the weeks that followed, Cristiani devoted much attention to satisfying the *mafioso*'s specifications, and he was finally proud of the sartorial results — until Holy Saturday, when he discovered an inch-long slash across the left knee of Mr. Castiglia's new pants.

Screaming with anguish and fury, Cristiani soon obtained a confession from the apprentice who admitted to cutting discarded pieces of cloth on the edges of the pattern under which the trousers had been found. Cristiani stood silently, shaken for several minutes, surrounded by his equally concerned and speechless associates. Cristiani could, of course, run and hide in the hills, which had been his first inclination; or he could return the money to the *mafioso* after explaining what had happened and then offer up the guilty apprentice as a sacrificial lamb to be appropriately dealt with. In this instance, however, there were special inhibiting circumstances. The culpable apprentice was the young nephew of Cristiani's wife, Maria. His wife had been born Maria Talese. She was the only sister of Cristiani's best friend, Gaetano Talese, then working in America. And Gaetano's eight-year-old son, the apprentice Joseph Talese — who would become my father — was now crying convulsively.

As Cristiani sought to comfort his remorseful nephew, his mind kept searching for some plausible solution. There was no way, in the few hours remaining before Castiglia's visit, to make a second pair of trousers even if they had matching material in stock. Nor was there any way to perfectly obscure the cut in the fabric even with a marvelous job of mending.

While his fellow tailors kept insisting that the wisest move was to close the shop and leave a note for Mr. Castiglia pleading illness, or some other excuse that might delay a confrontation,

Cristiani firmly reminded them that nothing could absolve him from his failure to deliver the *mafioso*'s suit in time for Easter and that it was mandatory to find a solution now, at once, or at least within the four hours that remained before Mr. Castiglia's arrival.

As the noon bell rang from the church in the main square, Cristiani grimly announced: "There will be no siesta for any of us today. This is not the time for food and rest — it is the time for sacrifice and meditation. So I want everybody to stay where you are, and think of something that may save us from disaster . . ."

He was interrupted by some grumbling from the other tailors, who resented missing their lunch and afternoon nap; but Cristiani overruled them and immediately dispatched one of his apprenticed sons to the village to tell the tailors' wives not to expect the return of their husbands until sundown. Then he instructed the other apprentices, including my father, to pull the draperies across the windows and to lock the shop's front and back doors. And then for the next few minutes, Cristiani's entire staff of a dozen men and boys, as if participating in a wake, quietly congregated within the walls of the darkened shop.

My father sat in one corner, still stunned by the magnitude of his misdeed. Near him sat other apprentices, irritated at my father but nonetheless obedient to their master's order that they remain in confinement. In the center of the workroom, seated among his tailors, was Francesco Cristiani, a small wiry man with a tiny mustache, holding his head in his hands and looking up every few seconds to glance again at the trousers that lay before him.

Several minutes later, with a snap of his fingers, Cristiani rose to his feet. Though barely five feet six inches tall, his erect carriage, fine styling, and panache lent substance to his presence. There was also a gleam in his eye.

"I think I have thought of something," he announced slowly, pausing to let the suspense build until he had everyone's total attention.

"What is it?" asked his most senior tailor.

"What I can do," Cristiani continued, "is make a cut across

the *right* knee that will exactly match the damaged left knee, and —"

"Are you crazy?" interrupted the older tailor.

"Let me finish, you imbecile!" Cristiani shouted, pounding his small fist on the table, "— and then I can sew up both cuts of the trousers with decorative seams that will match exactly, and later I will explain to Mr. Castiglia that he is the first man in this part of Italy to be wearing trousers designed in the newest fashion, the knee-seamed fashion."

The others listened with astonishment.

"But, maestro," one of the younger tailors said in a cautious tone of respect, "won't Mr. Castiglia notice, after you introduce this 'new fashion,' that we tailors ourselves are not wearing trousers that follow this fashion?"

Cristiani raised his eyebrows slightly.

"A good point," he conceded, as a pessimistic mood returned to the room. And then again his eyes flashed, and he said: "But we *will* follow the fashion! We will make cuts in *our* knees and then sew them up with seams similar to Mr. Castiglia's . . ." Before the men could protest, he quickly added: "But we will *not* be cutting up our own trousers. We'll use those trousers we keep in the widows' closet!"

Immediately everyone turned toward the locked door of a closet in the rear of the workroom, within which were hung dozens of suits last worn by men now dead — suits that bereaved widows, not wishing to be reminded of their departed spouses, had passed on to Cristiani in the hope that he would give the clothing away to passing strangers who might wear them in distant villages.

Now Cristiani flung open the closet door, pulled several pairs of trousers off the suit hangers, and tossed them to his tailors, urging a quick try-on. He himself was already standing in his white cotton underwear and black garters, searching for a pair of trousers that might accommodate his slight stature; and when he succeeded, he slipped them on, climbed up on the table, and stood momentarily like a proud model in front of his men. "See," he said, pointing to the length and width, "a perfect fit."

The other tailors began to pick and choose from the wide selection. Cristiani was now down from the table, the trousers off, and was beginning to cut across the right knee of the *mafio-so*'s pants, duplicating the already damaged left knee. Then he applied similar incisions to the knees of the trousers he had chosen to wear himself.

"Now, pay close attention," he called out to his men. With a flourish of his silk-threaded needle, he applied the first stitch into the dead man's trousers, piercing the lower edge of the torn knee with an inner stitch that he adroitly looped to the upper edge — a bold, circular motion that he repeated several times until he had securely reunited the center of the knee with a small, round, embroidered wreathlike design half the size of a dime.

Then he proceeded to sew, on the right side of the wreath, a half-inch seam that was slightly tapered and tilted upward at the end; and, after reproducing this seam on the left side of the wreath, he had created a minuscule image of a distant bird with spread wings, flying directly toward the viewer; a bird that most resembled a peregrine falcon. Cristiani thus originated a trouser style with wing-tipped knees.

"Well, what do you think?" he asked his men, indicating by his offhand manner that he did not really care what they thought. As they shrugged their shoulders and murmured in the background, he peremptorily continued: "All right now, quickly, cut the knees of those trousers you'll be wearing and stitch them together with the embroidered design you've just seen." Expecting no opposition, and receiving none, Cristiani lowered his head to concentrate entirely on his own task: finishing the second knee of the trousers he would wear, and then beginning, meticulously, the job on Mr. Castiglia's trousers.

In the latter case, Cristiani not only planned to embroider a winged design with silk thread that matched exactly the shade of the thread used on the buttonholes of the jacket of Mr. Castiglia's suit, but he also would insert a section of silk lining within the front part of the trousers, extending from the thighs to the shins, that would protect Mr. Castiglia's knees from the scratchy feel of the embroidered inner stitching and would also diminish the friction against the knee seams when Mr. Castiglia was out promenading at the *passeggiata*.

For the next two hours, everyone worked in feverish silence.

As Cristiani and the other tailors affixed the winged design on the knees of all the trousers, the apprentices helped with the minor alterations, button sewing, the ironing of cuffs, and other details that would make the dead men's trousers as presentable as possible on the bodies of the tailors. Francesco Cristiani, of course, allowed none but himself to handle the *mafioso's* garments; and as the church bells rang, signaling the end of the siesta, Cristiani scrutinized with admiration the stitching he had done, and he privately thanked his namesake in heaven, Saint Francis di Paola, for his inspired guidance with the needle.

Now there was the sound of activity in the square: the jingles of horse-drawn wagons, the cries of the food vendors, the voices of shoppers passing back and forth along the cobblestone road in front of Cristiani's doorstep. The window draperies of the shop had just been opened, and my father and another apprentice were posted beyond the door with instructions to call in with words of warning as soon as they caught a glimpse of Mr. Castiglia's carriage.

Inside, the tailors stood in a row behind Cristiani, famished and fatigued, and hardly comfortable in their dead men's trousers with wing-tipped knees; but their anxiety and fear concerning Mr. Castiglia's forthcoming reaction to his Easter suit dominated their emotions. Cristiani, on the other hand, seemed unusually calm. In addition to his newly acquired brown trousers, the cuffs of which touched upon his buttoned shoes with cloth tops, he wore a gray lapelled waistcoat over a striped shirt with a rounded white collar adorned by a burgundy cravat and pearl stickpin. In his hand, on a wooden hanger, he held Mr. Castiglia's gray herringbone three-piece suit that, moments before, he had softly brushed and pressed for the final time. The suit was still warm.

At twenty minutes after four, my father came running through the door, and, in a high voice that could not betray his panic, he announced: *"Sta arrivando!"* A black carriage, drawn by two horses, clangorously drew to a halt in front of the shop. After the rifle-toting coachman hopped off to open the door, the dark portly figure of Vincenzo Castiglia descended the two steps to the sidewalk, followed by a lean man, his bodyguard, in a wide-brimmed black hat, long cloak, and studded boots.

Mr. Castiglia removed his gray fedora and, with a handkerchief, wiped the road dust from his brow. He entered the shop, where Cristiani hastened forward to greet him and, holding the new suit high on its hanger, proclaimed: "Your wonderful Easter costume awaits you!" Shaking hands, Mr. Castiglia examined the suit without comment; then, after politely refusing Cristiani's offer of a bit of whiskey or wine, he directed his bodyguard to help him remove his jacket so that he could immediately try on his Easter apparel.

Cristiani and the other tailors stood quietly nearby, watching as the holstered pistol strapped to Castiglia's chest swayed with his movements as he extended his arms and received over his shoulders the gray lapelled waistcoat, followed by the broad-shouldered jacket. Inhaling as he buttoned up his waistcoat and jacket, Mr. Castiglia turned toward the three-sectioned mirror next to the fitting room. He admired the reflection of himself from every angle, then turned toward his bodyguard, who nodded approvingly. Mr. Castiglia commented in a commanding voice: "*Perfetto!*"

"*Mille grazie,*" responded Cristiani, bowing slightly as he carefully removed the trousers from the hanger and handed them to Mr. Castiglia. Excusing himself, Mr. Castiglia walked into the fitting room. He closed the door. A few of the tailors began to pace around the showroom, but Cristiani stood near the fitting room, whistling softly to himself. The bodyguard, still wearing his cloak and hat, sat comfortably in a chair, his legs crossed, smoking a thin cigar. The apprentices gathered in the back room, out of sight, except for my nervous father, who remained in the showroom busily arranging and rearranging stacks of material on a counter while keeping an eye focused on the fitting room.

For more than a minute not a word was spoken. The only sounds heard were made by Mr. Castiglia as he changed his trousers. First there was the thump of his shoes dropping to the floor. Then the faint whishing rustle of trouser legs being stepped into. Seconds later, a loud bump against the wooden partition as Mr. Castiglia presumably lost his balance while standing on one leg. After a sigh, a cough, and the creaking sound of shoe leather — more silence. But then, suddenly, a

deep voice from behind the door bellowed: "Maestro!" Then
louder: "MAESTRO!"

The door bolted open, revealing the glowering face and
crouched figure of Mr. Castiglia, his fingers pointing down toward his bent knees and the winged design on the trousers.
Waddling toward Cristiani, he yelled: "Maestro — *che avete fatto
qui?*" — what have you done here?

The bodyguard jumped, scowling at Cristiani. My father
closed his eyes. The tailors stepped back. But Francesco Cristiani stood straight and still, remaining impassive even when the
bodyguard's hand moved inside his cloak.

"What have you done?" Mr. Castiglia repeated, still squatting
on bent knees, as if suffering from locked joints. Cristiani
watched him silently for a second or two; but finally, in the
authoritarian tone of a teacher chiding a student, Cristiani responded: "Oh, how disappointed I am in you! How sad and
insulted am I by your failure to appreciate the honor I was
trying to bestow upon you because I thought you deserved it —
but, sadly, I was wrong . . ."

Before the confused Vincenzo Castiglia could open his
mouth, Cristiani continued: "You demanded to know what I
had done with your trousers — not realizing that what I had
done was introduce you to the modern world, which is where
I thought you belonged. When you first entered this shop
for a fitting last month, you seemed so different from the backward people of this region. So sophisticated. So individualis-
tic. You had traveled to America, you said, had seen the New
World, and I assumed that you were in touch with the contemporary spirit of freedom — but I greatly misjudged you . . . New
clothes, alas, do not remake the man within . . ."

Carried away by his own grandiloquence, Cristiani turned
toward his senior tailor, who stood closest to him, and he impulsively repeated an old southern Italian proverb that he regretted uttering immediately after the words had slipped out of
his mouth.

"Lavar la testa al'asino è acqua persa," Cristiani intoned. Wash-
ing a donkey's head is a waste of water.

Stunned silence swept through the entire shop. My father
cringed behind the counter. Cristiani's tailors, horrified by his

provocation, gasped and trembled as they saw Mr. Castiglia's face redden, his eyes narrow — and no one would have been surprised if the next sound were the explosion of a gun. Indeed, Cristiani himself lowered his head and seemed resigned to his fate — but strangely, having now gone too far to turn back, Cristiani recklessly, repeated his words: *"Lavar la testa . . ."*

Mr. Castiglia did not respond. He sputtered, bit his lips, but said not a word. Perhaps, having never before experienced such brazenness from anyone, and particularly not from a tiny tailor, Mr. Castiglia was too wonderstruck to act. Even his bodyguard now seemed paralyzed, with his hand still inside his cloak. After a few more seconds of silence, the eyes in Cristiani's lowered head moved tentatively upward, and he saw Mr. Castiglia standing with his shoulders slouched, his head hanging slightly, and a glazed and remorseful look in his eyes. He then looked at Cristiani and winced. Finally, he spoke. "My late mother would use that expression when I made her angry," Mr. Castiglia confided softly. After a pause, he added, "She died when I was very young . . ."

"Oh, I am so sorry," Cristiani said, as the tension subsided in the room. "I do hope, however, that you will accept my word that we *did* try to make you a beautiful suit for Easter. I was just so disappointed that your trousers, which are designed in the latest fashion, did not appeal to you."

Looking down once again at the knees, Mr. Castiglia asked: "*This* is the latest fashion?"

"Yes, indeed," Cristiani reassured him.

"Where?"

"In the great capitals of the world."

"But not here?"

"Not yet," Cristiani said. "You are the first among the men of this region."

"But why does the latest fashion in this region have to begin with me?" Mr. Castiglia asked, in a voice that now seemed uncertain.

"Oh, no, it has not really begun with you," Cristiani quickly corrected him. "We tailors have *already* adopted this fashion." And holding up one of his trouser knees, he said: "See for yourself."

Mr. Castiglia looked down to examine Cristiani's knees; and then, as he turned to survey the entire room, he saw the other tailors, one after another, each lift a leg and, nodding, point to the now familiar wings of the infinitesimal bird.

"I see," Mr. Castiglia said. "And I see that I also owe you my apologies, maestro," he went on. "Sometimes it takes a while for a man to appreciate what is fashionable."

Then after shaking Cristiani's hand, and settling the financial account — but seemingly not wanting to linger a moment longer in this place where his uncertainty had been exposed — Mr. Castiglia summoned his obedient and speechless bodyguard and handed him his old suit. Wearing his new suit, and tipping his hat, Mr. Castiglia headed toward his carriage through the door that had been pulled wide open by my father.

VICTOR ZASLAVSKY

Mystery in a Soviet Library

FROM PARTISAN REVIEW

AMERICAN LIBRARIES suffer from what Stalin would have called a "peasant leveling mentality." Simply anyone can walk in, go to the stacks and choose a book . . . simple as buying a piece of cheese. I suspect that these computerized cemeteries impart no respect whatever toward books, but rather depress readers. The will to write, to add yet another tome to the multitudes standing on the shelves, is completely dissipated. Soviet libraries are very different . . .

And I know what I miss in American libraries. It is that in many of them the traditions of Western individualism are obeyed to such an extent that the tables are big enough for only one reader. For this reason alone, I never would have had the chance to share a table at the Central Public Library with a certain reader registered under the surname Carrasco, whose real identity aroused in me an obsessive curiosity.

It was an opportunity arrived at after years spent traversing the capricious library-access hierarchy of the Soviet Union. When I was just ten years old, my school's head librarian noticed my love for books and co-opted me onto the Library Council. The council's first memorable act was purging books. Immediately after the war, textbooks were scarce, and my school received two hundred history textbooks printed in the mid-1930s. To purge the old edition of "the enemies of the people," we would open to page 181 and spill ink on the portraits of Marshals Tukhachevsky and Blucher.

The store of books in the school library was meager, textbooks excepted, and I read quickly. The librarian wrote me a recommendation for the district library for grown-ups. The district library was subject to almost military discipline. Books could be signed out three at a time and exchanged no sooner than three days later. The library had a catalogue but it was out of bounds. To sign out a book the reader had to name the author; if he could not, which was usually the case, he had to mention at least what kind of book he wanted. "Something about love," the women quickly said. The men often hemmed and hawed, their hands aflutter.

When I entered the university, I reached a new height. The student library was a department of the Central Public Library, which, despite its name, was open only to scientific researchers. It was not open to the man in the street either — a student pass was required. This was a real library with a large catalogue and specialized reading rooms. Books could not be signed out — a great defect, as the number of students seeking admittance easily exceeded the number of seats. One had to show up at seven o'clock in the morning and queue for an hour and a half. Those who arrived later waited even longer, until one of the early birds, done for the day, left a place.

After graduating I was finally granted the precious right to study in the Central Public Library. A "research pass" for the main reading room was required, and a university diploma was a prerequisite. It was the Olympus of libraries: millions of volumes, a gigantic collection of manuscripts accumulating over the centuries, even Voltaire's private book collection.

To avoid confusion, the readers were divided into three categories. The first and certainly most numerous had the right of access to "common reading rooms." These were homey and quiet. The walls supported heavy prerevolutionary shelves, so that the truly essential references were always at hand. The forty-five volumes of Lenin's *Collected Works* (fourth edition), in brown covers, went nicely with the three score light brown volumes of Marx and Engels, while the cool primness of the fifty-five blue volumes of Lenin's *Full Collected Works* (fifth edition) harmonized well with three dozen more assorted Lenin volumes in dull red. The modesty of the classics clashed with the vanity of the rather temporary guests: the thick volumes of current

Politburo members' speeches with their fashionable glossy, gold-stamped covers, looking *nouveau riche* and even opulently gangsterlike among the aristocracy of spirit. The common reading rooms are chronically overcrowded; the latecomers line the walls, marking time by leafing through the *Manifesto* or *What Is to Be Done?*

Reading rooms for professors and academicians are another thing altogether. Although the same brown-blue volumes populate the shelves and the tables are graced by the same green lampshades, there is always space for more among the famous linguists and literature specialists. There sits Vladimir Propp, past victim of the anti-cosmopolitan campaign, forever stiff with fear. Victor Shklovsky steps in like an old wrestler, pushing through invisible opponents. The common and professional reading rooms merge in the corridors, the smoking room, and the marble staircase, where open-mouthed graduate students peck at the crumbs of wisdom dropped by their supervisors.

The upper grade of readers inhabits a different realm still, having access to "restricted reading rooms" — *"spetskhran"* in Russian, or "spets" for short. Spets house the books defined as anti-Soviet and that require of their readers a greater political maturity. By definition, all of these should have been published after 1917, but there are also prerevolutionary works of authors who managed to write an anti-Soviet something even before the revolution. The majority of Western editions, except for technical and pure science texts, are found in the *spetskhran*.

To gain entrance into the spets one first obtains a supporting letter from a reputable research institute or university, signed by its troika of director, party secretary, and chairman of the trade union committee. But the decisive information characterizing the candidate's political maturity arrives through the invisible network that links the spets to the departments responsible for state security in every respectable organization. The supporting letter should contain the subject of the proposed research, lest the spets librarian hand out books on unrelated topics. Hence, those coveting the spets try to formulate their topics in the vaguest of terms. Almost everyone admitted to the spets examines all-encompassing topics, such as "culture and personality," "criticism of bourgeois ideology," and the like.

The *spetskhran* is located in Room 88. I would enter the spets
trembling and proffer my internal passport and pass to the
guard with a shaking hand, trying to appear exactly like the
photographs in my documents. I trembled openly, for I knew
the guards took pleasure in that. It was easy, as I really was
afraid: what if the guard should detect my political immaturity,
notice my moral infirmity, or simply observe in my eyes the
desire that he and his organization go to hell? To my good
fortune, the guards had not yet learned to read minds.

The spets room had space for no more than a hundred at a
time, but it was never full. Apparently, politically mature researchers were as hard to come by in the city as ripe pineapples
in its vegetable stores. To the newcomer the most striking aspect
of Room 88 was the high shelves on the walls, crammed not with
the habitual blue-brown volumes promising the last word on
every subject, but with endless rows of bright covers — the cry
of advertising, the chaos of the ideas market. The forbidden
fruit could be plucked directly from the shelves. A strange feeling would grip me, a mixture of confusion, elation, and, most
of all, the stupefaction of freedom.

The elation passed fairly quickly when it turned out that in
the spets freedom took the form of Engels's "recognition of
necessity." Almost any book could be chosen, but it had to be
registered in the reader's personal selection sheet. It was easy to
see that from time to time the overseeing organization would
peruse the books selected by a given reader over a year or two
and draw certain inferences about his interests and progress in
his studies. If the reader felt the need to keep his interests to
himself, great care had to be taken to conceal it. The simplest
tactic was to select as many books as possible, so that the true
choices were buried by the mountain of books registered as
ballast. But the method could backfire if a perusal of his choices
led the organization to draw spurious conclusions by fabricating
connections between the chosen books — and sometimes to
bring charges against the reader.

Somehow the atmosphere in the spets was always tense. The
readers did not speak to each other, even if they were acquaintances. People sat two to a table in their assigned seats, and even
if they shared a table for years they never exchanged words or

recognized each other. Each guarded his own secret, and when they left Room 88 it was as if their secrets ran along on a leash.

I got hold of a comfortable table by a window with a view onto Nevsky Prospekt, where a worried humanity could be observed queuing with shopping bags at the famous Eliseev food store. For a full year I had the table to myself and, having grown accustomed to solitude, was almost offended when one day a neighbor materialized. He carried at least two dozen books, embracing the stack like a bundle of firewood. He loaded the books onto his half of the table and apparently wanted to give me a friendly nod but cut himself short, understanding the impropriety of such a greeting. In response I shifted my chair slightly to the left. The exchange was the utmost in politeness given the circumstances: we acknowledged each other's existence in a place where people should not notice each other.

My neighbor showed up almost every day and came to interest me more and more. He was without distinguishing marks: simply a tall, broad-shouldered man, about sixty, with a stubborn chin. A Ukrainian, perhaps. Obviously he had been strong but had gained weight from lack of exercise. Then again, all the habitués of the spets gained weight at that age: there could not have been too many athletes in such a place. He dressed in Western style, but that was no rarity in the spets either. Nonetheless, my neighbor was markedly different from a typical spets reader, and it took me a while to realize why. Usually the *spetskhran* customer tried to shrink, hide, disappear. We all prayed for invisibility, wished to be forgotten, so that nothing threatened our fragile right to read forbidden literature. My neighbor, however, had some sort of inner confidence. He did not seem afraid to lose the precious privilege, nor did he appear to revel in his unique status. Even more surprising was his way of reading. An ordinary reader always remembered he was not alone and hence kept up an expression of distaste or boredom no matter how gripping the book — as if he were being forced to read or to chew on a lemon. It was our disagreeable profession, after all, that compelled us to read Western propaganda rather than join the rest of the populace and rejoice in optimistic Soviet literature. My neighbor, for his part, was obviously and completely captivated by his reading: he read and repeated to

himself, he smiled and smirked. Once, when he stepped out for
a moment, I could not help breaking the sacred rules of the
spets; quickly, thieflike, I riffled through his pile of books. The
opened one turned out to be *L'Affaire Toulaev* by Victor Serge
— neither the book nor the author meant anything to me. But
his other books struck me. They were by Trotsky or about him,
and almost all of them in French or Spanish. Even more amaz-
ingly, my neighbor disdained concealing his interest. In 1950,
during a search of the apartment of the father of one of my
friends, they found Trotsky's *Literature and Revolution*. At the
closed trial the prosecutor stated that "with every page the accused took another step toward betrayal of the fatherland." The
accused cried with joy after being sentenced to twenty-five years
— he had expected the firing squad. And my neighbor, he read
Trotsky as if it were the most ordinary thing! The only explanation was that he belonged to the dying breed of "anti-Trot-
skyist propagandists." But they all worked at an institution that
was privy to special sources of information and had no need to
visit the spets.

The urge to find out about my neighbor grew daily. To inquire directly was out of the question, but to wait for a lucky
accident to give away his name could take years. Still, I had some
special sources of my own. Natasha, my "almost sister," worked
in the library. She was not my sister, but ever since I had had a
brief affair with her older sister — for whom I pined hopelessly
for a long time — we had been trusting and devoted friends.
The youngest Ph.D. in the library, she was the head of a department and a person of influence. But even she had trouble
finding out the name. The first flash of information was puz-
zling. He was registered under the surname of Carrasco. "But
that's Cervantes," I said, surprised. "Remember, he had a
character named Carrasco?" "A pseudonym, maybe," Natasha
guessed. Her curiosity was also aroused.

Several days later Natasha called me and said that she would
come around in half an hour. I knew from her voice that something had happened. "I cracked it!" she blurted out in the doorway and then whispered: "It's Ramon Mercader." "Who?" I did
not understand. "Ramon Mercader!" And she added in my ear,
"The guy who killed Trotsky. But, for God's sake, don't tell
anyone. We'll both be jailed. And in different cells, at that."

I asked around a bit and scraped some "facts" together, although they were all based on rumors. They said Mercader spent twenty years in a Mexican prison. They said that for "exemplary success in an important governmental mission," Stalin made Mercader a Hero of the Soviet Union and that all those years the Gold Star awaited Mercader in a safe deposit box. He did not get much out of it. Mercader returned during the Khrushchev years, not a good time for him. Although the victims of the 1930s show trials had not been rehabilitated, the condemnations of Trotsky as a Gestapo agent and Bukharin as a Nazi spy were also out of fashion. The word of the day was to "forget and never mention!" Thus, Mercader was sent to Prague. They said that he later came to sympathize with Dubček and the Prague Spring and had to be shipped back to the Soviet Union. Now he shuttled back and forth between Moscow and Leningrad — more accurately, between two *spetskhrans*, supposedly writing memoirs.

From that day on, I could not work in the spets. I bombarded my neighbor with questions: "Is it true that you're the very same Mercader? Why did you take the name Carrasco? Do you mean Trotsky was insane, a new Don Quixote? Do your children know who you are? And how do you feel now, thirty years after the murder of Leon Davidovich?" Of course, all these questions resounded only in my mind. A direct question could end badly for me and for Natasha. But I could no longer sit quietly in my seat nor read nor concentrate. I exchanged books needlessly. I stepped out into the smoking room — although I did not smoke. All the while I kept up an imaginary dialogue with Mercader. It was a sort of curse.

Mercader took no notice of my agitation or, indeed, my presence. But he had a hard time reading as well. He obviously conducted his own endless dialogue with Trotsky or, perhaps, with the authors of books about Trotsky. He argued, he accused, he defended himself . . . Sometimes he would pace back and forth in the corridor or jump up clenching his fists. Did he feel he was squeezing the icepick's handle, about to strike? Could those tales about a victim's ghost pursuing the murderer be true?

Knowing and not being able to tell is torture. I could no longer work at the same table as Mercader, but I was reluctant,

even afraid to change my seat in Room 88. Thus, I trudged
through the common reading rooms, greeted friends, talked
about everything except what was on my mind, generally wasted
time. I was so disturbed by the persistent internal dialogue that
I lost all sense of caution. And I was swiftly punished.

If to gain access to the spets was like winning a lottery, to lose
it through carelessness was like losing the winning ticket. It
happened so rarely that the story is worth telling. Once, lost in
indecision, I was walking through the library and ran into an
old pal who had the strangest job in the world. He was a trans-
lator of nonexistent poetry from Central Asian languages. His
clients were poets from Central Asia, or sometimes from Cau-
casian republics, who absolutely had to publish in Russian. If a
translation then appeared in a central journal, the poet was
showered with goodies: membership in the Union of Writers,
well-paid book contracts with local publishing houses, official
positions, power. The creative process went like this. The poet
explained in less than lapidary Russian prose what poem he
would write if only he could. My friend nodded approvingly
and took notes. Only a few days later he would read to the poet
a flowing stream of verse in which Soviet rule triumphed over
the desert and the happy Kirghiz (Kazakh, or any other Central
Asian person) wrote a song about his newfound happiness. The
central journals had a quota for ethnic minorities: sooner or
later they published my friend's poems, for he was, after all,
a talented versifier. My friend sincerely admired his clients.
"What vitality!" he would exclaim. "Under a different regime
these people would play the stock market or join the Mafia.
Here they become poets and join the Union of Writers. Such
characters won't lose out in any place."

The translations commanded a princely reward. Grapes and
aromatic melons, Armenian cognac thirty years old, and Tur-
koman carpets — all on top of the honorarium. However, there
were also a few real poets who published real books — occasionally good books — and then the work took a serious turn. My
friend maintained a group of Central Asian language specialists
who made literal translations and got paid by the line. This
threw up another obstacle. Several copies of the text were
needed, but transcription of Central Asian texts was painful and

expensive. The library owned a Xerox machine, but it was guarded like a bank vault. Two trusted comrades — the head of the copying department and the Xerox operator — kept the two different keys to the machine, and both had to be inserted in the appropriate slots for the machine to function. A reader was entitled to ten pages of copy a day. Worse, to copy these ten pages one needed the approval of the department head, who knew no foreign languages, certainly no Central Asian ones. Thus, there arose the classic Catch-22: for permission to make the copies necessary for the translation, one had first to present the translation itself. My friend removed this obstacle by those same gifts of the grateful South; a good part of them found their way to those responsible for the Xerox machine.

That unfortunate day I met my friend as he mournfully lugged a whole heap of poetry to the Xerox room. Delighted to see me, he begged my help with the Xeroxing. "Two's company," he convinced me and promised to reward me with a copy of a small book of my choice. The temptation was great: for a long time I had coveted a collection of Mandelstam's poetry, *The Stone,* not to be found for any money. But surely in the end I agreed because Mercader made my life a misery and I was ready for anything to avoid returning to Room 88. Later Natasha reproached me for my complete loss of sanity and self-control. Everyone knew that the extraordinary powers of the copying department bred intrigue and denunciations by the envious. Whatever the cause, as we approached the end of our Xeroxing several inspectors barged in — surely alerted by a tip — and found us in the act: a copy of Mandelstam, a load of copies of poems in unknown languages; and no permit to use the Xerox machine.

The consequences were horrifying. A report arrived at my institute detailing my "breaking of library rules." To wit: "illegal use of Xerox machine . . . serious infraction against instructions concerning *spetskhran* materials — attempted bribery of library staff . . ." There were other paragraphs that now escape my memory. Altogether they certainly amounted to less than "treason" but sounded worse than, say, "armed robbery." As the head of the first department brusquely told me: "Lucky they were dusty poems, or else off to Siberia for you." I did not lose my job but was demoted and lost not only my access to the spets but also the use of the entire library.

I did begin a new ascent to the spets, but then my emigration made it all meaningless. In those years I completely lost sight of Ramon Mercader. Rumor had it that he contracted cancer and was allowed to die in Cuba. I would like to know what his gravestone says: Carrasco, Mercader, or, simply, the man who killed Trotsky. And did he ever finish those memoirs?

Biographical Notes

JULIAN BARNES is the author of *Metroland, Before She Met Me, Flaubert's Parrot,* and *Staring at the Sun.* In 1986 he was awarded the E. M. Forster Award by the American Academy and Institute of Arts and Letters and was recently made a Chevalier de l'Orare des Arts et des Lettres. His new novel, *A History of the World in 10½ Chapters,* will be published by Knopf in the fall of 1989.

FRANKLIN BURROUGHS teaches English at Bowdoin College. He is currently at work on a collection of essays. A previous essay appeared in *The Kenyon Review* in the fall of 1986 and was noted with commendation by *The Best American Essays* for that year.

FRANK CONROY, director of the Iowa Writers' Workshop, is the author of *Stop-Time* and *Midair.* His stories and essays have appeared in *The New Yorker, Esquire, Harper's Magazine, GQ,* and many other publications. He has worked as a jazz pianist and has often written about American music.

JOAN DIDION has written four novels, the most recent of which is *Democracy,* and several books of essays and reporting, including *Slouching Towards Bethlehem, The White Album, Salvador,* and *Miami.* She contributes to *The New York Review of Books* and *The New Yorker.*

ANNIE DILLARD is the author of *The Writing Life, An American Childhood, Teaching a Stone to Talk,* and six other books. *Pilgrim at Tinker Creek* won the Pulitzer Prize in general nonfiction for 1975. *An American Childhood* received a National Book Critics Circle Award nomination in 1988. She has received grants from the John Simon Guggenheim Memorial Foundation and the National Endowment for the Humanities. In 1983 she was the Phi Beta Kappa orator at Harvard. She lives in Middletown, Connecticut, with her family.

STANLEY ELKIN is Merle Kling Professor of Modern Letters at Washington University in St. Louis. A member of the American Academy and Institute of Arts and Letters, he has published a dozen works of fiction, including *George Mills,* for which he won the National Book Critics Circle Award. He is currently at work on *The MacGuffin,* his ninth novel.

JOSEPH EPSTEIN is the editor of *The American Scholar.* His essays and stories have appeared in *Commentary, The New Criterion, Harper's Magazine, The Hudson Review,* and *The New Yorker. Partial Payments,* his most recent collection of literary essays, appeared earlier this year. *Once More Around the Block,* a collection of his familiar essays, will appear in paperback from W. W. Norton in winter 1989.

RICHARD FORD is the author of three novels, a collection of short stories titled *Rock Springs,* and numerous essays. He lives in Montana and in Mississippi.

ALBERT GOLDBARTH, who was born in Chicago in 1948, is the Adele V. Davis Distinguished Professor of Humanities at Wichita State University. He is the author of many volumes of poetry, the most recent of which, *Popular Culture,* received the Ohio State University Press Award in poetry and will be published by that press in fall 1989. "Parade March from 'That Creaturely World' " will be included in his book of essays *A Sympathy of Souls,* due from Coffee House Press in spring 1990; also included will be "After Yitzl," which appeared in last year's volume of *The Best American Essays.*

PAUL GRUCHOW spent twenty years as a newspaper and magazine editor before becoming an essayist in 1985. Since then, he has published two volumes of essays, *Journal of a Prairie Year* and *The Necessity of Empty Places,* and he has contributed more than fifty essays to periodicals. He is at work on a new collection of essays and a book about American places named after the devil.

CHRISTOPHER HITCHENS is a columnist for *The Nation,* an editor of *Harper's Magazine,* and a book critic for *Newsday.* He is the author of *Prepared for the Worst,* a collection of essays, and of studies of modern Cyprus and of the Parthenon Marbles. His forthcoming book, *Greece to Their Rome,* is a discussion of Anglo-American ironies.

EDWARD HOAGLAND has published six collections of essays, most recently *Heart's Desire,* and five books of fiction, including *Seven Rivers West,* and two travel books: *Notes from the Century Before: A Journal from British Columbia* and *African Calliope: A Journey to the Sudan.* He also writes criticism and contributes to the *New York Times* editorial page. He is the editor of the Penguin Nature Library and is a member of the American Academy and Institute of Arts and Letters.

MARY HOOD is the author of two volumes of short stories, *And Venus Is Blue* and *How Far She Went*, and has published nonfiction in *Harper's Magazine, The North American Review*, and *Art & Antiques*. She is writing a novel, *Familiar Heat*.

WILLIAM KITTREDGE grew up on the MC Ranch in southeastern Oregon, stayed home with the farming until he was thirty-five, studied at the Iowa Writers' Workshop, and is a professor of English at the University of Montana. He held a Stegner Fellowship at Stanford University, received two Creative Writing Fellowships from the National Endowment for the Arts, two Pacific Northwest Booksellers' Awards for Excellence, and the Montana Governor's Award for the Arts. Kittredge has published stories and essays in *The Atlantic, Harper's Magazine, TriQuarterly, Outside, Rolling Stone*, and *The Paris Review*. His most recent books are a collection of short fiction, *We Are Not in This Together* (Graywolf Press, 1984), and a collection of essays, *Owning It All* (Graywolf Press, 1987). He was also co-winner of the Neil Simon Award from *American Playhouse* for his work on the script of the film *Heartland*. "Who Owns the West?" will be included in a book, *Hole in the Sky*, that he is writing for Simon & Schuster.

LEONARD KRIEGEL is professor of English and director of the Center for Worker Education at the City College of New York. His stories and essays have appeared in *The American Scholar, Dissent, The Georgia Review, Raritan, Partisan Review, The Nation, The New Republic*, and *The New York Times Magazine*. He is currently working on a collection of autobiographical essays, of which "Falling into Life" is one, and a series of stories that deal with the idea of neighborhood. His previous books include the memoir *Notes for the Two-Dollar Window* and the novel *Quitting Time*.

DAVID QUAMMEN is a science journalist and novelist who lives in Montana and travels on assignment, whenever possible, to jungles and swamps. In 1987 he received the National Magazine Award for essays and criticism. His most recent book is *The Flight of the Iguana*. At present he's a Guggenheim Fellow, doing research for a book about evolution and extinction on islands. "Strawberries Under Ice" appears in a slightly expanded form in *Montana Spaces*, a volume of essays and photographs in celebration of Montana.

JUDY RUIZ writes and lives in Fayetteville, Arkansas, where she is an assistant professor of English at the University of Arkansas. She teaches creative writing in the Adult Community Education program. Her second book of poetry, *Because the Swans Ballet So Hard,* is looking for a home, as is her first, *The Pepper Birds.* She is now working on a collection of essays. She directs a performance art group called Entourage, which made its debut during the Eureka Springs Arts Festival. Ms. Ruiz will read from her work as part of the Spoken Arts series at the Painted Bride Art Center in Philadelphia in the fall of 1989.

SHELBY STEELE is an associate professor of English at San Jose State University. He has published short fiction and literary criticism in several journals. His book on the subject of race in America, *The Recoloring of America,* will be published by St. Martin's Press in the winter of 1990.

ROBERT STONE is the author of *A Hall of Mirrors,* which won the Faulkner Award in 1967; *Dog Soldiers,* which received the National Book Award in 1975; *A Flag for Sunrise* in 1981; and *Children of Light* in 1986. His articles and short stories have appeared in many publications, and he has received the John Dos Passos Prize for literature and an award from the American Academy and Institute of Arts and Letters. He taught creative writing for many years at Amherst College and recently at the University of California at San Diego.

GAY TALESE is the author of such best sellers as *Thy Neighbor's Wife, Honor Thy Father,* and *The Kingdom and the Power,* as well as earlier works: *The Bridge, Fame and Obscurity, New York — A Serendipiter's Journey,* and *The Overreachers.* Born in Ocean City, New Jersey, he attended the University of Alabama, and after two years as a lieutenant in an armored division, he joined the *New York Times,* working as a staff writer from 1955 to 1965. Between the 1960s and 1970s he contributed many articles to magazines, principally *Esquire* when that periodical was edited by the late Harold Hayes. Mr. Talese spends his time between his homes in New York and Ocean City; he is married to Nan Talese, an editor, and they have two daughters, Pamela and Catherine.

VICTOR ZASLAVSKY, formerly of the University of Leningrad, is professor of sociology at Memorial University of Newfoundland, Canada. In addition to his academic publications — including *The Neo-Stalinist State: Class, Ethnicity and Consensus in Soviet Society* and *Soviet-Jewish Emigration and Soviet Nationality Policy* (with R. Brym) — he has published short stories in English, Italian, and Russian. He is the editor of the twentieth-century Russian literature series published in Sellerio, Italy.

Notable Essays of 1988

SELECTED BY ROBERT ATWAN

JAMES ATLAS
The Survivor's Suicide. *Vanity Fair,*
January.

JAMES AXTEL
Confessions of a Bibliolater. *Virginia
Quarterly Review,* Winter.

JACK BEATTY
Going Home to Dorchester. *New
England Monthly,* December.

SALLIE BINGHAM
The Wandering Eye. *Shenandoah,* Vol.
38, no. 1.

ROBERT BLY
The Grace of Indirection. *The Painted
Bride Quarterly, No. 35.*

JAMES BOGAN
An Idle Evening's Entertainment.
North Dakota Quarterly, Spring.

ANTHONY BRANDT
Incidents of Travel in South and
Central America. *Boulevard,* Fall.

JIMMY BRESLIN
Crack. *Playboy,* December.

NICHOLAS BROMELL
Quabbin. *Georgia Review,* Spring.

COLETTE BROOKS
Somewhere in the Eighties. *Georgia
Review,* Winter.

ROSELLEN BROWN
An Insider/Outsider in Mississippi.
Witness, Summer/Fall.

WILLIAM F. BUCKLEY, JR.
Why Spy? *Playboy,* February.

TOM CAHILL
On the River of Cold Fires. *Outside,*
August.

ANNE CARSON
Chez L'Oxymoron. *Grand Street,*
Summer.

GERALD CLARKE
Fame. *Fame,* November.

GEORGE HOWE COLT AND ANNE
FADIMAN
Grand Canyon Suite. *Harvard
Magazine,* July–August.

E. N. COONS
Blizzard. *American Heritage,* February.

BERNARD COOPER
How to Draw. *Georgia Review,*
Summer.

PAUL COWAN
In the Land of the Sick. *Village Voice,*
May 17.

DOUGLAS CRASE
How Emerson Avails. *Boulevard,*
Spring.

BENJAMIN DEMOTT
Rediscovering Complexity. *The
Atlantic,* September.

JOAN DIDION
Letter from Los Angeles. *The New
Yorker,* September 5.

ANNIE DILLARD
Making Contact. *Yale Review,*
Summer.

CARL DJERASSI
The Quest for Alfred E. Neuman.
Grand Street, Autumn.

GERALD EARLY
Her Picture in the Papers:
Remembering Some Black Women.
Antaeus, Spring.

GRETEL EHRLICH
A River's Route. *Harper's Magazine,*
December.

BURNS ELLISON
The First Annual Nelson Algren
Memorial Poker Game. *Iowa
Review,* No. 1.

JOSEPH EPSTEIN
Racial Perversity in Chicago.
Commentary, December.

BERNARD FARBAR
My Life Inside. *Esquire,* September.

PAUL FUSSELL
When Truth Gets in the Way.
Philadelphia, October.

FRANK GALUSZKA
Art and Inspiration. *Adolescent
Psychiatry,* Vol. 15.

WILLIAM H. GASS
On Thinking Through a Little
Problem. *Harper's Magazine,*
February.

VERONICA GENG
A Lot in Common. *The New Yorker,*
January 25.

ROBERT GIROUX
The Poet in the Asylum. *The Atlantic,*
August.

PAUL GLASTRIS
The Case for Denial. *Washington
Monthly,* December.

MARY GORDON
"I Can't Stand Your Books": A Writer
Goes Home. *New York Times Book
Review,* December 11.

STEPHEN JAY GOULD
In a Jumbled Drawer. *Natural History,*
August.

ROCKWELL GRAY
Autobiographical Memory and Sense
of Place. *North Dakota Quarterly,*
Winter.

PAUL GRUCHOW
A Backyard Sparrow, Ho-Hum.
Audubon, September.

DORIS GRUMBACH
On Growing Old. *American Voice,*
Summer.

DONALD HALL
A Ballad of the Republic. Afterword
to *Casey at the Bat: A Centennial
Edition* (David R. Godine,
Publisher).

LEAH HALPER
Many Hands. *Northwest Review,* Vol.
26, no. 1.

PETE HAMILL
Breaking the Silence: A Letter to a
Black Friend. *Esquire,* March.

O. B. HARDISON
The Disappearance of Man. *Georgia
Review,* Winter.

ELIZABETH HARDWICK
Mrs. Wharton in New York. *New York
Review of Books,* January 21.

DAVID HELLERSTEIN
Vectors. *North American Review,*
Winter.

DANIEL HILL
Dakota Journal. *North Dakota Review,*
Fall.

RICHARD HILL
Kerouac at the End of the Road. *New
York Times Book Review,* May 29.

EDWARD HOAGLAND
The Indispensable Thoreau. *American
Heritage,* July/August.

DAN HOFSTADTER
Omnivores. *The New Yorker,* April 25.

JONATHAN HOLDEN
American Male Honor. *TriQuarterly,*
Fall.

Guns and Boyhood in America.
Georgia Review, Summer.

WILLIAM J. HUGHES
Catching Up: A Time in Jail.
Massachusetts Review, Summer.

JOSEPH INGLE
Etiquette of Death. *Southern,* March.

MARK JACOBSON
God Knows. *Esquire,* March.

JEFF JOHNSON
On a Fuzzy Tree. *Twin Cities,*
November.

STEPHEN JONES
Snow Job. *Northeast* (in the *Hartford
Courant*), February 7.

PAT JORDAN
The House of the Three Sisters. *New
York Woman,* November.

E. J. KAHN, JR.
Hand to Hand. *The New Yorker,*
February 8.

GARRISON KEILLOR
My Life in Prison. *The Atlantic,*
November.

DANIEL KEMMIS
The Art of the Possible in the Home
of Hope. *Northern Lights,* October.

GWEN KINKEAD
An Overgrown Jack. *The New Yorker,*
July 18.

JOHN KNOWLES
Musings on a Chameleon. *Esquire,*
April.

HANS KONING
Memories Official and Unofficial.
Harper's Magazine, October.

PETER NAJARIAN
The Big Game. *Witness*, Summer/Fall.

MICHAEL O'ROURKE
A Perfect Place. *New England Review and Bread Loaf Quarterly*, Winter.

HEINZ R. PAGELS
The Instruments of Creation. *Gettysburg Review*, Spring.

SAMUEL PICKERING, JR.
Might As Well. *Chattahoochee Review*, Winter.
At Cambridge. *Southern Review*, Winter.

DARRYL PINCKNEY
On James Baldwin (1924–1987). *New York Review of Books*, January 21.

JOE PINTAURO
Algren in Exile. *Chicago*, February.

DAVID PLANTE
In Moscow. *Grand Street*, Winter.

DAVID QUAMMEN
Nuclear Dreams. *Outside*, November.

ROGER ROSENBLATT
The Dark Comedian: Richard Nixon at 75. *Time*, April 25.

MORDECAI ROSENFELD
An Election Year (1988) Fable. *New York Law Journal*, September 22.

BERTON ROUECHÉ
The Foulest and Nastiest Creatures That Be. *The New Yorker*, September 12.

RICK RUBIN
Praise Failure. *Clinton St. Quarterly*, Spring.

OLIVER SACKS
The Revolution of the Deaf. *New York Review of Books*, June 2.

REG SANER
The Magpie Scapular. *Ohio Review*, No. 41.
Snow. *New England Review and Bread Loaf Quarterly*, Winter.
Technically Sweet. *Georgia Review*, Winter.

RICHARD SELZER
A Mother's Fury. *New York Times Magazine*, October 23.

DANIEL SHANAHAN
The Cuban Missile Crisis: Memoirs of a Survivor. *North Dakota Quarterly*, Spring.

ROBERT SHAPLEN
The Long River. *The New Yorker*, August 8.

KEN SMITH
Wormwood Scrubs. *Antioch Review*, Summer.

MONROE K. SPEARS
Montaigne Our Contemporary. *Hudson Review*, Summer.

SHELBY STEELE
I'm Black, You're White, Who's Innocent? *Harper's Magazine*, June.

MICHAEL STEPHENS
The Poetics of Boxing. In *Reading the Fights*, edited by Joyce Carol Oates and Daniel Halpern (Henry Holt).

LAWRENCE TABAK
The Meaning of Tennis. *Racquet*, Summer.

JANE TOMPKINS
Fighting Words: Unlearning to Write
    the Critical Essay. *Georgia Review,*
    Fall.

SUSAN ALLEN TOTH
Shade in a Spring Garden.
    Minneapolis Star-Tribune Sunday
    Magazine, May 15.

CALVIN TRILLIN
Stranger in Town. *The New Yorker,*
    February 1.

MILDRED RAYNOLDS TRIVERS
The Storm God. *Virginia Quarterly*
    Review, Spring.

GEORGE W. S. TROW, JR.
Subway Story. *The New Yorker,*
    February 22.

JOHN UPDIKE
The Writer Lectures. *New York Review*
    of Books, June 16.

NICHOLAS VON HOFFMAN
Voting Rites. *Grand Street,* Autumn.

DAN WAKEFIELD
James Baldwin: Friend and Mentor.
    GQ, August.

TOM WICKER
Rough Passage. *New York Times*
    Magazine, July 24.

JOHN WIDEMAN
The Black Writer and the Magic of
    the Word. *New York Times Book*
    Review, January 24.

PETER WILD
Among Spies and Spooks: Saving
    Myself. *North Dakota Quarterly,*
    Spring.

NANCY WILLARD
Telling Time. *Prairie Schooner,*
    Spring.

JOY WILLIAMS
I Led a Totally Unrequited Life. *New*
    England Monthly, May.

LAWRENCE WRIGHT
The Sins of Walker Railey. *Texas*
    Monthly, January.

ERIC ZENCEY
Apocalypse and Ecology. *North*
    American Review, Fall.

WILLIAM ZINSSER
The News from Timbuktu. *Conde*
    Nast's Traveler, October.

Readers will also find essays of
    interest in the following special
    issues of periodicals that appeared
    in 1988:

Agni, "Mentors and Tormentors,"
    edited by Sven Birkerts and Askold
    Melnyczuk (No. 26).

Antaeus, "Journals, Notebooks and
    Diaries," edited by Daniel Halpern
    (Autumn).

Antioch Review, "The Peking Express:
    China Today," edited by Robert S.
    Fogarty (Spring).

Georgia Review, "The Kingdom of
    Kitch in American Culture," edited
    by Stanley W. Lindberg (Summer).

North Dakota Quarterly, "North Dakota
    Centennial Issue," edited by Robert
    W. Lewis (Fall).

Sewanee Review, "Sallies of the Mind,"
    edited by George Core (Fall).

Witness, "The Sixties," edited by Peter
    Stine (Summer/Fall).

Yale Review, "Encounters, Part III,"
    edited by Kai Erikson (Summer).